THE
Olive Readers

In September 2004 *Richard & Judy*'s Executive Producer, Amanda Ross, approached Pan Macmillan: her production company, Cactus TV, wanted to launch a major writing competition, 'How to Get Published', on the Channel 4 show. Unpublished authors would be invited to send in the first chapter and a synopsis of their novel and would have the chance of winning a publishing contract.

Five months, 46,000 entries and a lot of reading later, the five shortlisted authors appeared live on the show and Christine Aziz was announced as the winner with her debut, *The Olive Readers*.

But there was a surprise in store for the other four finalists. On air Richard Madeley said, 'The standard of the finalists is staggeringly high. All are more than worthy of a publishing contract.' Pan Macmillan agreed and published all four: *Tuesday's War* by David Fiddimore, *Journeys in the Dead Season* by Spencer Jordan, *Housewife Down* by Alison Penton Harper, and *Gem Squash Tokoloshe* by Rachel Zadok.

CHRISTINE AZIZ has worked as a shop assistant, dental receptionist, factory packer, singer, cleaning lady, actress, journalist, community worker and English teacher. She now works as a homeopath and freelance journalist. This is her first novel.

CHRISTINE AZIZ

THE
Olive Readers

PAN BOOKS

First published 2005 by Macmillan

First published in paperback 2006 by Pan Books
an imprint of Pan Macmillan Ltd
Pan Macmillan, 20 New Wharf Road, London N1 9RR
Basingstoke and Oxford
Associated companies throughout the world
www.panmacmillan.com

ISBN-13: 978-0-330-43963-3
ISBN-10: 0-330-43963-4

Grateful acknowledgement is made to the James Baldwin Estate
for permission to reprint lines from *Nothing Personal* by James Baldwin.
Collected in *The Price of the Ticket* © 1985 by James Baldwin,
published by St Martin's Press.

1 3 5 7 9 8 6 4 2

A CIP catalogue record for this book is available from
the British Library.

Typeset by Intype Libra Ltd
Printed and bound in Great Britain by
Mackays of Chatham plc, Chatham Kent

For Dad, Mum and Malcolm

With special thanks to
Diana Morgan

One must say Yes to life and embrace it wherever it is found – and it is found in terrible places ... For nothing is fixed, forever and forever and forever, it is not fixed; the earth is always shifting, the light is always changing, the sea does not cease to grind down rock. Generations do not cease to be born, and we are responsible to them because we are the only witnesses they have. The sea rises, the light falls, lovers cling to each other, and children cling to us. The moment we cease to hold each other, the moment we break faith with one another, the sea engulfs us and the light goes out.

JAMES BALDWIN

Acknowledgements

This book's inception and how it came to be published were both unexpected. It started as a blank piece of paper and a woman at a typewriter who did not have a clue what to write. The first sentence came from nowhere and was originally intended as the start of a short story. The emerging characters took over and told me their story.

The book's publication is the result of winning a nationwide novel-writing competition, and must be every unpublished writer's dream. I am still pinching myself. I am indebted to Diana Morgan, who persuaded me to enter the competition and who always raised my spirits when the going got tough and provided invaluable and wise insights.

The competition was brought about by a team of people with a passion for books. I thank them all, particularly Amanda Ross of Cactus Films, who originally came up with the idea as a way to encourage new writers. I am indebted to Maria Rejt, my editor at Pan Macmillan, for her unwavering faith in *The Olive Readers*, and her patience with a novice who wrote the first half of the book intermittently over eighteen years and the second half to a two-month deadline. Her assistant, Anna Valdinger, was a much-valued, reassuring voice throughout the editing process.

ACKNOWLEDGEMENTS

Heartfelt thanks to my daughter, Shola, who has always encouraged me and had faith in my writing abilities, and to my son, Tariq, who completely understood the impact of this book's publication upon my life and what it meant to me.

Without the assistance, encouragement and generosity of my friends, I doubt this book would have been written. I cannot name everyone – you know who you are – but my warm appreciation goes to Annette Gartland, Marlene Edmonds, Margaret Kitchen and Vikki Baron for their practical, objective input. Special thanks also to Vivienne Greenwell, Diana Walters, Christina Artemis, Nicola Lockey, Barbara Holloway, Diane Von Der Muhl, Ria Longuet, Gurdev and Amarjot Singh-Dhoot, Melanie Friend, Frederique Delacoste, Caroline Penn, Jenny Matthews, Rachel Carter, Wendy Simpson and Liz Coutts. Also thanks to members of the Artemis Theatre Group of Bournemouth, who kept me sane and were kinder than they know.

Zoe Linsley-Thomas read the first half of the novel and offered helpful criticism. Sadly, she did not live to see me finish it. I am indebted to her for her support and outrageous zest for life.

Thanks to Tanya, Claudia and Annette for their healing.

The pioneering ideas on natural energy by the remarkable Viktor Schauberger (1885–1958), are a thread that runs through this book. He was a man before his time, as was Dr Jean Beneviste (1935–2004), whose controversial research on the 'memory of water' has also provided some of the impetus behind the story.

My lovely grandchildren, Ruby and Sena Aklotsoe,

are part of the next generation to inherit the earth. They were the inspiration behind the emerging story, long before they were born.

Christine Aziz, July 2005

Prologue

This restaurant where I wait to meet Hephzibah is decorated in a style inspired by the period in which you live – a wash of terracotta on the walls, bare rustic wood, ornate candelabra, elegantly fashioned wrought-iron chairs made comfortable with cream linen cushions. The style is restrained, but to my eyes is like a stage setting from another era – to be precise, your era.

I am here speaking to you from your future. Strange that, as far as you are concerned, these events have not yet occurred, yet can be viewed by you in your present. Before your very eyes they are transmuting into the future. Imagine you have moved to another star on the edge of the universe. You peer back at your home star through a telescope. Thanks to the equations of time, speed and light, you witness events that have already taken place in your absence.

What does it matter? A story, no matter how fast it hurtles through space, remains a story and the play of electrons does not dilute passion.

I have to keep reminding myself that our universe is probably expanding. Does this mean we will always have further to travel?

JEPHZAT Q, Olea, February 2295

Book I

Don't tell me the moon is shining;
show me the glint of light on broken glass.

ANTON CHEKHOV

Book 1

I

I don't know how long it is since I last saw Hephzibah. It could have been when our country shifted its borders, or when the old woman, Sengita, saw snow for the first time. Memory makes time wanton, fills it with hapless corners and dead ends. To divert myself I turn time into an abacus and try to count the days, months, years that have divided us.

It started with the war, but when was that? It wasn't a war that passed us by with faint rumblings and the smell of smoke above the hills and olive groves. It walked into our house and seduced us all, even though its cause hardly mattered to us. It was the axis upon which our memories now turn and yet, as with all wars, it solved nothing, merely shifting a heavily guarded border thirty kilometres further south. The villagers have ceased weeping for those murdered by the bands of passing soldiers, but are still mourning for the ancient olive trees that were blasted from the earth, their wood dissolving silently in the air.

I place my fingers on the table to count the years that may have passed since Hephzibah and I last spoke, and find that I am drumming soft thuds that fall like bare feet on wood as each finger rises and falls in turn again and again, until they pause, and I see her, as she was then, walking along the jetty, turning to watch me as I step into

3

the small boat alone. I can still hear the heartbeat of her footsteps muffled by the hot, still afternoon.

Mercifully, the bright flare of a pre-twilight sun had prevented me from looking up at her, but I knew she was watching me cast the boat adrift and then row, the oars slicing the estuary's taut sheen. We said nothing to each other, and I heard her footsteps again as she walked away from me up the incline above the jetty. She stopped and turned and I saw her shade her eyes against the sun to watch me as the boat moved slowly forward, its cargo pushing the hull deep into the water. I strained at the oars and felt the evening sun burning the back of my neck. Hephzibah turned to continue walking towards the house and did not look back. I tried to concentrate on rowing, directing the boat towards the open sea, away from the shore, where the village rose pink and white against the feathered silver of the olive trees.

By the time I returned and reached the path leading through the citrus groves to my parents' house, clouds had moved across the sun and a hot wind raised dust from the path. When I arrived at the high and heavy front door, the shutters were closed and the dogs were barking. Hephzibah and the soldiers had gone.

2

And Lomez, what has become of Lomez, the son of Pesh, the fisherman? He should have emptied his net back into the sea that night. Where is he now and does he still carry that nightmare in the pockets of his sleep?

Pesh had been killed by the soldiers and it was his mother, Tulu, who was to introduce Lomez to the whims of the open sea a year earlier than was the tradition. Half the village's fishing fleet had been destroyed by the war – boats had been blown out of the water and many of the village fishermen lined up against walls and shot and then gutted like fresh mackerel on the harbour wall. It took a furious storm finally to clear the tides of the lingering blood and the awful smell. Young boys were taking the place of lost fathers, and their mothers were sailing with them, teaching them the art of navigation and the ways of snaring fish. I would watch them sometimes, the women still wearing the white of mourning, hauling their petti-coats over the hulls, passing on what they had learned from their husbands' accounts of their expeditions. As children they had sat at the quay with their own mothers, cleaning and scaling the fish as they came in, watching their fathers and brothers at work on the boats, tying and untying nautical knots, spreading and folding the nets. As small children they had slept in the hot afternoons curled up in the cool hulls of the boats. Later, as women, they fell asleep at night in their husbands' arms, listening to their whispering voices speaking of the sea's mood that day, its textures, its tides, its fickleness. This was how they learned the ways of the ocean, just as a woman might know the intimate details of her husband's mistress without ever having met her.

Barely past childhood, but with the strength and height of a grown man, Lomez thrilled at what seemed to be the weight of a full harvest in the net he and Tulu had cast hours before. It was a good omen for his future. His friend, Pedro, had pulled his first net on the previous night of the full moon, and hauled in only a scaggle of eels.

The weight of the net broke his reverie as it hit the hull underwater and sank lower. His man's body strained, as it had never done on land, yet his child's heart was fearful. What could it be in the net that defied his strength? He had heard stories of sea monsters that came too far into coastal waters, to ensnare themselves in the nets and drag fishermen from their boats into a watery hell. The muscles in his arms felt as though they were about to split his skin. Lomez bit hard on his lower lip until blood came. He could hear his mother singing to the fish as she bent over the boat's port side, pulling them up towards her, grieving still for her husband. Her vast white skirts billowed over the deck and her headscarf slipped over her brow, almost covering her eyes, but she could not push it back for fear of losing the net. The night was warm and she could feel the scarf and her blouse begin to soak with sweat and stick to her skin, but she was happy. Pesh would be proud of her. By working his boat and fishing and sailing in waters he said he knew better than his own body, she felt closer to him. It was as if he stood beside her, guiding her every move. Since his death she had never felt his presence on land, but here in his rocking boat he was with her, reminding her that she was not alone.

Lomez was comforted by his mother's deep, measured voice, which occasionally broke into an unnerving chuckle, but he still wished his father was there to see him becoming a man, harvesting his first catch. The thin, coarse twine of the net split his palms and the moon felt cold, hard and heavy on his back. His strength was waning. He felt the net pulling away from him, gaining momentum as it fell. If he could not pull harder it would be lost for ever. He called to Tulu, who was now busy bringing up boxes from the hold for the fish. She heard her son call and ran over to him. Her fingers, thick as eels, curled around the neck of the net and she fell forward with its weight. 'What the hell is this?' she cried, and would have crossed herself (an old superstition that no longer had meaning) had her hands not been so busy. 'Lomez, what have you caught? It has half the seabed in its belly!'

Lomez imagined the full fat fish about to emerge – a swordfish perhaps, worth a lot of money in the market. Tulu wondered why such a catch hung so heavy yet so still upon her fingers. She called to Pesh as she struggled with her son to heave the net out of the water. The moon was already drifting to the horizon by the time it was pulled over the boat's side and on to the deck. Small fish twisted and turned like sequinned acrobats. When Lomez loosened the neck of the net, sea snakes, snails and weed poured over their feet in a thick spill of slime.

As they stood gathering their breath, a hand suddenly broke through. Its long white fingers pointed at Lomez and Tulu, now both crossing themselves in horror. Tulu bent closer, making sure her skirts did not touch the creature, and tried to clear the weed. There was enough blue silk to indicate a skirt and a bodice. Much of the body's flesh had been eaten away, leaving only patches of bone that gleamed tooth-white in the early morning light. Even in the corpse's decomposed and bloated state – it was clearly that of a woman – Lomez could see how beautiful she had been. Her hair lay dark and heavy upon the deck. The one eye that remained was open and shone iridescent green and blue like a fish's scale.

'She's not one of us,' Tulu said quietly. 'This is an ill omen.'

Lomez begged his mother to return the body to the sea, but Tulu chastised him, saying it had been lifted out of its watery grave for a reason – so that it could be given a death ritual, the way any body should be. She stood up, wriggled out of one of her petticoats and wrapped it round the body like a shroud. Normally she would have waited for a dawn wind to gather, or would have tacked her way slowly to shore, but this time they needed to get home quickly before heat rose with the sun. She switched on the engine and the boat surged forward. Tulu, normally a lively woman with a fondness for talking, steered the boat in unaccustomed silence, staring grim-faced ahead of her. Lomez busied himself with the rest of the catch, packing the fish into boxes and putting them in the hold where it was cooler. He kept one eye on the shrouded body, wondering if it could be a magical creature with the power to return to life. Then, when Tulu's head was turned, Lomez bent to kiss the drowned woman's slightly parted lips. He smelled the thick, ancient stew of the sea's bed, and tasted salt and a fetid sweetness. The taste was to remain in his mouth for the rest of his life.

3

The villagers sent a child to our house. She was welcomed by Manos with hot, sweet tea and almonds. Manos was the only servant who had dared to return to us since the soldiers left. She spoke to the child in a low voice and lifted to her lips the quartz that hung from her waist, kissing the crystal as she received the news. Then she sent the child upstairs and busied herself boiling huge pots of water and steeping bunches of herbs. Later, she would serve the brew as a tranquillizer for grief, and when my mother wasn't looking, sprinkle it around the house to rid its many rooms of the Evil Eye.

I was there when the child told my parents about the body, its silk and mutilation, its resemblance to my sister, Hephzibah, who had been missing for many days now. The child spoke with a heavy local accent and they kept asking her to repeat words, which unnerved her. She began to weep softly, burying her face in her hands. When the girl could think of nothing more to say about the discovery of the body, Father told her to go home. She ran quickly down the elaborate carved staircase, her foot-steps echoing on the cool marble.

My parents sat beside each other, silent and still. They looked pitifully crumpled and lifeless. Father stared at the clock opposite him, which had stopped years ago and which no one had bothered to rewind. My mother, who always preferred me to call her Dolores, seemed to be sleeping, her head slumped forward on her chest. I retreated into the shadows and stood watching them. Father sighed and glanced up. His bent back seemed even more pronounced as he rose and walked with difficulty towards the clock. I was shocked by how old he looked; he seemed to have aged in the several hours since I had last seen him. He stood gazing at the clock, while my mother raised her hands to her face and bent over into her lap, shaking with grief. I noticed how thin the crown of her once luxuriant hair had become.

Even though Dolores was crying she made no noise, except for a slight hiccuping. Theirs was a polite, mannered grief – displays of emotion were always firmly bounded by etiquette. I had never seen either of them cry before – my mother's swallowed sobs were the first indications of any real emotion I had witnessed in this house since Father blasted the ceiling with his gun after Hephzibah's birth, but hers was to be a dry, disciplined sorrow. In a voice that was strained she said, 'Your sister just brought up from the sea like a poor fisherman's catch, and all you can do is stand there.' It was the first time Dolores had spoken to me since the soldiers had left. I flushed with anger, and neither my father nor I went to comfort her.

'Leave her alone,' Father said sharply. 'I blame you, Dolores. You and Hephzibah cavorting around with the soldiers under this roof like a couple of whores. I knew that, one way or another, it would end up like this.'

He couldn't control the disgust in his voice, but Dolores mustered a defiant half-smile. I paused by the door to give Father time to reach me; he had begun to walk slowly and painfully across the room and seemed to have difficulty finding his breath. He insisted on holding the door open for me, even though it was a struggle for him to do so. As he opened it, we heard the faint sound of villagers calling to one another as they harvested the olives in the terraces behind us.

'You must go to the village and identify the body. Be careful,' he whispered.

4

I could tell that my presence had unnerved my parents. Hephzibah and I were always together; now I served only to highlight the tragedy of her disappearance. I was pleased that we did not look alike. I did not want to be a constant reminder of her to my parents and thus a source of their sorrow. Hephzibah had inherited our mother's high cheekbones and forehead. But my full lips and strongly defined jawbone came from our father. My eyes are light brown but Hephzibah's were bright green, flecked with blue. Their colour overwhelmed her face, even her wonderful thick mane of burnished copper tendrils, which hung down her back. My dark hair was prematurely laced with grey and I was tall, long-limbed and sparsely fleshed. I still am, and, even as a child, was always taller than other children in the village. People of my size and shape are usually associated with grace and ease of movement, but in those days I moved quickly and gawkily, frequently banging into furniture or twisting my feet on uneven paths as if I was never sure which direction I was taking. I envied my sister, and although I don't want to give the impression that I was ugly (I am attractive in my own way), Hephzibah had beauty. Perhaps she still does.

I can't imagine that she has lost that luxuriant smile

which devastates the onlooker. As she grew out of child-hood she used it sparingly and the young men in the village worked hard to bring it to her lips. She used her smile like money – spent it only when she wanted something, used it as a long-term investment. When her smile was absent, her features settled into an alert stillness. Her eyes stared sharply, missing nothing, only occasionally working with her full, expressive mouth to betray the emotions that lay behind them.

She was shorter and rounder than me, but moved with athletic grace. She walked with a sense of purpose, even if she had none, and always seemed to have a destination, even when she did not. She said she liked to walk with me because I kept up with her, although she usually became irritated by the number of times we had to stop to look at toes I had stubbed on some object or other en route. Some said her beauty was marred by the faint scar that rose from her lip to her nose. I thought it enhanced her face. It transfixed the onlooker like an out-of-step dancer in a chorus line of perfectly synchronized movement. The scar was a barometer of her emotions – when she was upset it twitched, even though the rest of her face revealed no emotion at all.

Hephzibah had been born with a split upper lip and a slightly cleft palate. I remember her pitiful mewling after her birth. Sengita, the village midwife, known as the Guardian of Secrets by the villagers, had been called for the confinement. When she arrived, Father sent me to my room.

'Don't come out until I tell you,' he said gruffly, as if

I had done something wrong. I was too young then to associate this gruffness, as I later did, with consternation and fear. I used to believe I was the cause of it and assumed that I had displeased him in some way. I stood looking up at him. Surely it wasn't my fault that a baby was about to be born.

'Why not?' I demanded, although I knew the answer already.

'Your mother is having a baby, and we mustn't disturb her.'

'Can't I watch?'

Father seemed taken aback by the question. Impossible, he replied, little girls didn't watch things like that; it was a secret, something only for grown-up women. Who would be with my mother to help her, I asked, suddenly aware of doors banging, water running, and the hurried swish of skirts up and down stairs. 'The baby must be coming soon,' he said as an explanation of the disturbances that had clearly alerted me, and then added, 'Sengita is delivering the baby.'

'But Mother doesn't like Sengita,' I said. 'She says she's a witch.'

'I think your mother is a little afraid of her.' He spoke gently.

'I'm not,' I replied staunchly. Sengita didn't dress like the other local women. Instead of the single traditional round earring, she wore several through each ear and had a strange mark tattooed on her forehead. She wore her hair long, while the other women kept theirs short to show off the indigo patterns on the nape of their necks – a part of the body their men considered sensuous, perhaps because the back of the neck never seems to age. Sengita's waist was thick with plaited scarves and she always wore a red waistcoat decorated with coins, shells and small bells. When she moved they clinked and tinkled together. Her thick, bushy eyebrows and aquiline nose worked together to give her face a stern expression that nevertheless did not intimidate me. She was different with children, and we often saw the kindly twinkle in her dark, deep-set eyes, which the adults did not, and I loved her low, mischievous chuckle. It was only when I grew older that I noticed how her eyes served as mirrors, uncomfortably reflecting deceits and untruths. It was her voice, calm, smooth and quick, that reassured and told me by its tone alone that she had not judged, no matter what she had seen.

Father knelt down beside me and looked me directly in the eyes.

'You're not afraid of anything,' he said.

5

Father closed the door behind him and I fidgeted, listening for sounds that might tell me how babies are born. I decided to go and find my new sibling. I made my way across the landing to my parents' room. The door was firmly shut. I could hear Sengita telling my mother to push, but push what? Push her stomach, Sengita or the baby? A village woman came running up the stairs with a pile of clean, hot towels. I quickly hid behind a chest, and watched as she entered the room and then left, leaving the door slightly ajar behind her. I peeped in and saw my mother lying, not on the bed, but on the floor, the hem of her nightdress pulled up around her shoulders, her legs apart, her knees bent and her head on Manos's lap. Her breasts were huge, with dark nipples the size of saucers. The shutters were drawn and the room was gloomy. Manos was leaning over my mother and massaging warm oil into her huge stomach, while Sengita was on all-fours pulling blood-soaked towels from underneath, replacing them with clean ones and wiping my mother's thighs with wet rags. I was shocked by their luminous whiteness (her arms and face had always been sunburnt) and by the blood running dark to the floor.

I had not seen my mother naked before, but I knew what a grown woman's body looked like – I had bathed with the young women in the estuary. Now to see her vagina like a gaping wound filled me with horror and pity. I could not understand why it was the focus of the room – my mother's pain-filled face and occasional heart-rending screams should have preoccupied us – but this raw heart of grimacing flesh seemed to possess a power that was all its own.

Dolores strained; her face turned red and her vulva widened, vermilion and bloodied. Sengita lowered herself as if ready to stick her face between my mother's thighs. 'It's coming. I can see it,' she said calmly, sweat now gathering on her forehead. My mother lay back exhausted. Manos stopped massaging and began to bear down on her stomach. 'Push, my little one!' Sengita commanded. Dolores heaved herself up from the floor on her elbows and strained again. Sengita wiped the blood away and moved aside. I glimpsed flesh that was not my mother's. It was darker, purplish, its head covered with what looked like the damp feathers of a newborn bird.

'The head is coming. Push again!' Sengita urged impatiently.

My mother screwed up her face – every feature seemed to meet at the tip of her nose – and let out a great scream, not of terror, but of frustration and release. It hit us all like a hard smack. She tried to look over her belly, but her eyes slid across to me standing in the doorway. The mother I knew had slipped away, and in her place I saw this striving primeval beast.

I took advantage and stepped brazenly into the room. Dolores seemed to forget me as Sengita slipped a hand beneath her. 'One or two more pushes and it's over,' she said, glancing anxiously at my mother. 'I can't, I can't,'

Dolores cried. Manos bore down harder, but my mother tried to push her away.

'Leave me alone! Leave me, you evil cats!'

Her insults were suddenly taken over by the power of her pelvic muscles. She strained as if her life counted on it and I watched in horror as a head slipped out between her legs, red and purple as if with rage. It was an image that came into my dreams for a long time afterwards – the small, moist head, like a cyst, between Dolores's long pale thighs.

Sengita gave one of her chuckles.

'Welcome, little princess,' she said, grabbing the baby's tiny ankles. Then she winced as she glanced at the newborn's face. To my consternation she hung the baby upside down and slapped its bottom until it let out a strange, strangled cry.

'It's a girl!' Dolores gasped, falling back into Manos's lap with a long, low moan. Sengita held the baby in her arms and stared down at a face I could not see. She looked over at Manos.

'What's the matter?' Dolores asked, noticing the expression on Sengita's face.

'She has a harelip. It is not good. She will not suckle.'

Dolores closed her eyes and whispered, 'I don't want to see her.'

Sengita turned to me as if she had known I had been there all the time.

'Come,' she said, holding the baby out to me. 'Here is your sister.' I walked over and Sengita laid her in my arms. She was heavy for a four-year-old to carry and wriggled like a caught fish in my arms. The cord was still attached. I looked down at my sister and her dark eyes held mine with an unfocused gaze as if looking through thin gauze from another land. She was like a newly minted coin, a stranger, and yet I felt as though she had always been with me. Her little fingers played with the air and I was lost for words. She smelled of fresh butter and I knew in an instant that I loved her more than anyone else in the world and that I would do anything she asked of me. At that moment my heart was delivered into slavery.

6

Suddenly we heard a loud bang. I recognized it as one of Father's antique guns firing in the distance. When we moved into the house, he had found a box of them hidden under the floorboards of an unused room. He had oiled and greased each one, but rarely fired them. The baby jumped in my arms and immediately turned her head and looked at me as if for protection. I stroked her head gently, my heart beating fast. After cutting the cord, Manos helped my mother to the bed and told me not to look. She took the baby while Sengita bent over my mother and pressed her palms flat on her stomach. I helped Manos fill a bowl with warm water, and when I turned back again Sengita was wrapping something that looked like raw liver in paper.

'Is that another baby?' I asked.

Sengita and Manos laughed.

'You mustn't touch this,' Sengita warned. 'It has to be buried if your sister is to have any happiness.'

'Did you bury something for me as well?' I asked.

'I wasn't around when you came into the world, sweet thing. You were born a long, long way from here in a country where they do things differently, so I don't know what the nurse did with this,' she said, handing the bloodied package over to Manos.

'Does that mean I can't be happy?'

Sengita bent down and rested her large hands on my shoulders. 'Now, look over there at that darling sister of yours. How do you feel when you watch those little feet kicking away like that?'

'Happy.' I beamed.

'Well, there you are then. Burying the afterbirth just helps things along a bit and this little one is going to need all the help she can get.'

Sengita took the baby, and Manos went out with the afterbirth, which was beginning to drip blood over the floor. I helped Sengita wash my sister with damp towels and then she was handed over to my mother. I hovered by the bedside, looking up. At first my mother looked coldly at her daughter, and then she seemed to be hypnotized by her and couldn't take her eyes from her face. Mother and daughter gazed at each other for a long time and then my mother began to smile at her and play with her tiny fingers. It was a long time before she turned to Sengita and asked her to fetch my father.

Sengita fussed around the room, talking in a heavy local dialect of Federese to Manos, who had returned breathless. I could follow their conversation, but Dolores understood little of what they said.

'Someone must have cursed them to have a daughter with a lip like that. By rights she should have been drowned; it is no good having a baby that can't suckle from the mother. But they are foreigners, and have their strange ways.'

I moved protectively towards my mother and sister.

'You won't drown her, you won't,' I screamed, and began to kick Sengita.

'Get out of here,' Dolores said angrily to her. 'It was bad enough having to have you deliver my child without your superstitious babbling!'

Sengita's eyes began to twinkle. 'Well now, look at her and her uppity ways,' she said to Manos. 'It's going to be me and my so-called babbling that are going to keep this mewling thing alive. How are you going to feed her, my madam? How are you going to keep infections out of that mousemeat-from-the-cat mouth? Sengita has her ways and means and, if I were you, I would keep quiet.' She turned and winked at me.

My mother sank petulantly into the pillows, looking down at my sister, who had by now begun to mewl and splutter. 'She's hungry,' Sengita said, and, turning to me, asked, 'Bring me one of your father's ink pens.'

Feeling proud to be asked to do something so important, I rushed to his study. I chose the largest, most beautiful pen.

Moments after my return, we heard my father coming up the stairs. Sengita quickly covered up my mother's breasts.

We heard him shouting delightedly, 'A daughter! A daughter! Well done, Dolores! Two girls!'

He burst into the room, brandishing his gun in triumph above his head. 'Double luck today. I've just bagged myself that wretched wild cat. She won't be at the chickens again. A good omen, eh?'

There was silence, and I knew that Sengita was trying to find the words to warn him that all was not well. She began to speak, but Father would have none of it. He dropped the gun and whirled me up in his arms, laughing.

'Let's look at your new sister, shall we?' he cried, and bent over the bed with me still in his arms.

I could feel his arms tightening around my waist.

'What's wrong with her?'

'She has a harelip and a slightly cleft palate.' Dolores looked up weakly. 'She can't feed from me.'

Father put me down on the bed and carefully took Hephzibah in his arms, staring closely at her. He explored her little mouth gently with a finger.

'This is nothing that Frederick can't fix,' he said with confidence. 'When she's stronger we'll take her to see him and she will be as beautiful as she is meant to be. All the men in the village will be after her, won't they, Sengita?'

'No,' Sengita said firmly. 'They will consider it a curse, even if your jiggery-pokery doctors use their magic on her and the disfigurement disappears. She was born with it, and that's that.'

'You and your superstitions. This is what I think of your nonsense.'

My father handed Hephzibah back to Mother and, picking up his gun, aimed it at the ceiling and fired. We all jumped at the blast. Plaster fell around us while Sengita and Manos rushed under the bed, pulling me with them. Dolores disappeared under the bedcovers with her baby. There was silence and then we all came out of our hiding places and gazed up at the ceiling. Thick flakes of plaster drifted down and dust filled our noses and mouths.

That was how Hephzibah was welcomed into the world.

7

Hephzibah grew strong on my mother's milk fed to her through Father's pen's nib, and when she was six months old my parents finally received permission from headquarters to travel to Ferat, a heavy manufacturing Company in the north, for the specialized surgery she would need. I did not know then that it was unusual for anyone to get permission for such a journey, nor that most people in the Corporate Federation were confined to a small world that measured no more than the distance between the place of their labour and their home.

It must have been around this time when my parents told me in hushed voices that Ferat had, long ago, been part of an empire. This particular region had once been home to our ancestors until it was taken over and shared between a number of multinational corporations. Its population was deported to other regions of the new Corporate Empire. My father told me that the chairmen of these corporations became presidential dictators overnight and carved the old empire up between them. This patchwork of production centres became work camps; then they were established as countries in their own right, run by the corporations and their subsidiaries, and known to us now as the Companies. The old fallen empire, he said seriously, had been called America.

Vast numbers of people were moved from one 'camp' to another, or held in special training centres to acquire new skills for the Companies that now effectively owned them. This was long before I was born, of course, but some of these Companies already existed in your time, their corporate tentacles reaching into your politicians' pockets and sending you into a deep trance with their cheap gadgets and entertaining propaganda. You thought you were free then, didn't you? But it was just the first step.

The displacement occurred worldwide, and no one was allowed to keep anything that reminded them of the lives they had once lived. Even our villagers were descendants of a random huddle of survivors from all corners of the old empire, brought there to work the olive terraces. None of them knew from which tribe, which land, which city, which river bank, which mountain – which family – their ancestors had been torn.

All forms of information and art, other than Corporate propaganda, were destroyed. The books, discs, recordings, music, art and cartography of your time disappeared, burned in vast incinerators. No one had a past to return to and so the present became more precious, the future anchored only by its monotonous certainty.

When I was told this I puzzled, even at my young age, as to how my parents, unlike everyone else, had information on their origins. I tried to ask, but Dolores put her finger to her lips. She and my father swore me to secrecy. I could not even discuss it with my sister. Such knowledge, they said, was punishable by death.

My parents were lucky. My mother was an eminent

physicist and this had previously earned her certain privileges, including permission to live and work in Ferat for several years. The country in which we lived was responsible for the processing of the world's olives and all their ancillary products. All olive-producing regions were obliged by the Federation to send their olives to the Olive Country, which itself produced more olives than anyone. My father, a biochemist, was given permission by the Ferat authorities to transfer to the Olive Company along with Dolores, to work on a project researching the use of the olive in pharmacy. As I showed an aptitude in science at the Company schools we attended, I was later allowed to work alongside him as an assistant.

This is how we came to live in the village, but I remember little of our original home in Ferat, as I was very small at the time we left it. But sometimes I dream of tall, brightly lit buildings with shining spires, and stairs climbing upward to an open sky.

For several weeks after her birth I did not know what to call my sister, as my parents had not been able to agree on a name. My father wanted to call her after his mother, but as Dolores had never liked her mother-in-law, she would not agree. In the end they settled on the name Hephzibah, after a woman they had once known who had a beautiful singing voice. I asked where this woman was now, but my parents weren't too sure. Dolores thought she had been sent to one of the retraining camps when she reached adulthood. Her Company didn't have much need for singers.

Now, six months later, when the day came for their departure to Ferat, I dreaded being without my sister and implored my parents to take me with them.

'The Company has only given permission for the three of us to leave. With you left behind, little one, it knows we won't try to hide elsewhere. You guarantee our return.' Father then explained how Uncle Jacobius, who still lived in Ferat, had a doctor friend who would be able to mend Hephzibah's lip.

'In the old days, we would not have had to travel all this way with such a small baby. But, with these ridiculous restrictions and the lack of local medical care, what else can we do? I suppose we have to be grateful that we are being allowed to leave at all.'

'You might forget you have her with you,' I said.

Father laughed. 'We are only going home for a short visit.'

'Home? But isn't this our home?'

Father paused. 'Remember, little one, we are strangers here. You were born in another country, our country. You must not forget that. And you must never tell anyone where we are from. It is dangerous to know these things.'

'What's home like?'

'It's beautiful.' He was whispering. 'We lived in a big city with huge old buildings and grand parks. That was where you were born. It was raining that day. I remember it very well, and it was cold, very cold, not like here. Your mother and I, we had a huge apartment with old lights – they were called candelabra, made of tiny bits of glass – and we had many friends who often came to visit us.'

This surprised me. My parents rarely had visitors now, apart from the Commissioner, who occasionally searched through the house, laboratories and gardens. Once, I remember a strange-looking man dressed in a black suit with a wide, happy smile and a loud laugh who came to stay. Father first introduced him to me as my Uncle Jacobius, although he called him Frederick. He was the man they were now going to visit.

Uncle Jacobius jumped me up and down on his knees until I cried with joy. He told me stories of how things were before, and my parents would nod their heads sadly and click their tongues. In our family, then, there was a sense of merely passing through; one day we would return to that big city and life would continue as before, as if there had never been an interruption. At least, that is what my parents led me to believe. Their dream always made me aware of the differences that separated us from the villagers – descendants of people who had been allocated to the village at the whim of a Federation employee following the collapse of the American empire. Unlike my parents, they had no memory of an ancestral home. Their geography, customs and language had been wiped from all records. All they were left with was the village, their olives, one another, and a past slowly creating itself.

When my parents left with Hephzibah, I did not know what to do with myself. After lessons at the Company school, I used to run immediately to the nursery to be with my sister. She was always waiting for me, cradled in Manos's arms or playing in her cot. She would try to smile as much as her harelip allowed. I made up funny stories while she watched me, chuckling as though understanding every word. I helped Manos feed her with the pen, squirting milk into the back of her throat. I was surprised by her strong will – she knew how to let us know when she had had enough and when she wanted to be picked up, and she knew how to seduce you into cuddling her. Dolores didn't like me near her when she was looking after her. She wanted the baby all to herself, but, luckily for me, she was quite often tired and would leave Hephzibah with Manos.

The doctor stitched and repaired the tiny mouth, leaving only a delicate seam where her flared lip had been, and later a soft lisp. The villagers thought a miracle had been performed but did not believe the surgeon's skill had sliced away the curse. When my parents returned I looked for signs of change in Hephzibah – she had grown plumper, bigger and now, instead of mewling, cried like any other baby. She held out her arms to me when I met her, and cooed and gurgled and smiled.

'I think she loves you more than anyone,' Father said.

She sucked voraciously on a bottle and began to take food, which I sometimes fed her. I noticed changes in Dolores too. She had lost weight and hardly spoke. My father was also quieter, and spent more time hunting or in his laboratory. It was during this time that Dolores instructed me to stop calling her Mother. She gave no explanation, and I did not consider it strange as filial titles were not considered important. But Hephzibah was never asked to call her Dolores, which I considered unfair.

Eighteen years later we were confronting Hephzibah's death. I could see that Dolores found it painful to look at me. She lowered her eyes, but not before she had given me a sharp glance, which said, 'Why did it have to be your sister? Why couldn't it have been you?' And I promised myself then that one day I would answer her question with something more than the defiance with which I then briefly held her gaze.

8

I had to follow Father's bidding immediately: in the heat the body would not last long. The village Commissioner met me in the main street that ran down to the harbour. He had somehow acquired the clothing of a priest who, it was said, had been executed two decades before following the discovery of an ancient computer in his cellar. There weren't many priests left in the Federation since all the old religious buildings had been closed down or converted into Company offices. But, by then, people had already lost interest in faith as they realized that the Federation had allowed what remained of the old religions to continue only as another means of control and surveillance.

Most people would have nothing to do with the Commissioners, high-collared men and women who knew little of the old religious practices, yet maintained a status that gave them disproportionate power in their communities. I knew, from my visits to the villagers' homes, that they preferred to keep tiny secret shrines dedicated to a woman called Maya, who they believed had saved our planet from extinction. Offerings of flowers, salt and olives were regularly placed on shrines that were kept carefully hidden on rafters, in cupboards or under floorboards.

Maya had been born before the creation of the Federation and lived in a time of great climatic upheaval that you, reader, have yet to see. Huge tracts of land were washed away by rising seas, countless people were suffocated by the air they breathed, and vast numbers died of hunger and thirst. Those in power locked themselves in impregnable fortresses of clean air and privilege, ignoring the cries of those they purported to serve, and justifying continual armed conflict. Most wars were fought, then as now, over the ownership of dwindling and increasingly valuable resources. Eventually all these resources – all, that is, except water – were owned by five megacorporations run by people from no more than three Old World countries. Their global reach and power were like those of Old World empires, and their tools of exploitation and organized scarcity were applied with little regard for the consequences of their greed.

Maya's charisma and formidable energy enabled her to build a worldwide following from millions tired of their political and environmental subjugation. At first the movement remained underground. Small cells of supporters existed in all the world's major cities. As support for Maya increased, she openly confronted the governments, who by then were entirely dependent on the support of megacorporations for their power. At mass meetings, Maya harangued the politicians for maintaining the causes of relentless global warming. She accused them of benefiting from what she called the 'toxic profits' of the entrepreneurs, and failing to serve the interests of the people. She published the Green Charter, and created an army of Green Revolutionaries who held corporate leaders hostage and sabotaged industries heavily reliant on the old fuels. The spirit of the movement was unstoppable. During the Green period, 100 billion trees were planted and aircraft dropped mineralized rock dust on reclaimed forests to fertilize them. Agricultural needs were tended by machines operated via satellite control. The transportation system was revolutionized and cars began to operate on magnetic energy, or on water, producing oxygen as a byproduct. Fields of cannabis and hemp were grown to replace oil and timber products. Water was drawn from the oceans and desalinated.

Scientists sympathetic to Maya began to develop technologies that had been suppressed for generations because they were considered a threat to profit and jeopardized the balance of world power. Does any of this sound familiar to you? But out of fear, and in a desperate bid to strengthen their positions, the corporations and governments fused their alliances and became one ruling elite.

Maya's followers oversaw the installation of fusion reactors, which safely simulated the nuclear forces at the heart of the sun. Her movement supervised the manufacture of solar panels the size of small cities, and a global grid system which is still in place today, distributing clean power around the world along superconductor transmission lines.

Some saw Maya's Green Charter as ecological fundamentalism. Her code had to be strictly adhered to and controlled all aspects of life, from defecating to bathing, from what people wore to how they ate and how food was cooked. Air travel was restricted, nothing was thrown away, everything was recycled and food choice was limited. Meat soon became a rare delicacy. As a consequence, many people, mainly the privileged, resented the fact that their previous lifestyle had been snatched away. They

THE OLIVE READERS

didn't want to live like their great-great-great-grand-parents had.

Maya died mysteriously in 2170. The Companies claimed she died of old age, but she was little more than a hundred years old, which by then was not considered old. She had set the world on a course that calmed the seas, tamed the winds and harnessed the power of the sun. By using the Earth's natural energies, which did not wound either the atmosphere or its inhabitants, she had set a sustainable precedent. But the old corporate habits remained festering below the surface. The corporations had been forced to adjust their industries to the philosophy of the Green Charter and had embarked on a new era of profit and growth despite its restrictions. Once Maya was dead, they became powerful and expansive once more by developing and monopolizing new and more efficient energies of their own that remained sustainable. The fear that the Earth might again wreak its own havoc remained.

Despite the fact that Maya herself despised the corporations, the Green Revolutionaries eventually became another element of propaganda for the Companies. Her successor, one of her former lovers, was mysteriously murdered and Maya was added to the list of those whose names could not be mentioned. The Federation had taken over her legacy. It was as if she had never existed.

I doubted that the Commissioner knew of the secret Mayad shrines in the village: if so, there would have been several disappearances of families and public reprimands.

He was far too preoccupied promoting his own image and refurbishing his grand offices. No one seemed to mind as it meant he neglected his own work as Commissioner. Commissioners were not popular people. They were employed by the Companies ostensibly to ensure that the welfare needs of the workers were met and that efficient production was maintained. In reality, they were Company spies making sure there were no thefts from Company properties, and that employees did not have access to illegal means of communication and information. They also made sure that no one reproduced anything copyrighted by another Company. Occasionally we heard stories of villagers elsewhere, in another faraway Company, producing oil from local olives and selling it, instead of shipping it to the Olive Country. Once caught, these people were never seen or heard of again.

The Commissioner knew where I was going, yet made no reference to Hephzibah. He looked nervous, and his soft, carefully manicured hands rested on my arm as if in sympathy.

'Now that the soldiers have left the village, life can start returning to normal,' he said. 'Of course, it will mean a lot more work for me. Conflicts like these always do. People take advantage of the chaos and get up to all sorts of tricks the Company wouldn't like.' His eyes narrowed and he stared suspiciously at me.

'I think they have other more pressing things to do, such as organizing death rituals for their butchered loved ones,' I countered, and walked away quickly, heading for the tiny white house built on to the harbour wall.

This was Sengita's home. Only she knew how to keep dead flesh sweet in the heat. In her lifetime she had brought many villagers into the world and then later prepared them for another journey. She lived on the harbour wall with her orphaned grandson, Joachim. Joachim, who would always have the body of a child, followed his grandmother everywhere. He spoke in a strange tongue that only Sengita understood, and sat underneath her petticoats, scratching and gnawing at her legs until they bled. His parents, Sengita's only son and his young wife, had been marched to a boat along with other villagers and taken out to sea by soldiers who had passed through the village when the conflict began. The soldiers had returned alone, spattered with blood. One or two bodies were later washed ashore, but Sengita's son and daughter-in-law were never found. From that day she kept a light in the window overlooking the estuary to guide him and his wife home. She never gave up hope.

Sengita opened the door to the tiny room built onto the side of the main wall where the water lapped. It had been some time since I had seen her. Her eyebrows had grown grey but her hair remained thick and black and she had on the same red waistcoat she had worn at Hephzibah's birth.

She greeted me warmly and I smiled at her.

'Don't be afraid,' she said, taking my hand. 'There is nothing to be afraid of.'

She ushered me into the room. It was here that Sengita fought the sun. The door was made of a special hard wood that only grew on the north side of the hills, and had been cut to fit the doorway perfectly without letting in a chink of light. The only window was shuttered and any gaps between the slats were stuffed with threadbare shawls. The stone floor was splashed with lavender water and even the roof, upon which the sun beat mercilessly, seemed to keep the room cool. It was as if death itself had conspired with Sengita and sprayed its icy breath upon the walls.

Any light that had managed to filter through the roof tiles reflected on the lime-washed walls and fell on the white sheet draping the body, which lay on a crude table in a corner of the room. Sengita closed the door, leaving her grandchild outside, and took me to the body. As she lifted the sheet, her sun-scarred face smiled as if greeting a guest. I gagged on a strong unfamiliar scent and later, whenever I smelled frankincense, cedar or myrrh, I was reminded of untimely death.

Sengita began to comb my sister's long hair with her fingers so that it hung in loose strands to the floor. The face, with its filament of fine white bones and bleached flesh, was like a mask. The right eye remained open with its iris like a planet fixed in orbit. It seemed to stare straight at me wherever I stood.

'Can't you close it, Sengita?' I asked, unnerved. My voice echoed around the room as Joachim began to rattle frantically at the door.

'Sometimes the dead need to watch the living,' the old woman replied.

There was no skin beneath the nose to show the scar that had once risen from Hephzibah's mouth. I stared down at the half-eaten face and felt nauseous. I turned to Sengita. She knew what I was seeking.

'It's not there,' she said knowingly.

'Of course not,' I replied abruptly. 'But beyond doubt this is my sister.'

Sengita pulled the sheet back over the body and smoothed it over as if preparing a bed. As she closed the door behind me, she whispered, 'It's not me you need to convince.'

She led me through a kitchen full of jars and drying herbs and onto a small stone terrace that extended out from the harbour wall and looked over the sea. On the terrace stood a rickety table and two chairs shaded by a large red umbrella.

'I'm sure you need a drink after that,' she said, inviting me to sit down.

I nodded enthusiastically and she went back into the kitchen to return with a tray containing a bowl of plump, green olives, two glasses, a large bottle of whisky, cut lemon and a bowl of ice.

'Let's start with this,' she said, unscrewing the top of the bottle and filling both glasses to the rim. 'Never say die.' She winked, then held her glass up to the sun and threw back her head, pouring the amber liquid down her throat. Then she dropped into one of the chairs, her skirt and petticoats puffing up around her like a mushroom, and Joachim scuttled under them. Light filtered through the umbrella, reddening our skins.

'This is a sorry business, Jephzat. I know how close you were to your sister. I remember when she was born. You held her before her mother did and the two of you grew to be inseparable. This must be very hard for you.'

She poured herself another glass while I sipped from mine, staring out beyond the mouth of the river to an impassive shimmering sea. A gentle wind carried the faint hum of the energy fields that floated like islands beyond the horizon.

Sengita took the second glass more slowly. The terrace was full of pots of herbs and flowers, jars containing flakes of dried serpent skin and powders of all colours. Fishing nets hung over the wall.

'Now that the soldiers are gone things will get back to normal. They won't be returning again as some sort of agreement is being worked out. At least, that is what the Commissioner is saying.'

I remained silent.

'I know it's hard for you, Jephzat, and I know what went on in your house.'

'You don't know, Sengita. You're like the rest of them; you don't know anything.' I rounded on her viciously. 'You think you do, but no one knows what has been going on in our house. Who offered to help us when the soldiers arrived? No one. I came to the village and begged for help. I might as well have been speaking to the dead. We were left alone with the enemy and now everyone is going to say we collaborated, just because we fed them. But it was either that or we died. All of us. We wouldn't be much use to the Company then, would we? Who else in this village would have done differently? What would you have done?'

'Poisoned them,' she screeched, slapping her thighs and bursting into a raucous laugh that sent nearby seagulls into flight. Then she fixed her dark, shrewd eyes upon me.

'You and your family must be careful now. Peace will bring recrimination and you are obvious targets. You're still considered strangers here, unlike the villagers who have been here for several generations now and created their own community. They resent the fact that, except for your sister, you have kept yourselves separate and aloof. But since the village heard about her and the soldiers she would have stood little chance – had she stayed alive. Even with your sister's death, you should still fear the anger of the village. Go into hiding with your parents until emotions have cooled.'

'How can we leave? The Company will support the villagers and will not give permission for us to leave. Anyway, I don't want to go. Everything I know is here.'

Sengita's skirts shifted as Joachim fidgeted. She reached over and put her arm around my shoulders.

'My darling child, calm yourself.' She rummaged in one of the pockets in her waistcoat and gave me two tiny pills from a glass phial, instructing me to place them under my tongue. 'Ignatia. It will calm the grief.'

She was right. I wasn't getting upset about the soldiers. I didn't care about them any more. I was grieving for Hephzibah. She had gone, and how was I going to live without her? I sobbed miserably in the old woman's arms.

'These are hard times, Jephzat, very hard times. But they are lost on those as young as you because you have no memory of how things used to be. You have no access to anything which can tell you how it was, and if you try to find out, you're risking your life.'

'I know how things were. My parents have told and shown me.'

I knew revealing such things could be dangerous. After all, I wasn't sure if Sengita could be trusted. She was known for her noisy disagreements with the Commissioner, although that alone did not make her trustworthy. But what

I had confessed didn't seem to register with her. She merely rubbed her forehead and then, in a movement that surprised me, pulled at her hairline and clawed back her wig. Her beautiful black hair lay on the table. She was bald.

'That bloody wig has been annoying me for days now in this heat,' she said, scratching at her bare skull. 'I only wear it so that I don't look too different. I'm already in the Commissioner's black books. I don't want to give him any more excuses to brand me subversive.'

She turned and looked at me. 'You know what I'm talking about, don't you?'

I nodded, and knew then that Sengita was reliable. Like us, she had precious books carefully hidden somewhere in her house. Like so many of us, when she felt safe, she picked one out, blew off the dust and began to turn the pages. We exchanged knowing looks and laughed and laughed until Joachim crawled out from under his grandmother's skirts to see what the joke was about.

'I was right,' Sengita said suddenly, banging her glass on the table so that its contents spilled. 'Your sister had a bad start with her split lip, but the worst is yet to come.'

She turned to me and ran her fingers along my mouth. 'Thank heavens you weren't born with a disfigurement like that. With your obstinacy and honesty things would have been a lot worse. Your sister was bad enough.'

This did not offend me, because she said it fondly as if I were a daughter, but I still thought it ridiculous to believe that a physical defect implied an inherent curse.

'Normally I feel very close to those I help bring into this world, but with your sister I felt nothing. It is for you I have these feelings even though I did not attend your birth. From the moment Hephzibah was born I knew something was wrong, and this was before I saw her lip. It was as if she was sucking all my energy from me. I was weak and drained after her birth and felt none of my usual exhilaration when a new child comes to us.'

She shrugged her shoulders and examined her glass. I wanted to defend Hephzibah but knew in my heart that Sengita's observations touched on the truth.

I drained the last drops from my glass and rose to leave. Sengita escorted me to the front door. She embraced me warmly and wished me luck. I left a coin on the step of the doorway, as is the custom here for those who keep the dead, and turned to walk back, bracing myself to meet the hostile stares of those I passed.

9

I did not go back through the village. Instead, I took a path which skirted the side of the citrus groves and led to the summerhouse. It stood by what had once been a small lake but which the heat had since turned to dust; we could now no longer afford the cost of the water needed to fill it. I had not been to the summerhouse since Hephzibah's disappearance and found it difficult to approach the small, dilapidated building, as it held so many memories. The summerhouse had always seemed newly painted to us as small children: its white wood exterior once shone in the sunlight and Dolores had planted damask roses and jasmine, whose green shoots had entwined around the latticework and smothered the roof. Seen from the house, it hardly looked like a building at all, more a bank of foliage. Now, flaked paint hung like fingernails from the wood, and some of the latticework was rotting, throwing a tracery of distorted light upon the floor.

When the heat was unbearable we used to eat as a family in the summerhouse. Manos spread a bleached white tablecloth over a garden table and brought us freshly baked bread, cheese, olives and tea. The summerhouse was open on all sides and caught the breezes coming in from the sea. Hephzibah and I often used to lie on the floor by the wide door to catch any air that moved. She would jab at flies in the air, which irritated me. Sometimes we would sleep there on mattresses, always waking up the next morning in each other's arms.

I pushed away a threadbare cushion stained with what looked like blood and lay on a wide bench built into the summerhouse around its seven angled walls. Each wall was open above the bench, presenting a different view of the house. From where I was sitting I could see the turret of the east wing rise above the trees, and beyond it caught glimpses of villagers shaking the olive trees for the fruit to fall onto the nets they had spread along the terraces. No one really knew the exact origins of the house. Like everything else from the past, it had its own fiction that was now accepted as truth.

The origin of the village was also unknown, but it is likely it began as a small settlement of fishermen and their families. When the Companies took over the empire, the village was emptied of its original inhabitants. No one knows where their descendants are now. Their successors were brought to the deserted village by the Olive Company to be trained to tend the olives, harvest them and produce olive oil.

These refugees walked into their new homes to find cups of coffee still half drunk, maggots in pots of food about to be served, dishes still to be put away and cots whose covers hinted at the hasty snatching of babies from their sleep. Small pieces of illegible scribbled paper were found folded behind shelves and pressed into cracks in walls. The new arrivals packed the belongings of the previous inhabitants into boxes and stacked them in attics ready for their return. It was less an act of kindness than an expression of the hope that one day they would also be able to return to their former homes.

It was the olive that united this group of individuals whose ancestors would have spoken different languages and whose looks indicated their disparate roots. A new hybrid tongue – a sort of dialect – grew out of their desire to communicate with one another, which they used alongside official Federese. They took to wandering through the olive groves, aimlessly at first. They stroked the ancient gnarled trunks and spent hours gazing up at the thick, spreading branches, the leaves shifting grey and green against the sky. For them, the olive tree provided comfort in its permanence and solidity. These new arrivals had been uprooted and taken as Company property to a strange country, but surrounding them were the sentinels of time, witnesses to a vanished era of inheritance and belonging.

They grew to love the trees, and each villager had a favourite. Long neglected, the olives were tangled with undergrowth; many had grown ugly tumours, others had weakened from years of disease and their leaves curled from infestations of olive fly and mould. Out of love, but in ignorance, the new arrivals pruned badly and set about hacking away at waist-thick branches. The Company had initially forgotten the village and as a result the first harvests were sparse. Finally, Company advisers arrived to test soil and give instructions on how to maintain the ocean of silver-leaved trees that spread over the surrounding hills and terraces. They trained the inhabitants in propagation and pruning techniques, gave harvest targets and oversaw the production of the oil until the villagers could manage on their own.

At first, the villagers did not know the names of the varied species of tree so gave them family names of their own. Soon afterwards, a beautiful old carving of an olive tree was found on the back of a small cupboard door in the tiny home of a young couple. Words in a strange and elegant script had been carved into the tree's branches and trunk. Beneath each word was a translation in Federese. People crammed into the poky room at all hours, eager to discuss the meaning of the woodcut and marvel at the mystery of it. How could it be that the tree appeared to have been carved before the creation of the Federation, and yet words in Federese had also been found on it? Some put it down to Company subterfuge or a mysterious shift in time, a trick. Others were more intrigued by the meanings of the mysterious words, as even in Federese they meant little. Were they the names of the families who lived in the village previously? Were they directions for harvesting or pressing? The cupboard door was taken off its hinges and placed in the square. Every morning after the daily salutation by the villagers to the Company, its president and directors, people crouched down before the door and examined it minutely. They incanted the words, feeling their breath rise up from their bellies to be shaped and moulded by their tongues into sounds that began to comfort them: Santa Caterina, Mortatele, Kosino. One morning, when a Company Commissioner at one of the daily salutations had harangued them for failing to meet harvest quotas, they stood closer than usual to the carving. Each villager, out of fear for their lives, was asking the carving to bless the village with a good harvest for the next year. United in their meditation, they did not hear the cry of the small child clinging to her mother's skirts.

'Why do trees have names? Are they like humans?' she asked. Her mother tried to quieten her but the little girl persisted until someone in the crowd let out a yell: 'That's it. These are the names of the families of trees.' So the trees growing around the village were given the names from the carving – and while it was accepted that these names probably did not match the trees as originally intended, there was pleasure in giving back to the olives what was believed to be theirs.

Some of the new inhabitants mended the boats that had been left behind, and took to fishing to supplement the villagers' diet. If their harvest more than met their needs, the extra fish had to be dried and sent to the Company that dealt in all fish-associated products. It was illegal to sell to private buyers, but of course it happened, despite the countless number of spies from the Fish Country that hung around the harbour, conspicuous by their idle hands.

In the absence of any known history, the villagers also began to create stories that gave them a make-believe inheritance, which I embellished further, mainly for Heph-zibah's sake. She loved to hear me tell stories and would always beg me for more. Some I made up, or I would visit Pesh, one of the fishermen and the best storyteller in the village – until the soldiers killed him.

Centuries ago, no one knows exactly when, a huge parcel of land overlooking the mouth of the estuary was given as a gift to a troubadour by his doting king. The young man was said to be more beautiful than any woman in the court, and the king loved him more than all his wives. The troubadour's music wove spells and whole banquets were said to drift into the air when he sang, so that flanks of venison, huge bowls of fruit and jewel-encrusted goblets of wine hung over the heads of the diners, who finally left sated by song.

Unfortunately the troubadour neglected his land, preferring to concentrate on court dalliances. When he died, a distant relative from his mother's side came to claim the land and planted the olive groves. He built a house, befitting that of a landowner, away from the village and overlooking the estuary. It was a grand building, fancifully overworked. The owner took to seducing every woman far and wide, regardless of their age or marital status. Within a few years he had sired twenty-six sons and daughters, all left abandoned as babies on his doorstep. He had not the heart to reject them, and handed them over to local women to wet-nurse and later employed a fleet of tutors, cooks and guardians to look after his growing brood. After his death, the children, unable to agree on one sole heir, all left the house, and it was taken over by a succession of wealthy families, who each built their own stylized addition to the original buildings. It became the temporary headquarters of the Olive Company, but before they moved on they ripped out their technology and left it empty. When they gave it to my parents it was on the understanding that they lived in only a small part of the house. The rest was callously abandoned to the dust and spiders' webs.

The turret of the east wing rose in gothic splendour above the pines. Hephzibah and I called it the Turret of the Red Scarf because of a story Manos had told us when we were small. A previous owner, she said, had spent his life trying to end it. He locked himself away in his study, obsessed with engineering the perfect suicide. Many of his attempts involved strange contraptions made up of pulleys and timing mechanisms that wrenched his body this way and that, or machines that looked like the inside working of a clock, with cogs that sliced a man's anatomy with the precision of a surgeon's knife. He inadvertently made a fortune from the patents on these deathly creations during the Environmental Revolution, when they were discovered to serve more useful functions in kitchens and bathrooms because they used little energy. But his suicide attempts always failed, and left his body grotesquely patterned with scars.

Despite their wealth, the man's wife grew weary of her husband's strange obsessions. The longer he shut himself away in his study, the more she hated him and the more she brooded on revenge. One day he abandoned his complex mechanical inventions and asked his wife to knit him a red scarf. He gave her the precise measurements. It was to be a handspan wide and one foot shorter than the height of the turret in the east wing. The cotton thread was brought over in huge skeins by boat and soon the house was filled with the rhythmic sound of clicking knitting needles. The wife's fingers lost their skin to the bone and bled heavily, staining the thread a deeper red. Finally, she took the completed scarf to her husband. He climbed to the top of the turret, fixed one end of it around a stone statue and tied the other end around his neck, then jumped. As he flew through the air he realized that his wife had not followed his instructions accurately and had knitted the scarf to within only a few inches of the turret's full height. The extra inches were added by the weight of his body stretching the scarf. He crumpled as he hit the ground and his wife found his broken body. He was still alive but now in her power; it was just as she had planned.

He spent the rest of his days prone and paralysed in the east wing's old schoolroom, while his wife squandered his money and petted her young lovers.

This was Hephzibah's favourite story and she would drag me around the forbidden parts of the house looking for the red scarf. 'Don't be silly, it's only a story,' I chided, not even sure of its true meaning. It would take days for us to explore one wing and then move on to another, our tiny feet echoing in long, vaulted corridors. Finally we reached the east wing and entered the abandoned school-room, and above our heads, woven through the rafters, hung a long rust-red scarf.

I didn't tell Hephzibah, but I was convinced Manos had put the scarf up there herself. Later, I wasn't so sure. Who in the village would knit such a long scarf just to surprise two inquisitive little girls?

Excited by our discovery, we spent even more time exploring. There was never an end to the rooms in the house. No sooner had we discovered one than it seemed to lead into another. Some had high, vaulted ceilings with rafters, like the interior of a barn, while others had ornately plastered ceilings and high, heavy doors and walls clad in worm-eaten wood panelling, which made them gloomy and dusty. None of the rooms we found was locked, except one. Once we thought we heard someone moving inside, which made us even more determined to open the door. We poked all manner of things into the lock until it finally creaked open, hindered still by its weight.

CHRISTINE AZIZ

We were confronted by hundreds of boxes piled on top of one another, almost filling the room. We began to open one of them, speculating on finding hidden treasure, gold and jewels, playthings. Instead, it was full of freshly harvested violet-black Maraiolo olives. The implications of this find were lost on Hephzibah, who was instantly disappointed and soon lost interest. Maraiolo olives were nothing special – they grew plentifully around the village because of the trees' tolerance to wind and salty air. But I knew, even then, the penalty for siphoning off a Company's product and did not want our family to be held responsible for this. From my reaction Hephzibah knew something was wrong and wormed the reason out of me.

'Then what we must do is find the person who's taken these olives in the first place.'

As she said this there was a faint shuffling behind some of the boxes. Hephzibah rushed to peer over them and screamed. I joined her and saw a man crouched down behind them. He raised his head and gazed directly at me. I flinched at the startling brightness of his blue eyes.

'Don't report me to the Commissioner.' He stood up to his full height and frowned.

I was about to reassure him when Hephzibah suddenly dived straight for him. He fell backwards, banging his head against the edge of a box, and lay there stunned as she flew at him, her fists pummelling his chest. He tried to fend off her blows in a way that would not hurt her and I leaped over to pull her off him.

'Leave me,' she screamed. 'He's a thief! He's putting our lives into danger just so that he can sell a few stolen olives.'

I knew how hard it was for most of the villagers to

earn enough to eat and did not blame them for storing a few olives for themselves. The Olive Country had millions of olive trees. Father said we had more olives than cockroaches. What difference would a few missing olives make? I looked across at the young man, who was now dusting down his clothes and trembling slightly. He stood in dignified silence as I urged my sister to leave the room with me.

'Hephzibah, we must forget we ever saw this person. Who is ever going to find out? Dolores and Father never come to these rooms, nor does Manos.'

I put my arm around her shoulders and looked at the intruder with sympathy.

'I think the best thing to do is to leave you here,' I suggested, and asked him for the key. As I did so I glanced quickly up at the high windows, which he could easily reach by climbing the boxes. He paused for a moment, gave a half-smile and handed me a large brass key. Hephzibah snatched it and flounced out of the room. I turned to the man. 'I will do my best,' I said and whispered, 'Leave as soon as we are gone.'

We locked the door behind us and ran quickly through the maze of corridors. Hephzibah reached our parents first. They were sitting together on one of the verandas. Both were dozing, taking advantage of the cool, soft rain that had begun to fall. Hephzibah woke them with a start and gabbled out what had happened.

Dolores jumped up, clearly alarmed, while Father woke slowly, trying to take stock of the situation.

'Is this true?' he asked me.

As the oldest, I was expected to verify everything my younger sister said, and up until now I always had, whether she told the truth or not, but an image of the man's startling blue eyes would not leave me.

'No. She's lying.' I did not dare to look at Hephzibah.

'What do you mean, I'm lying? How dare you? You're the liar.'

She suddenly pounced on me in much the same way she had attacked the man. Both our parents pulled her off.

'There are olives in this room, stacked in boxes as high as the ceiling. They're hiding them there and selling them off from our house. Jephzat said we would all be killed if the Company finds out. I don't want to be executed, even if she does. I recognized the thief. They have already started pruning the trees and I'm sure he's one of the pruners. We can go early tomorrow to the terraces and catch him.'

Father looked at me intently and when he saw me shake my head settled back in his chair.

'I tell you what, let's have something to eat and then we'll go and search the rooms for boxes.'

My mother, who always settled for the easiest option, rang a little bell summoning Manos.

I dawdled over tea, chewing my food slowly, chattering non-stop about nothing in particular, all the while playing for time, while Hephzibah glowered at me across the table and fidgeted.

'We must go to the Commissioner immediately and tell him before it's too late,' she pressed. 'He might discover it himself; you know how often he comes snooping to this house.'

'As soon as we have finished eating,' Father said, winking at me.

This only annoyed Hephzibah further, and she jumped up, violently knocking back her chair, and ran off before any of us could say anything more. Dolores looked across at me.

'Are you sure this has all been made up?'

'Yes. You know what Hephzibah's like; she loves to hear stories. And it was one of my stories that I told her days ago. I must have told it so well, she believed it.'

This seemed to satisfy Dolores, but my father rose from his chair, took the key from me and suggested that I show him the room.

An hour later we were still looking and poor Father was getting irritated. I had told him the room was in the east wing, when really it was in the west.

The next day he continued to search with me. When finally we reached the west wing and stood outside the room, Father turned the lock and my heart beat fast as the door opened. I could barely disguise my sigh of relief as sunlight fell from the high windows to illuminate an empty room.

10

In the summerhouse I felt a chill creep over my shoulders even though the early evening sun was still warm. There was a rich, syrupy smell of fermenting fruit and sulphur, as if a match had been recently extinguished.

I did not want to tell my parents what I had seen at Sengita's, needing to delay the moment for as long as possible, so I lay down on the bench and closed my eyes, trying hard to recall my sister's voice and the events that preceded her absence.

This war had been nothing more than a skirmish compared to those that took place in the early days of the Federation. But the Olive Country should have known better than to have taken on such a powerful neighbour. It amounted to nothing more than a small dog snapping at a monster's heels. This particular 'monster' was the most powerful of all the Companies within the Federation, changing the landscapes it had taken over beyond recognition. You would not recognize it as the poor, scrubby region it was in the last millennium. Its dry savannah is now full of huge covered reservoirs, and more fertile than you could imagine. The land this Company covers is relatively small, but its power comes from its ability to manufacture potable water. Once it was called Aqua, but we now refer to it as the Water Country. As with any product that guarantees unlimited profit, its means of manufacture remains a closely guarded secret.

The discovery of a water-making formula changed the old balances of power, especially since it followed on from Maya's Green Revolution, which had outlawed fossil and nuclear energy and turned incontrovertibly to the elements for energy. From what I was told there was little choice. These old fuels were poisoning the planet and there was little time left to save it. After the terrible floods, water became scarce, despite the desalination plants, and vicious wars were fought over the control of its sources. The secret formula enabled water to be produced in vast quantities and at the time this was seen as a blessing. Tired of thirst and war, people were eager to see an equitable distribution of the manufactured resource, even though they complained it did not have the sweetness of water that sprang naturally from the earth. Vast tracts of land were turned into reservoirs and once-moribund lakes teemed with life, resurrecting the communities that had lived around them before. Then Maya died, and for a short while her rules for the equitable distribution of water remained. But the takeover of the empire made this status quo impossible to maintain. Those who held the formula fought amongst themselves to form a Company – knowing that being able to produce such a valuable resource could make it the most powerful member of the Federation and the leader in the eventual colonization of space.

Once formed, the Water Company held back its supply to force up the tariff, and ignored the grumblings of fellow Federation members who were made to pay. There was an unspectacular skirmish when the Olive Country, squeezed by the high prices, tried to siphon off some of the water produced by its Superpower neighbour. Despite calls for restraint from the Federation, the Water Company sent its soldiers to take over a patch of Olive land that ran along the borders. The water theft was a rare act of disobedience in the Federation and unsettled those privileged enough to know about it. Naturally, we fought back.

But I knew enough of the past for the fighting to hardly matter.

During the last skirmish the Water soldiers had forced their way into our home and demanded that they stay. There were fourteen of them and they were on their way to capture the estuary's main port, forty kilometres from the village. They had to wait in our village for reinforcements before moving on, having already burned and blasted their way through other settlements. Now they held their weapons to our heads. There was little my parents could do, although my father insisted they ate alone. These were simple men who knew their place, and they took their war technology to the kitchen. The two officers insisted on eating upstairs at the vast mahogany table with silver cutlery and crystal goblets, but they, too, ate alone.

Manos and the others refused to come to the house once the soldiers arrived, so Dolores and Hephzibah cooked for them. Father spent most of his time in the citrus groves and the laboratory and only came to the house for meals. I locked myself in my room to avoid them, coming out only when hunger forced me to.

I hated the soldiers and what they represented. I loathed their smell, the oil they rubbed on their shaven heads, the coarse cloth of their uniforms. Their pale, moist eyes repulsed me, as did their puffy skin, which made them look as if they had been underwater for a long time.

I recalled one of my previous visits to the summer-house. I had gone to be alone but found Hephzibah already there. She looked startled. It was as if she was expecting someone and was disappointed to see me. I can still see her sitting on the summerhouse steps, her head leaning against the archway, knees drawn up to her chest. She was chewing on a sweet that one of the soldiers had given her.

I sat beside her and remained silent for a long time. She knew I despised the way she communicated with the soldiers, and for some days now we had been avoiding each other. I missed her, but their arrival had shifted family alliances. I had become complicit in my father's silent defiance. The two of us had shut ourselves away from the rest of the house, while Hephzibah allied herself to my mother, serving the soldiers and meeting their every need. I blocked my ears whenever I heard Hephzibah's slow, sleepy laugh rise up from the kitchen, and felt betrayed when I noticed how Dolores had begun to wear lipstick again.

I had no choice but to remain in the same house as the soldiers. It would be dangerous to go elsewhere, and besides I loved Hephzibah and could not think of life without her. Watching her long, lean back in the protective shade of the summerhouse, she looked more beautiful than ever. I wanted to share her betrayal and the consequent intimacy this would have brought, but could not. Instead, I tried to unite us through my hatred of these strangers. But what she told me then was to drive us even further apart. She bragged how she played a game with the men. She explained how she had given each one a number and during the day tried to bring the number of the soldier she desired into her conversation. I suddenly remembered the strange questions she asked me on my infrequent visits to the kitchen and which I ignored. 'Is Joachim Twelve yet?' 'Do you really think Thirteen is an unlucky number?' Sometimes she found herself with two men waiting for her in the summerhouse, as in some sentences she had inadvertently mentioned two numbers. 'You only have Five buttons on your uniform. Have you lost One?' She had really wanted Five that night, but One had appeared too.

I buried my head in my knees as she told me everything, suddenly seeming so grown-up. Although I could feel the familiar warmth of her body close to mine, I could smell wine on her breath and I felt a distance, like a vast arid plain, lying between us. Her voice seemed faint as if she were in another room. One lover, she said, had a small penis, but his exquisite hands ran over her like water, seeking out the secrets of her body with the gentle expertise of one who knew where his treasure lay. Another cried and shivered in her arms after he came, calling the name of the lover he had left behind. Hephzibah had not minded.

'Affection has its own deceits, and if there is comfort in the calling of a missed lover to escape the tragedy of war, then why not?'

One of the officers had been injured, his groin and part of his left inner thigh sliced away. She had not been afraid of his scars, and kissed what was left of him there. 'Nobody undresses me the way he does,' she murmured. 'It takes him a long time, and even on the coolest evenings I never feel cold. He leaves my slippers until the end and as he slips them off I come.'

I let out a burst of scornful laughter.

'It's funny thinking of you having your feet licked. When they run their hands over you, don't you think of who they have killed – Pesh and his friends, people we know and love? Look at that smoke over there. That's the work of their comrades. Soon it will be us.'

At first I thought she had not been listening to me but then she spoke quietly.

'Yes, I have thought of those things. It changes nothing. This war will not last long. Their country will flood us if we do not capitulate. All this is just a game to the Water people. They know they are powerful. Imagine having the capability to flood this planet and hold everyone to ransom. We are on the wrong side, Jephzat. But you and Father always will be.'

I suddenly felt very hot and my stomach ached. It seemed as though everything liquid inside my body would drain away. I thought of the man with his red scarf tied to his neck leaping from the turret. This was how it must have been for him when he jumped – a dreadful lurching in the stomach, then floating downwards as time stood still until the terrible snapping of bone.

'Afterwards we eat oranges,' Hephzibah went on dreamily, as if in a trance. She moistened her lips with her tongue. I could think of nothing more to say. I looked at the orange peel covering the summerhouse like a golden carpet and walked quickly towards the house. When I reached my room I could smell oranges on my hands, as if I, too, had lain with the soldiers.

11

I did not come out of my room for a long time. One evening, as I lay on my bed, staring out of my window and over the thick branches of the olive trees, Hephzibah stood outside my door. Her voice was low and urgent and she refused to go away. I opened the door a crack.

'What, run out of numbers?' I asked sarcastically.

She was holding a plate of peeled oranges, olives and thick slices of ham.

'I'm sorry, it's all I could find.'

I ignored her offering as she pushed through the door and placed the plate beside the bed before retreating again.

'You've got to help me. I'm in terrible trouble.'

Her eyes were bright and nervous as she hung back in the room. 'I have to leave as soon as I can. But I have to leave in such a way that nobody notices, not the Company, nor our parents, no one. I can't be held prisoner here.'

'What do you mean?'

She put a finger to her lips and when I began to shake uncontrollably she ran to me and held me to her.

'Sengita's boy, Joachim, saw me with one of the soldiers in the summerhouse. He had been watching us. He ran away when he knew he had been seen, but goodness knows how long he's been spying on me. He's bound to tell Sengita, and then the whole of the village will

CHRISTINE AZIZ

know. She's never liked me. They will come for me. They will turn against all of us. I have to leave soon. I can't stay here, Jephzat, I can't.'

I felt a heavy chill of dread.

She was right, she had to go. But where?

'The borders are too heavily guarded to leave the country now,' I said. 'But you could stay in hiding somewhere further up the estuary, and wait until the war is over, and then we could leave together.'

I don't know why I suggested this. I didn't want to suddenly uproot myself in this way and live the life of a fugitive, which is what would happen. Unless we had permission from the Company to move, residency elsewhere would be illegal. I had heard of those who had fled and spent the rest of their lives running like hunted animals from one hideout to another, hungry and trusting no one.

'I can't leave them,' she said desperately. At first I thought she meant our parents, and then realized she was referring to the soldiers. 'I can't bear to be without them. I love them all. What will I do when they are gone? Wait for the villagers to come and kill me? If I go into hiding it puts the whole village in danger. The only solution is to leave with them.'

I was puzzled. Hephzibah was not normally so concerned about the consequence of her actions upon others. There had to be another reason for leaving. Her arms were still around me when she whispered, 'Whatever happens I have to leave. I'm pregnant and I want this child. It's mine. It's the only thing I've ever had that's truly mine, and no one is going to take it away from me. I want to have it the old way, growing inside my body.

I don't want it developing in a birth-centre along with lots of other numbered foetuses in tiny glass cubicles, its cells harvested to grow limbs and organs for complete strangers. I want to have it the way women used to have their children, you know, like Mother, like it says in the . . .'

She checked herself and broke off. Then she explained how one of the officers had told her that the reinforcements would be arriving tomorrow and suggested she leave with them.

'Somehow I have to be seen to die,' Hephzibah said with a stubborn tilt of her chin, 'so that I can be released for ever. So that there will be no recriminations against anyone once I am gone . . .'

Her voice trailed off again, but there had been a defiance in it that I had not heard before. It filled me with both pride and fear: she was planning the impossible.

12

The reinforcements came early. I heard the sound of wheels on the gravel in front of the house. Men's voices greeted one another. Then I heard a woman's voice with an accent I did not recognize. I rushed to the other side of the house and peered from Father's room, which overlooked the front gardens. I could see the tops of several armoured vehicles, which were lining the drive outside the house, and more soldiers climbing out of their domes. They looked tired and were covered in a thin layer of fine grey dust.

Hephzibah was with them. I couldn't see her face as her back was turned to me. She had changed into a long skirt of rough brown material with a white scarf tied round her head in a style I had not seen before. She must have sensed someone was watching her because she turned around and immediately looked up at me, revealing a stranger's face. This woman's face was longer than Hephzibah's, she was darker, too, from the sun, but her hair was the same length and had an identical copper sheen.

When I walked past the kitchen, Dolores looked surprised but said nothing. She was busy cooking food for the new arrivals, some of whom were sprawling in chairs around the table, drinking coffee. I headed for the front of the house, my feet echoing on the marble floors. On the veranda, the heat smacked me with such force that for a moment I felt dizzy and swayed a little as I walked down the steps leading into the garden.

'Are you all right?'

A pair of cool hands steadied me and a woman's voice spoke softly and gently. There was a faint scent of roses about her.

'I'm fine. It's just the heat. I'm not used to it. I've been keeping cool in the house,' I mumbled. My vision cleared and I saw the woman I had spotted from my window standing beside me. Her likeness to Hephzibah faded slightly on closer inspection, but there was still a strong resemblance. She did not have a scar rising from her upper lip, but her eyes exuded the same iridescence. Her smile did not devastate in the same way as Hephzibah's, but instead was charming and warm.

'Would you like some coffee?' I asked.

She nodded and looked nervously over her shoulder at the soldiers as we went inside, but they appeared not to notice her. She seemed to relax a little as we took our coffee back into the garden, and I invited her to sit in the shade of a eucalyptus while I brought her some food. She seemed grateful and moved wearily over to the tree, sitting down with a sigh. I turned towards the house again and saw Hephzibah standing in the doorway with one of the officers she had 'befriended'. She was carrying a tray of bread and olives, and was clearly surprised by what she saw. Both women stared at each other as if suddenly accosted by their own reflection. The few soldiers who dallied around the vehicles remarked upon the resemblance of the two women while I waited uncomfortably. Hephzibah said something to the officer, then walked steadily towards us. She set the tray before us and without acknowledging me turned around and returned to the house.

She stood for a moment on the veranda before calling me over. The officer had gone, and I excused myself from our visitor.

Hephzibah could not conceal her excitement. 'Riffa has said I can join him with the soldiers when they leave.' She curled a finger through my hair and nodded towards the woman. 'He says I can take her place. No one will know the difference until afterwards and then it will be too late to do anything. He's the senior official and high up in the hierarchy back home. He says he can sort things out with the Water Company. Everyone will think I'm her, if I wear her clothes.'

'But you'll become a prisoner of war! You can't leave her behind. What will she do here? The Company won't permit it. They'll execute her.'

Hephzibah stared at me and her finger tugged at my hair until I winced.

Full of foreboding, I returned to the woman, who had been watching us. 'Who is that?' she asked.

'My sister.'

'She could be my sister too,' the woman said with a half-smile. 'But they say everyone has a double somewhere in the universe. If that is true, then I've just met mine. I wonder if this is a good omen.'

'Do you need one?'

'I do. I want to go home to my family.'

She leaned back against the tree and studied me as I poured olive oil over the salad and dribbled some on to my bread. Its fresh pungency – medicinal almost – was a comfort.

'It's so good to rest. We've been travelling for a long time and have been under attack. I'm lucky to be alive,' she said, and smiled again, revealing perfect teeth. Both of us were hungry – I hadn't eaten for a long time and neither, it seemed, had she. Eating was a good excuse to remain silent.

When she had finished, she brushed the crumbs from her skirt. To avoid conversation I found myself quickly clearing up the dishes and offering her more coffee. She preferred water, so I returned to the kitchen with the tray. There I saw Hephzibah standing amongst the soldiers, looking radiant in a blue silk dress that skimmed her breasts and hips. One of them had an arm around her waist and I glared at him as I reached for a jug and placed it under the tap.

'Remember that you only drink that stuff thanks to us,' he said to me as the water fell clear and sparkling.

'Not all the water we use is produced by you. Some of it's natural, thank goodness. Your stuff tastes like poison.'

He removed his arm from around my sister and moved over to join me at the sink, running a hand beneath the flowing water.

'That's what your Company will have you believe. But the truth is, if you had to rely on water as a natural resource, you and everyone else in this miserable little country would have died of thirst by now and your scabby little olives would be more withered than they are now.'

His companions laughed.

'Most of this planet is covered in water and there's still a way to make salt water sweet. We are not as dependent on you as you would like to think,' I retorted.

'Salt water? Sweet? What kind of a fool are you?

Which Company prefers to spend money on making salt water potable when it's cheaper to buy it from us?'

'Why don't you make the formula available to everyone so we could all produce our own?'

The kitchen fell suddenly silent except for the sound of water splashing over the jug's rim. Hephzibah lowered her head and turned away from me.

'It's obvious, isn't it, why you don't. Because without it you'd have no power. Look how you've managed to subordinate this Company, just by threatening to flood us. It's easy, isn't it? Send out the soldiers, let them kill a few people, burn a few houses and olive groves and then threaten to open the floodgates on us. This little war is just a bit of muscle-flexing to show the Federation who's boss.'

I am sure the officer would have punched me if he had not been so surprised at my daring. His fists were clenched and sweat had broken out in greasy drops on his forehead.

Dolores pushed through the soldiers and drew me angrily away from the sink. 'Take your jug and shut up! You endanger all of us with your talk,' she hissed. 'Go to your room.'

'I've spent enough time in my room, thanks to you,' I said coldly, and stormed out into the garden, upset that Hephzibah had not defended me. I could hear Dolores apologizing for my behaviour with fear in her voice. 'She's not well. The heat and the war have been too much for her.'

Someone roughly grabbed my arm, and I swung round expecting to see the soldier. But it was Hephzibah.

'Take no notice of them in there. They just want to go home,' she said. Then she looked over at the woman. 'Get her to the summerhouse as soon as you can. I'll meet you there.'

'What are you going to do?' I asked, still agitated.

'Swap clothes.'

The woman was lying down on the grass. 'Let's go to the summerhouse,' I suggested, 'it's cool and very peaceful there. You can have a rest for a few minutes before setting off.'

I sat on the bench and invited her to lie on the cushions scattered on the floor. Hopefully she would fall asleep, but it seemed she preferred to talk, and she told me how the soldiers had captured her while on an author- ized visit to the Olive Company headquarters.

'They just stormed the house, killed everyone in it and took me. They seemed to know I was from another Com- pany further north and I suppose they didn't dare kill me without orders. I don't know why. Perhaps the orders never came – or they'd had enough of killing. They didn't seem to know what to do with me, so I've just been travelling as their prisoner, doing the odd jobs that no one else wants to do. One of the officers has promised that I'll be released when we reach the port. I won't believe him until it happens. They could turn on me at any moment.'

Then she began to tell me how she tried hard not to think of her family because it upset her too much. They did not know where she was and she feared they assumed the worst. I could feel the heat stinging the back of my neck and suddenly felt nauseous. I noticed how long her fingers were and that she wore gold rings. She must be favoured by her Company, I thought, and said, 'You have beautiful hands.'

She spread them out over her legs. 'I'm a musician,'

she said proudly. 'I play for the Company Presidents and their friends at their parties.' Presidents were the most powerful people in the Federation and generally remained hidden from the public eye. 'When I first did it I thought I would have to play the usual Company stuff – patriotic anthems and product songs, but I'm always asked to write music especially for each of them which has nothing to do with the Company. I play a keyboard and sing my own songs, music that comes from my heart. You have to be careful, though; you can't sing anything which might get you into trouble.'

She paused, and cleared her throat as if getting ready to sing. 'It's an eye-opener, it really is. You see how they live – the President and his friends, and the directors. It's not like us. They eat their food from gold plates, and there's always enough to feed an army. It's disgusting really, when you think how most people are hungry. They drink, too, until they can't stand.'

She laughed then, until I thought she was going to cry. Embarrassed, I turned away and looked through one of the windows; Hephzibah was standing motionless amongst the lemon trees, staring directly at the summer-house.

'What does your country produce?' I asked nervously, hoping Hephzibah would leave us alone.

'Wheat, fields and fields of it. You can walk for ever and only see wheat. It's lovely in the spring when it's all green, and lovely in the summer too, when everything is gold. Just like the Company plates,' she added bitterly.

We lapsed into silence, until she sighed and I followed her gaze out towards the estuary. 'There's music every-where – can you hear it?'

I shook my head.

'Listen to the trees, and the tap-tap of the roses on the roof and the birds calling. It's all music.'

'I suppose it is. I never thought of ambient sound as music.'

'That's how I create my songs. I go for walks and listen to everything – the insects, the wind blowing through the wheat. Sometimes I think I can hear the clouds move through the sky.'

'You make it sound very romantic.'

'It's not romance, it's work,' she said, suddenly sounding tired. 'I just wish the rest of the world could hear my music, but I'm only allowed to play it to those monsters.'

I was surprised at her frankness, and realized it was a sign of the trust she had already placed in me.

'Are you close to your sister?' she asked suddenly.

'Yes. We're very different, but I adore her.'

'You're lucky. I don't have any siblings. My mother had more children, but they were all taken away, some directly from her womb. I don't know where they are now – probably in some camp somewhere, or being experimented on. Sometimes, when I'm at the parties, I think of approaching the President and asking him to find them for me, but my mother begs me not to. She says I might disappear as well. She must be sick with worry now that I haven't returned. I was allowed to travel here because a special request had been put in by your President for me to play at one of his receptions.'

'Why don't you have a little nap?' I suggested as kindly as I could. 'It's a long way to the port and you need to be fresh for the journey.'

She nodded in assent and stared out across to the

estuary. Her eyes skimmed the sky and the horizon, and she smiled.

'Maybe things aren't so bad after all.'

With these words she closed her eyes and I watched as her breathing slowed and she slipped into the unconsciousness of sleep. She was lying on her back and her arms rested by her side. Suddenly Hephzibah appeared at the entrance, a flash of blue and copper. She did not look at me, but stared down at the sleeping woman, humming, almost in a trance. It was as if I were not present. She moved slowly and carefully, put down the sheet she had brought with her and picked up a large cushion from the floor. She clutched it to her chest and for a moment stared down at the perfect face and long, relaxed body. I thought she would bring the cushion to sit beside me and I moved to make space for her. I was not prepared for what happened next. Hephzibah's body suddenly jerked as if shot, and she dropped to the floor, pinning the woman's arms down with her legs and violently slamming the cushion onto her face. The woman resisted immediately and twisted and turned and tried to push Hephzibah's knees away with such force I thought she would succeed. I heard her muffled screams as she kicked violently at the air. Her beautiful, ringed hands fluttered like a bird's wings.

I rose quickly and began to pull at the cushion to get it off the woman's face, but Hephzibah only pressed down harder, her fists like stones. She looked at me, sweat gathering along her top lip, which was clenched in merciless fury. I pulled at her hands and arms, but she would not give an inch.

'Let her go, Hephzibah,' I screamed. 'Let her go!'

Pummelling her back, I braced my arm tightly around Hephzibah's neck, trying to pull her away. She released one hand from the cushion and jabbed an elbow hard into my ribs, winding me. I loosened my grip and she bit my arm.

Beneath us the woman struggled for life. She kicked her legs and heaved her body, so that Hephzibah rose and fell as if riding a storm. She tried to move her arms from underneath Hephzibah's knees, but could not. I tried to help her and moved round to pull at Hephzibah's legs, but it was as if she had become one with her victim, and nothing could tear them apart. I rolled round to face her.

Her hair hung like a curtain between us. 'Hephzibah, please stop this,' I cried, tugging at the cushion, knowing that I could not match her demented strength.

'Shut up,' Hephzibah screamed, and looked at me with such venom that I was suddenly paralysed. The woman's body began to twitch and Hephzibah ground her fists into the cushion even harder.

After what seemed a long time, the woman lay motionless beneath her. For a moment I thought she had fallen back to sleep but I could see that she had stopped breathing. Hephzibah continued to press down on the cushion, making strange animal noises. I tried to stand up but felt too weak, as if all my energy had haemorrhaged away. My legs were numb and I saw that my hands were trembling. I stared at my sister but felt nothing.

'Stop it. She's dead,' I whispered, and mustered enough strength to pull her off the body. Hephzibah lifted the cushion and we both stared at the horror of the contorted face suddenly revealed to us. The woman's battle for life was evident in every feature and her eyes stared, still terrified. The cushion had ground her nose into her face and pressed her mouth into her teeth. Her lips were moist and swollen with dark blood. Hephzibah took a knife from her pocket.

'What are you going to do?' I asked hoarsely.

'Just watch – and say nothing.'

She prised the woman's top lip away from the teeth and sliced away the flesh beneath the nose with the efficiency of a hunter. 'The eels will do the rest,' she said.

Blood dripped down each side of the dead woman's face and gathered in pools upon the purple cloth of the cushion she had lain upon.

'Quickly,' Hephzibah commanded. 'The soldiers are leaving soon and you have to take advantage of the tide.'

I don't know if it was fatigue or shock which prevented me from speaking, but I remained silent as we undressed the woman. The faint perfume of roses drifted up from her body, reminding me of how she had been when alive.

'Look, she had a baby,' she said as she stripped the woman of her underclothes, revealing a tiny scar above her mons pubis.

While I dressed the body in Hephzibah's blue silk, I shut out the picture of a small, beautiful child running with outstretched arms towards a woman in a wheat field. Sentiment would not get me through this, I told myself as brusquely as I could.

Hephzibah took the woman's rings and put them into her skirt pocket. 'I might need these,' she said, bending to help me roll the body in the sheet that she had brought.

Then we carried the body down the path towards the jetty and onto the boat. We found some large stones by the shore and placed them inside the sheet, then secured it carefully around her with rope.

'Will you be able to get her over the side?' Hephzibah asked me, tying the woman's white scarf around her head.

'Yes,' I choked, hardly believing that this was the last time I might ever see my sister. I wanted to embrace her but the disabling darkness which had slipped between us in the summerhouse prevented me from doing so. She stood before me, then squatted down on the jetty to wash the blood from her hands.

'Get rid of the knife,' were her last words to me.

I climbed into the boat, wondering how I would find the strength to row so far out. Voices rose from behind the house.

'Mariam, Mariam,' they called. 'We're leaving now.'

I looked down at the weighted shroud beneath my feet and wished with all my heart that I did not know the dead woman's name.

Book II

The moment we cease to hold each other,
the moment we break faith with one another,
the sea engulfs us and the light goes out.

JAMES BALDWIN

13

And now Mariam had been caught like a fish. She had broken free from her shroud and floated into Tulu's nets. As Hephzibah had predicted, the sea's scavengers had done their work and no one who saw the body would be able to deny that it was my sister. We had not intended that her body be found, but its discovery could prove an advantage. With Hephzibah's death confirmed, probably murdered by soldiers, it might make the villagers less likely to seek revenge on my parents.

I didn't care what happened to me. I deserved the worst. What I had done was unforgivable, and in my quietest moments I heard the keening of a thousand mothers.

Rain began to fall in slow, heavy drops. I thought of Hephzibah, happy with her entourage of devoted men, sitting amongst them, staring straight ahead, anticipating a new life. I knew she would not look back. But I did not envy her. I had heard about the Water State, its perfumed, uniformed workers, its glass water towers, and cities of high, narrow buildings, with strict surveillance and a network of waterways.

I did not quicken my pace when the rain grew heavier, ripping through the trees' branches and flattening the bushes and flowers. I savoured the gathering coolness and the water soaking through my clothes. I stood still before the front door and closed my eyes, imagining every trace of the woman I had helped kill being washed away. The rain drenched my skin and weighted my clothes. I knew that, no matter how much I longed to cry, I could not. Sorrow settled in my throat like ash.

A violent smack of thunder reverberated through the darkening sky and the still air as I ran up the stone steps into the house. I searched for my parents to tell them that the body dragged up from the sea's tides was their daughter. To lie to my mother out of necessity would not be too difficult, but facing Father and telling him news that I knew would break his heart was a different matter.

He approached me in the long corridor leading to the kitchen, holding two glasses of brandy. He looked at me and from the expression on my face knew that his worst fears had been realized. Silently, I took both glasses from him and led him back to the room where I had left him with Dolores. She was still there, her face grim and prepared as she glanced up, clearly expecting the worst.

'There is no doubt it is Hephzibah,' I said quietly.

Her expression did not change as she threw the brandy to the back of her throat and then coughed. I did not expect her voice or demeanour to be so calm when she spoke. 'Was there any evidence of violence?'

'None. It appears she drowned.'

'But how? She was in the kitchen one minute and then she disappeared.'

'Maybe she went for a swim and got out of her depth. You know how the tides are.'

'It just doesn't make sense. She was always disappearing, but I assumed she wanted to visit friends in the village,' Dolores said, smudged lipstick staining her mouth like a faded bruise.

'She didn't have any friends in the village, certainly not after the soldiers came here. I don't think we'll ever know what happened to her,' Father said as gently as he could. 'And in a way it doesn't matter. She's dead, and that's the only important thing.'

'Although there's nothing to suggest it, I think she was killed by one of the soldiers.' I spoke quickly, eager to get the lie over with. 'I knew you should never have let them into the house.'

'What choice did we have?' Dolores said, agitated.

After a long pause, Father asked me if I had made arrangements for the death rites. 'I don't think any of us should be seen going into the village, Jephzat,' Dolores said. 'You know what the villagers think about us. Manos has told me that feelings against us are mounting day by day as they learn the full extent of what the Water people have done to this part of the Olive Country.'

I wanted to say that she was partly responsible and should send Manos home, rather than encourage her visits and place her in danger by association with us. Instead, I argued that it would be better if I went to Sengita and arranged for the disposal of the body. It wasn't something we could do ourselves, despite what Dolores thought.

She rose unsteadily to her feet. We knew she would be heading for her bunker in the garden. She would climb down into the darkness, activate her computer and lie down to watch images of the child she had lost.

There was a resigned look on Father's face as Dolores shut the door behind her.

'Well, we won't be seeing your mother for a while,' he said quietly.

'Don't you be doing the same and holing up in that laboratory of yours.'

He smiled and took me in his arms. 'How could I leave you alone like that? You'll be lonely without your sister,' he said, his voice breaking. I held him tight as he cried into my arms. I was surprised at how frail he felt, and how his sobs matched the vigour of the storm that was now directly above us.

'Hephzibah,' I groaned inwardly, feeling wretched. 'How could you do this to your family?'

A loud noise startled us both. At first I thought it was the thunder returning. Unable to peer through the windows because of the closed shutters, I headed for the front door, tripping over boxes and rubbish that the soldiers had left behind.

I peered through a crack in the door and glimpsed what seemed to be a wooden cross against red cloth. The visitor banged again on the door. I ran back to Father.

'It's the Commissioner. What shall we do?'

'Why the fuss? He's probably come to pay his condolences. I am sure word has got out by now. Let him in.'

Once inside the house, the Commissioner's face arranged itself in an expression of sympathy. 'Very bad news. Very bad news indeed,' he said pompously. 'Yet another casualty of this terrible war. Thanks be to everyone that it has ended.'

Father and I stared at him gloomily from the other side of the room, both of us wishing his rictus mouth would shut and he would leave. I wondered if Hephzibah could return now that the war was ending – she must have reached the port by now – but knew in my heart that she never would.

14

'Jephzat, Jephzat!' My father's voice brought me back to the room. 'Are you listening to what the Commissioner is saying?'

I had to admit that I wasn't. I apologized but offered no excuse.

'I have just told your father that Sengita came to me a short while ago, concerned for the welfare of you and your parents. She says that the villagers are directing all their anger at this house, mainly because you took in the soldiers, and also because they have no one else to blame. There is talk amongst some of them of burning down your home – with you all in it.'

'Don't they realize we've suffered enough? We didn't want the soldiers here. They forced their way into the house and they probably murdered my daughter . . .' Father sounded crushed, defeated.

'There are rumours in the village that Hephzibah was sleeping with the soldiers,' the Commissioner said, narrowing his eyes.

We sat quietly as he watched us closely. Perhaps he was interpreting our silence as confirmation. I crossed the room to open up the shutters and let in the light. Gazing out across dripping foliage to the roof of the summer-house, I reluctantly decided to speak.

'Commissioner, there is no proof of that. We were forced to accept these men into our house on pain of death. It is a possibility that my sister was forced to have sex with them, but certainly neither I nor my parents had any inkling of it. Hephzibah hated them as much as we did.'

'This is beside the point. Your sister is dead, and as far as the Company is concerned there are more important things to be considered now with regard to your family.' The Commissioner spoke dismissively, his sallow skin yellowing further in the light. 'The point is that your father's work is of great importance to the Company and we do not want to lose him to a rabble of ignorant hooligans. Your mother, too, is valued, but let's say for different reasons. I have constantly updated the Company on the ongoing situation and the latest word from them is that your parents must leave. They will be settled temporarily in another region of the country.'

'What about Jephzat?' Father asked, clearly alarmed. 'She must come too.'

The Commissioner fingered his crucifix nervously. 'Jephzat is instructed to remain in the house. She will look after the laboratory here because there may come a time when you'll both be able to return.

'You'll be expected to leave tonight,' he continued, lowering his voice. 'It has all been arranged. A vehicle will pick you up at eight p.m. Be ready. Take little with you. Everything you need has been taken care of.'

'I have already lost one daughter. Must I lose another?' was all my father said.

15

I felt cheerier after cleaning the kitchen. It was reborn. I had scrubbed away all evidence of the soldiers; I swept away strands of their hair and the dirt brought in on their boots and the crumbs that had fallen from their mouths. I scrubbed away the coffee stains on the table and around the sink. There were dirty fingermarks around the door and I rubbed them away vigorously with my cloth. If I could not maintain control of events going on around me I could at least cleanse my environment of dirt, arranging kitchen utensils like a Company official arranging employees.

Shortly after the Commissioner's departure, Father had fallen asleep on the sofa. I wanted to leave him in peace for a while, so after my manic clean I headed for the bunker. I raised the lid with effort: I never knew how Dolores managed to lift it alone. She was lying down, and I climbed down several rungs, then squeezed up beside her. She was smiling, and while I sat there, held out her arms as if reaching out for something.

'Come to Mummy, darling,' she said, cooing. 'You're such a sweet little thing. Look at your little feet. Let's see how fast they can run. Come on.'

She was talking to Hephzibah the way she used to when she was a small child.

I poked her shoulder. 'Dolores!' I shouted, the warmth of the bunker already beginning to stifle me.

'What's the matter?' she said, as she lightly touched the wall. A panel made a faint popping noise as it went back into the impacted earth. It was the only indication in the bunker that electronic media equipment of any kind existed there, but I knew that energy-controlled panels were secreted behind the earth walls, accessible only by invisible pulses.

I told her of the Commissioner's visit and that she would have to prepare to leave. She was apparently not disturbed by the news, but looked relieved.

'Did the Commissioner say anything else?' she asked.

'He said something a bit odd. He said you were being moved because the Company valued your and Father's research. I've been working with you, but have you been deceiving me, and working on something else I don't know about? What are you doing that's so crucial they want to make sure you're safe?'

She looked at me earnestly. 'Listen, Jephzat. You must not speak of this to anyone. I was planning to tell you and Hephzibah soon, but things have changed so much now.' She dropped her voice to a whisper. I nodded in assent and surprise. 'I can't tell you everything, there's not enough time. But the reason your father and I were moved to this village was because the Federation wants to discover the water formula for itself. It's afraid that the Water Country will take over the Federation, and doesn't trust its ulterior ambitions. Your father and I have been working to find the formula.'

I gawped at her in amazement, not knowing whether to feel betrayed, or terrified by the secrecy and importance

CHRISTINE AZIZ

of the project. Nothing my mother had ever said before had prepared me for this.

'It's not possible. It's not your field.'

'Listen carefully. This is all I can tell you for the moment. The discovery of man-made water was a revolutionary development. Desalination plants had proved vulnerable during the wars and became inefficient. Nature was dying, then thanks to this discovery land stripped of its flora and fauna became forest again, teeming with life. People no longer died of thirst, and transport became available to all again, powered by hydrogen cells. Until water production was discovered conservation laws were so strict that their transgression carried the death penalty. All this ended with the accidental discovery of the formula.'

'But how?' I asked.

'A team of scientists were about to finish their shift on board a deep-space ship when they accidentally discovered a phenomenon in space which began to produce and then replicate its own water. What happened to those scientists who discovered the formula we do not know – we can only assume they were assassinated by those who realized its potential. The Federation wanted the formula for itself, and offered a huge price to those who had acquired it illegally, but they refused, and after much argument they formed a company of their own and were admitted into the Federation. The Federation believed the Water Company to be less threatening within its ranks than as a renegade on the outside. It was allowed to carve out a piece of land, some of which had been secured for olive production by the Olive Company. The rest was wasteland. Water workers uprooted thousands of olive trees

90

and used the land to store water. They built cities on water, and brought in people from all over, often to the detriment of the other Companies. The Olive Company has never forgiven the Federation for that. Hence our continual skirmishes.'

'So where did the Water Company get their workers from?'

'Some came from the retraining camps while others were given special secondment by other Companies. The work was so important to the Federation; access to unlimited supplies of water would be beneficial to everyone. There was also a lot of backhanded dealing, with vast amounts of money paid to other Company personnel to keep them friendly. And now the Water Company is intent on colonizing space. Then they really will be rulers of the universe.'

'Are you anywhere near discovering the formula?' I asked eagerly. Dolores remained silent for a long time.

'There are many scientists from different disciplines working secretly on this project throughout the Federation. But I don't think any of us are anywhere near discovering it.' She clicked her tongue impatiently. 'All I know is that the ship I've mentioned, the *Olympia*, was part of a deep-space exploration programme and that the operatives accidentally discovered specific conditions that prompted water to keep replicating itself. One early drawback, however, was that people would explode if they came close to the source while it was producing water. The water in their own bodies would begin to replicate.'

She had still not answered my query.

'Water has memory, you see,' she added impatiently, as if I had asked a stupid question.

We fell into silence, both considering the implication of what she had said, until the bunker began to vibrate. Someone was walking in this direction.

'It's your father,' Dolores said, her ears accustomed to his familiar step.

We checked the monitor and saw Father walking slowly through the trees. I started to climb up and Dolores followed. We emerged, squinting to protect our eyes from the bright shards of light that followed the storm, and returned to the house to get ready for their journey.

They refused my offers of help, and packed minimally. I prepared food for them to take, and when I came out into the hall their two little bags were already waiting. Father had gone off to his laboratory to make hasty, abbreviated copies of his crucial notes and write a list of instructions for me.

Dolores had sorted out some small gifts and money for Manos. I then heard her upstairs in Hephzibah's room and knew that she was looking for something that belonged to her. She came down the stairs with a long floating scarf in her hand that Hephzibah often wore around her shoulders in the evening. In an instant I saw my sister again, sitting on the veranda staring out across the garden, the thin green material sliding down her shoulders and pleating at her elbows so that the green darkened to the colour of grass. Dolores held it to her face, inhaling deeply.

'It still smells of her,' was all she said.

16

The atmosphere in the village had changed since I last saw Sengita. It was eerily quiet now except for the noise of the gulls. Normally children ran along the harbour wall to frighten them away, but today the birds had been allowed to fly further inland than usual. One of them dived at me, its yellow beak wide open in a violent shriek.

As I walked down the main street, women came out of their houses and stood in their courtyards and stared at me. I kept my eyes fixed ahead on the little white house on the harbour wall and saw a tiny figure step out and run towards me. It was Joachim, and it was the first time I was pleased to see him. His stunted legs struggled towards me as if missing the momentum of Sengita's skirts. He grabbed my hand and pulled it, urging me to walk faster. Some of the women began to hiss menacingly at us and then their men joined them. The hissing grew, angry and steady. Joachim urged me on, but I did not want to show them that I was afraid, so I pulled away from him and slowed down to meet the gaze of those who watched us. But their stares remained unfaltering and hard.

When we reached the house Sengita pulled me in and slammed the door loudly behind us. She drew the bolts and, once satisfied the door was firmly locked, ushered me into her kitchen.

I sat down with relief, suddenly realizing how weak I felt. Joachim scuttled to the top of the house, where he would keep watch unnoticed behind a window.

'Why did you come here?' Sengita's face was flushed and her wig was listing slightly to one side. 'I was just getting ready to come to you. I heard that your parents were leaving, and did not want you to risk coming here alone. You see how the villagers are. Emotions are rising very quickly.'

'I came to see you about Hephzibah and explain what my parents want to have done with her body. They want her incinerated, not buried.' The word 'incinerated' was still used even though the practice had ended. Traditionally, most bodies used to be incinerated until the procedure was outlawed for environmental reasons. Outside the cities people took to burying their dead, but this was not possible for the bulk of the Federation's population. Luckily, plants were discovered that held precious water. When broken open they revealed a porous interior holding the liquid, which could be drunk. These days they were dried to serve a different purpose; when scattered over a corpse they drew out all the moisture, desiccating the flesh until it turned to powder. In the process the plants began to look like crystals the colour of fire, hence their name. The powder and the fire crystals were then handed over to relatives or friends. Some people made necklaces from the crystals and thus wore the remains of their loved ones round their necks.

'Then I must look for the fire crystals.'

I gazed around the kitchen as Sengita rummaged in a cupboard. The shelves were full of different-coloured glass jars. A cornucopia of nature's healers – seeds, bulbs, leaves, roots and powders all stood alongside one another. Each jar's contents were meticulously labelled with instructions for dosage and date of acquisition. If Sengita's claims were true, every item in her kitchen had the ability to heal – or worsen – a malady. The medicines given by the Company doctors did nothing more than make people oblivious to their ailments, so that they grew worse. As a result people turned to women like Sengita who practised their healing in secret, relying on the energy of their natural medicines and the body's unique ability to heal itself.

I watched her with affection. Her large backside filled the cupboard as she searched through pots and sacks. Her muffled voice rose from the dark. 'There is not much call for fire crystals here. This lot prefers to bury their dead. They probably think it's good for the soil. I know I put them somewhere, but where?'

I offered to help her in her search but she did not hear me. Suddenly she gave an excited cry.

'Found them. Knew they were in here somewhere.'

I helped her drag the sack from the bottom of the cupboard. She undid the string and rummaged though its contents before holding out several thick-stemmed milky plants.

We dragged the sack into the room where the body lay. Since my last visit it had been wrapped in a thick blue cloth and a small bunch of fresh flowers placed upon it. The smell of pungent essences and herbs was stronger than before, but still failed to mask the sickly-sweet odour of decomposing flesh.

'We must do this very quickly,' Sengita said, handing me a piece of cloth to tie around my nose and mouth before loosening the shroud and placing the plants inside. We worked silently, covering the body entirely. Poor Mariam, I thought. This may not have been her family's choice of disposal for her. And then I thought of her little child.

'You mustn't look so worried, Jephzat. You're doing your sister a service and should feel honoured by it.'

She drew the cloth tightly around the body.

'We must leave the plants to do their work for several hours now, but you must stay here until the process is finished. I will make you food and then you must sleep. You look exhausted.'

We returned to the kitchen and I watched while Sengita gutted three mackerel and prepared vegetables. She refused my offers of help and placed a bottle of wine before me.

'Let's celebrate the end of the war,' she said briskly.

I poured the wine and relaxed into the chair. The kitchen was beginning to fill with cooking aromas and I could feel my eyes drooping as the alcohol entered my bloodstream. If only I could sink into a deep sleep and wake to everything as it had been before the soldiers arrived.

'I am thinking that maybe you should come and live with me.' Sengita's offer startled me. 'I'm sure the Commissioner would agree to this. You will be safe here and you could visit the house to sort out your parents' things when the situation becomes calmer.'

I knew I would miss my parents, my father especially, but also knew I couldn't accept, however vulnerable I felt.

'It's kind of you, Sengita, but I must stay in the house. I need to be alone for a while and I also have to finish off some of Father's work in the laboratory.'

'Excuses,' Sengita snapped.

'No, they're not.' I walked over to her and put an arm affectionately around her so that her waistcoat jingled like tiny bells in the wind.

'I heard talk in the village about Lomez,' she said, changing the subject. 'People say he's gone mad since he fished your sister from the sea.'

I was uncomfortably aware of Sengita's eyes searching my face, but surely this was not the first time that a body had been caught up in the nets.

'I told your mother that her daughter's affliction was a curse on us all,' she continued with some relish.

'That's rubbish. Do you really believe that a life is cursed by the chance development of a few renegade cells in a foetus?'

'Of course not,' Sengita chided. 'Your sister was not the way she was because of what she was born with, it was merely a clue. It can be an indication of something special, but that girl had nothing special about her. I'm sorry to speak so frankly, Jephzat, but it's the truth. We may all be displaced people who have forgotten our past, but this doesn't mean that somewhere deep inside us some truths don't linger. The Companies may have tried to wipe out our histories, but perhaps memory lives on outside us, in things ancient that talk to us in our dreams and in the precious moments that we do not give to the Company.'

'What on earth are you talking about, Sengita? You'd better not let the Commissioner hear this sort of thing.'

She ignored me and continued. 'Lomez says it wasn't your sister. He says it was another woman.'

My laughter was prompted by panic and surprise.

'How can that be? I should know my sister when I see her, dead or alive.'

'He says he had seen your sister often in the village
and played with her as a child. Many of his friends fell in
love with her as she grew into a beautiful woman, but he
did not. He said there was something about her that
repelled him. When the woman he fished up was laid on
the deck of the boat he says he looked at her and immediately fell in love with her. If it had been Hephzibah he
swears this would not have happened.'

I was determined not to panic again and maintained
as cool an exterior as possible. The smell of baking
mackerel filled the kitchen and I tried to change the subject
by saying how hungry I was. Sengita was not fooled.

'Death cannot hide the living,' she said mysteriously,
and I dared not ask her what she meant.

'What will become of Lomez?' I asked flatly.

'I have some remedies for him, but who knows what
the long-term prognosis will be? He says he kissed the
body and still tastes her in his mouth. I have given him
eucalyptus to chew, and cardamom and clove, but the
taste remains. Tulu is beside herself with worry.'

I busied myself finding plates and cutlery, fearing a
reply would give me away.

'I wish you would pay attention,' Sengita was scolding.

'I'm sorry. My mind just keeps wandering off. I can't
seem to concentrate.'

'That's because you are tired.' She placed the steaming
fish on the table and called Joachim. We could hear him
climbing noisily down the stairs. Sengita listened carefully
to his strange babble as she served the meal.

'He says the villagers have gone back into their homes,
but thinks they are only waiting for you to come out. He
says they wouldn't dare attack this house.'

'What does he know? He is only a child,' I snapped irritably.

Joachim kicked his chair, clearly understanding what I had said.

We ate in silence, all of us feeling tense. Afterwards Sengita removed my shoes and took my feet in her hands, rubbing crushed garlic into their soles.

'This will help you sleep,' she said, sending me upstairs to lie on her bed.

I sank into the soft mattress and gratefully closed my eyes. The smell of the sea drifted in through the open window and I slept a deep and merciful sleep without dreams. Even the raucous cries of the gulls did not wake me.

17

I awoke early the following day thinking it was still evening and that I had slept for only a few hours. But this was a clear dawn light that filled the room, not the purplish haze of twilight. There was no sign of Sengita and the house was quiet. I stretched lazily and stood by the window breathing in the cool sea air.

Downstairs I opened the shutters in the kitchen and searched for bread and eggs. I thought I would prepare breakfast for us all to eat outside on the terrace. I wanted to do something that would please Sengita, but as I cut the bread and cracked the eggs I began to wonder if she had already left the house. I crept upstairs to see if she had perhaps fallen asleep there. But Joachim was alone, sleeping on the floor and snoring loudly.

I finally found Sengita lying on a mat on the scented stone floor in the mortuary. She lay on her side with her knees drawn up to her chest and her wig snuggled up against her like a pet. She did not stir as I entered the room. A long thin pile of dust scattered with fire crystals covered the wooden table where Mariam's body had once lain.

Without moving or opening her eyes, Sengita muttered, 'There was a thunderstorm last night. Did you sleep well?'

'Like the dead,' I said, and she laughed as she sat up.

'You mean, like this one. She didn't move while the crystals were doing their work.'

'Were you expecting her to?'

'You can never tell. I always stay with them if they have fire crystals. I feel that someone should be there. It's not right to be alone at this time. Some of them stir and creak as the moisture leaves the body. It's a bit like the drying of wood when all the bugs crawl out.'

'What do you mean?'

'All the parasites; the worms, the larvae: they all leave the body as if it's a sinking ship. You can hardly see them but I know they're there. I always give the room a good scrubbing and fumigation when it's all done.'

I didn't want to linger so told her breakfast would be ready soon. I went straight to the bathroom and washed my body several times to rid it of any of the deathly dust. I also resolved to burn my clothes the moment I returned home.

Sengita sat with her grandson on the terrace while I served them breakfast. She had placed the fire crystals in a glass jar on the table, which disturbed me.

'You must always keep the fire crystals where you can see them, but the powder has to be buried.'

I said she could bury the powder wherever she wished and she replied that she would give it to Lomez. She did not seem surprised that I did not object, nor did she appear suspicious. Her bald head shone in the morning light, its armour of skull bones visible under the skin and a faint fuzz of grey hair at the nape. She began to plan my departure from the house.

'We will wait until siesta time. There are fewer people

around then in the streets, and Joachim and I will escort you through the main street to the house. I will stay with you for a few days to make sure you are all right. Here, take more Ignatia.' She pushed two tiny pills into my mouth and I let them dissolve on my tongue. 'Soon I'll take the dust to Lomez and do a little research. Maybe things will have calmed down since yesterday.'

The sun was already fierce in the sky, promising a very hot day. I wished it would be cooler – tempers would not fray so easily then.

Sengita busied herself with her morning routine while I swept and cleaned the kitchen and terrace, all the time ignoring the bright glare of the fire crystals. She sang mournful tunes dedicated to her son as she sorted through parcels of herbs and powders. Occasionally she gave Joachim an errand and he flew around the house babbling and saluting with his little arms as if passing through cheering crowds. He refused to do anything I told him to, either because he did not understand me, or because he did not want to.

Later, Sengita set off to Tulu's house to give the dust to Lomez. She thought it might help heal his grief. I did not want the crystals either, but had to keep them for my parents. My mother had told me about the soul and what it was once believed to be, although the word in Federese does not exist.

I sat on the terrace and stared at the crystals. Their fiery glow was not warm, but cold against the skin, and they did not catch the light in the same way as precious stones. In the light the colours appeared to move and flicker, giving the impression of burning flames. I wondered if the fire effect would have differed if they had devoured Hephzibah's body – would it have been paler or more intense?

Sengita returned and found me hunched over the jar.

'I wouldn't get too close. You never know what might happen,' she joked. I looked up at her.

'I was wondering whether, if the soul really existed, it could have been sucked into the fire crystals.'

'And you accuse me of nonsense?' Sengita laughed.

I lowered my voice. 'I thought you of all people might still cling to some of the ways of the Old World.'

Sengita whispered in response, 'The purpose of death is freedom. For a person to be sucked into a handful of coloured pebbles and held there for ever is not *my* idea of freedom.'

'Do you believe in the existence of the soul?'

'Who told you about the soul?' Sengita asked sharply.

'Mother, just once. She didn't go into any detail.'

'Huh. I doubt she has a soul.' Sengita spat, ignoring my look of chastisement. 'Lomez said it'd be better for you to lie low for a while. The villagers are still angry. They're convinced Hephzibah was a spy for the soldiers and are now saying that perhaps one of the villagers murdered her and that you should be finished off as well. He reckons they will have forgotten all this by the time your parents return.'

'Was he pleased with the dust?'

'Of course. He kissed the packet when I gave it to him. He says he'll bury it in the garden and mark it with a flowering oleander.'

I stared at the crystals, wishing I could be rid of them

as well. At least Mariam's dust was in the hands of someone who'd finally cared for her.

'I'm not going to wait several days to leave. I'll go
back to the house now.'

Despite Sengita's protestations I insisted I return alone:
I did not want to put her in any danger. If I left now while
the villagers were hiding from the sun, I would have a
good chance of returning unharmed.

Sengita shook her head. 'I respect your wish to leave
now, but I'm coming with you. You must walk beside
me.'

18

We stepped blinking into the harsh noonday sun. The main street stretched before us, lazy and empty. Where the village tapered off into shaded vegetable plots it turned abruptly east to join the main road to the port, and at its bend spawned a number of pathways that led into olive groves, pine forests or to the estuary shore. One of these pathways led directly to our house, which I could see rising above a tiny grove of ancient olives that the Company did not bother to harvest any more. The summer-house was hidden from view, but the minarets of the house, its domes, spires and towers were clearly visible and gave the impression of many buildings rather than one.

The fire crystals were heavy. The sun was at its highest point in the sky, leeching colour from our surroundings. I waited as Sengita closed her door quietly and then walked alongside her with Joachim trailing behind. After a few steps we began to sweat. The weight of Sengita's skirt and petticoats slowed her down. I was glad of my thin cotton sarong, but longed to leave the crystals behind and pick them up later when it was cooler. Sengita had insisted I carry them, out of a ridiculous belief that they would protect me.

As we walked further down the street, pushing

through the heat as if it were a heavy curtain, a small crowd began to move towards us. Suddenly, villagers jostling to get closer surrounded us. Sengita took my arm as we were forced to stop and face those who barred our way.

'Give her to us,' a woman cried angrily from the back of the crowd, which had begun to murmur like distant thunder. Sengita's grip tightened on my arm and I flinched.

She addressed the crowd. 'What has she done to you? She has already lost her sister and now her parents are gone. She is one of us.'

'She does not belong to the village,' someone shouted. 'Ever since her family arrived here there's been trouble. The Company watches us more carefully and they sent the Commissioner. Before they came we were free to do as we pleased. Clearly the Company does not trust these people, and neither do we.'

'Her sister may have played with our children and tried to be one of us, but her split lip has been a curse on us all. She fucked the men who killed *our* men. She has betrayed us and her family with her.' A man pushed his way to stand before me.

'Joab, you know that is not true,' Sengita said. 'Whatever her sister did has gone with her death. She was probably killed by the same soldiers who murdered our own. Isn't that revenge enough?'

Tulu was standing beside Sengita now, her white petticoats frothing at her feet. 'Look at my son,' she wailed, pulling Lomez before us. His handsome face was expressionless and his eyes glazed as if drugged. He did not seem to know where he was. Tulu began to sob, holding on to him, 'He has gone mad since he dragged up your sister from the sea. He is constantly brushing his teeth and rinsing his mouth. He has no skin left in it, and cannot eat. Even in death she is evil.'

'What has she to say for herself?' an old woman asked, squinting up at me.

'Whatever I say is not going to make any difference to any of you,' I replied, surprised by the confident ring of my voice. 'My family has always worked to help the village. Like you, they did not choose to come here; it was the Company's bidding. We have done nothing to betray you. We were held at gunpoint and had little choice but to let the soldiers stay.'

'Did she fuck the gun too?' called a young man. Sengita swung round and landed her fist on his chin. He swayed backwards and the crowd gasped in unison like a stunned animal.

'If anyone touches her, they will have me to answer to,' Sengita shouted, her face contorted in fierce fury. 'How many of you have I brought back from the dead? How many of you have I brought into this world? Do you think my medicine will be available to you if you do anything to this girl? I will pack my bags and leave you to the mercy of the Company doctors and their lethal experiments.'

Sengita was ready to make another swing at the crowd when we became aware of someone pushing their way towards the front. The crowd parted easily for the middle-aged man who finally stood before us. He wore only a sarong. He smelled strongly of olive oil and his arms were glistening. His long, stubbled face was familiar to me but I could not remember where I had seen him before.

'Go home, the lot of you,' he shouted in a baritone voice. The crowd shrank back. 'This girl has done nothing. Killing her will not solve any of the wrongs that have taken place in this village.'

His bright sapphire eyes looked directly into mine and suddenly I realized he was the man Hephzibah and I had discovered all those years ago in the abandoned room with the boxes of olives.

'She was the one who allowed me to escape many years ago. She could have reported me to the Commissioner and then the whole village would have been in trouble. It is thanks to her that we are here now.'

A collective memory had been stirred. Clearly the entire village had been involved in storing the contraband olives in our house.

'I think we owe her a favour. It was her sister who wanted to betray me, but Jephzat stopped her. Her sister is dead now and her parents have been taken away on the orders of the Company. Who knows what is to happen to them? Don't you think that is punishment enough?'

The crowd turned in on itself, each villager whispering to another. Heads started to nod.

'Go home!' he shouted, and people began to walk slowly away from us.

'It's over,' Sengita said, and Joachim wriggled out from under her skirts. I was soaking as if I had been standing in a downpour of rain. Sengita handed the man a cloth from one of her pockets and he began wiping the oil from his arms.

'I don't know what to say. Thank you is not enough,' I said to him.

'Then say nothing,' he replied with a shy smile.

'What's your name?'

'Homer.'

'Thank you, Homer. You and Sengita saved my life.'

Sengita tutted through her teeth and started to walk up the emptied street. 'Come on,' she said. 'I haven't got all day.'

I left Homer standing in the middle of the street, staring after us. When we reached the part of the road where it bends I turned to wave to him but he had already gone.

I was not looking forward to seeing the house again, and wondered if I should have taken up Sengita's offer to stay with her. But once she had sat me down on the veranda and returned with mugs of hot sweet tea, I was glad to have returned. I did not know how I would spend my days alone, but knew I had to be there for when my parents returned.

Sengita kept disappearing while I sat staring out over the gardens, amazed at how quickly any signs of the storm had disappeared. A thick tangle of jasmine grew up one of the veranda posts, its perfume vaporizing in the heat. The crystals had returned to their fiery state and glowed before me, a reminder of Mariam and what had been done to her. I pushed them under my chair.

Sengita bustled around me.

'Why did everyone obey Homer so quickly?' I asked her.

'I thought you might be thinking about him.' She smiled.

'I wasn't thinking about him, as you put it. I was just

wondering how an olive picker had such an easy author-ity,' I said defensively.

Sengita sat down beside me. I could hear Joachim's feet echoing through the corridors of the house.

'He knows a lot. More perhaps than is good for him.'

'Like what?'

'Oh, this and that.'

'That's no answer at all, Sengita.'

She leaned to one side so that she was looking directly into my eyes, and held my hands in hers. They were warm and comforting.

'Homer can tell from the shape of your head, your height, your skin colour and sometimes by your dreams where your ancestors came from.'

'That isn't possible,' I gasped.

She drew nearer and whispered into my ear. 'He has studied these things.'

'How can he tell? It's not possible. There has been so much genetic interference – designer genes chosen many generations ago by parents to make their offspring clev-erer, healthier, more beautiful, or by the Company to produce compliant workhorses. And what about those genes from years ago that were harvested from complete strangers, and which we have now inherited? I agree there is something of our ancestors left in all of us, but how can we tell what has been borrowed, manipulated or what is original?'

'Homer senses these things. He says your people were originally wanderers in the desert. My ancestors were horse warriors of the western savannahs.' She seemed amused by this and laughed. 'Imagine me on a horse!'

'Seems a bit far-fetched to me. And does it really

matter? I mean, the information is useless. What if my ancestors wandered the desert hundreds and hundreds of years ago? It doesn't help the person I am now. I've never seen a desert. I wouldn't know where to go to find one, although I have heard say that one remains.'

'Don't you feel the loss, Jephzat?' Sengita's voice was earnest. 'For thousands of years your people – if Homer is right – had the desert as their kingdom. Everything about them was shaped by it, and that knowledge lives on in you. Not in your genes, but somewhere else, deep inside you, a part of you that cannot rest until you have taken back from the Companies what belonged to your ancestors.'

'This is heresy, Sengita.' I sounded like the Commissioner. 'So here am I, doomed to unhappiness because I can't find a stretch of hot sand to wander, while you're frustrated because you can't ride a horse into battle. Let's have another war over it, Sengita! The idea of an ancestral home is exactly that – it exists only as an idea now. How can we dare speak of it when so much effort has gone into alienating us all from homelands and families – everything that was familiar to our predecessors? Our histories have been wiped out. Look at the villagers! None of them knows who their immediate forefathers are, let alone where their ancestral home is. Some of them don't even know where their journey began and how they came to be here, yet they have made the best of things.'

'You don't understand the significance of all this, do you?' Sengita said impatiently, scratching her forehead so that her tattoo darkened. She pulled me closer to her. 'Listen, it's subversive to speak of a homeland – let alone lay claim to one. Think of the hordes of people who would want to return and the upheaval that would entail. The Companies couldn't have that, could they?' A small, brightly coloured bird that skimmed the grass briefly distracted our attention, and Sengita smiled.

'Does that make Homer a revolutionary?' I wondered aloud.

But Sengita chose to ignore my question. The conversation had gone far enough. She had given me as much information as she dared.

19

Sengita tried to insist that she stayed, but I shooed her away. The dogs emerged from under the veranda and barked as she took off down the path to the village, with Joachim stumbling behind her. My regret at seeing her go was overshadowed by a strong desire to be alone.

I rose from my chair, picked up the crystals and entered the house, unused to its silence. At least in the kitchen there was always the sound of Manos at work, but as I entered it now I could hear only the sound of mice scurrying away.

I climbed the stairs and opened the door to Hephzibah's room. It was as she had left it: clothes were thrown across her unmade bed. It appeared she had taken nothing with her. Her brush lay on the dressing table, strands of hair threaded through its bristles. An uncapped bottle of perfume threw out its familiar scent of mimosa so strongly I thought she was standing beside me. The flowers beside her bed hung dry and heavy over their vase and several pairs of sandals lay discarded on the carpet. Underwear and shawls spilled out of drawers that had been pulled out. Anyone who did not know Hephzibah's untidiness would have thought the room had been burgled. The air was hot and stuffy, but I did not open the window because I did not want to lose the smell of her. I placed the crystals on the dressing table and curled up on the bed. It was warm from the sunlight that streamed across its covers and I buried my head in her clothes and wept until the sun moved away from the window and it grew cold. I was weeping not only for Hephzibah but for Mariam, too. I left her crystals looking out from the window awaiting the night.

My limbs felt heavy and stiff as I made my way to my own room, where I took off my clothes and rolled them in a bundle along with the ones I had worn the day Hephzibah left. I washed in the bathroom with jugs of warm rainwater collected from the storm and dressed again in warmer clothes.

In the garden I built a small bonfire and threw the bundle onto the flames. A thin strand of smoke rose up and settled in a dark pall over the garden. I knew the villagers would see it, but doubted if any one of them would care enough to come and find out if I was burning with the house. So it came as a surprise when I heard the sound of footsteps and saw a figure heading towards me through the dusk's gloom. He had a box balanced on his head. It was Homer.

I did not greet him, and he placed the box on the ground and squatted down beside me.

'I've brought you some food,' he said. 'It's nothing much, but I thought you might not be in the mood to shop in the village. Manos says she'll come, but not until things have calmed down a bit.'

'I don't need Manos,' I said tersely. 'I can manage on my own.'

We stared in silence at the fire, which had reduced the clothes to ashes. I glanced at him shyly. The dying flames gave his serious face a golden lustre and I noticed a small scar above his left brow.

'The provisions were just an excuse to come and see you,' he said quietly. 'I saw the smoke and thought you might be doing something silly.'

'I don't think my parents would appreciate it if I did.'

I liked his laugh. It was warm and quiet, rising from deep inside him, and I was surprised to find that I immediately felt at ease in his company.

I was usually inhibited and uncomfortable in the presence of men. Hephzibah was always much more at ease with them; I could not smile and toss my head at them in the way she did. She would say things that she knew would please them, but which meant nothing to her. She even talked to the Commissioner as if he were an old friend and I knew he liked that. I, however, felt that every man, except Father, restrained me. Each man's gaze robbed me of myself. I had seen this in the eyes of the soldiers, and knew that for a woman to believe in seeing the self reflected in such glances was dangerous. I had seen what it had done to Hephzibah and how it had briefly also turned my mother into a stranger.

I prodded the fire with a stick until sparks flew into the air. One twinkled briefly on Homer's moustache and then faded to a tiny ember. I surprised myself by spontaneously flicking it off. He did not acknowledge the gesture, but stood up and straightened his long body above mine, so that I had to bend my head back to see the full height of him. He offered his hand and pulled me up.

'What are you going to do in this big place now that your parents have gone? Has the Company told you what it expects of you?'

'I'm to look after my father's laboratory until he returns. I may continue with some of his work. He's left instructions for me. Then there's the garden and the citrus groves, the house itself to upkeep. I'm sure that the Company expects me to maintain everything, although no one has said as much.' I shrugged my shoulders carelessly as if my future was not the lonely burden it was beginning to feel.

'In time, what's happened will be forgotten by the villagers and they'll be rushing up here to offer help. Not all of them feel hostile,' Homer said as if to comfort me, aware of my anger.

'They've never done that before, so I see no reason why they should do it now,' I responded stiffly.

'But you're alone now and that makes a difference. Your parents liked to keep themselves apart from the village and did not make people feel welcome. But you can change that.'

'Do I seem like a big socializer to you?'

'No.' He scuffed at the earth with the edge of his sandals and looked worried.

'I miss Hephzibah very much,' I said quietly, 'and won't be in the mood for visitors for a long time.'

He said nothing. The fire was no more than a few glowing embers. It was time for him to go. I smelled newly crushed olives as he kissed me lightly on my cheek and left me standing beneath a high full moon obscured by dark clouds. I heard him whistling as I kicked earth over the embers and wondered why I had not seen him in the village since Hephzibah and I had startled him all those years ago.

20

I remained in my room for what seemed many days, only leaving it to eat, fetch water and visit the bathroom. Homer's box remained unopened and I ignored the occasional knocking on the front door and footsteps beneath my window.

In my room I did nothing but watch the light as it rose like a thermometer's mercury through the day, finally collapsing into shadows. Nothing distracted me from my vigil. The house spread around me with a life of its own that had nothing to do with me. My room had become a carapace and at night as I lay awake I could hear my heartbeat pulsing through the corridors like blood through extended veins.

The nights varied as much as bolts of ravelled fabric. Some nights were brittle and metallic like embroidered silk and set the teeth on edge; others settled lightly like muslin over the body, warming and protective. My favourites were those that hung like canopies of thick velvet, shutting out the world. There were nights so oppressive that even on waking I could not shake off a cloying sense of foreboding. As my eyes closed, my ears became my sentinels. Even the sound of a fly settling on a window caught their attention, as did the rustle of pigeons' wings in the eaves and the swish of a mouse-tail across the floor many rooms away. I heard bats unclamp their wings in the attic rafters and summon the dusk. They swarmed around the house like black clouds of vampires, glossy in the moonlight. Armies of cockroaches adjusted their armour in a series of clicks and I heard termites feasting on the rafters, their jaws ticking like clocks. Pupae fidgeted in their cocoons and spiders rustled their webs like ladies in silk. There was the muffled sound of tiny paws padding through the labyrinthine rooms above and below me.

The more I closed my eyes, the more I heard, until I thought each of these creatures had invaded my skull. My trips to the kitchen became less frequent. I felt hot and feverish and always awoke soaked in sweat. The light hurt my eyes, but I was too weak to draw the curtains. The sounds became louder and I imagined the spiders spinning webs the size of hammocks. Desperate for silence, I hid under the pillows, but the explosion of a thousand pupating caterpillars bursting from their cocoons filled my head. Huge creatures with bright, gossamer wings flew towards me.

A voice called, 'Jephzat, Jephzat,' and I felt the pillows being lifted and a cool hand placed upon my brow. My tongue felt thick and large in my mouth and I could not answer.

I heard water being squeezed from a cloth and someone washed my body. I could smell lemon and wondered if Sengita was ministering to me. It was not until some time later that I was able to open my eyes and saw Manos sitting by the side of my bed. My head hurt as I struggled to sit up.

'Manos, why are you here? It's not safe for you.'

'Things calmed down in the village after the Company people were seen there. They didn't say anything, just came and went.'

'But why?' I asked, intrigued.

'Obviously it was a warning. They clearly don't want any trouble in the village. They had a word with the Commissioner, and then zoomed off and up in those space buggies of theirs, making sure they took a load of fresh fish with them, leaving nothing for us. The boats are out again.'

I asked her how long I had lain in the room. She said she didn't know, but that Sengita had sent her. When I asked why Sengita had not come, Manos shrugged her shoulders.

'How would I know what that woman is up to? There's a strange illness going around causing rashes and headaches, and any other ailment you would care to think of. She's got some new concoction, and to be fair, it seems to have contained the bug. I don't know how she gets away with it. The Company must be terrified of her. It's either that, or she's on their payroll.' Manos lowered her voice. 'You know that she once cured the Company Director of a bacterium that had begun to eat him alive from the feet up? Apparently his toes are new. All the best Company doctors had seen him, but they could do nothing for him. She was his last port of call, so to speak.'

'I don't think Sengita's on anyone's payroll except her own. She's obviously allowed to do what she does because she saved the Director's life. We get away with a lot more in this village than anywhere else because of her. Look at the Commissioner the Company has sent us. He neglects his duties and hardly cares about what goes on. Sometimes

I think he's a decoy, and that someone else among us is reporting to the Company as Commissioner.'

Manos sighed and stood up, smoothing down the dark brown tunic she always wore. Her thin black hair was captured in a wispy bun and strands of it hung around her face. Her skin was pink and pinched. It was unusual to see such pale skin – most people chose to be dark because it afforded greater protection against the sun and was considered more attractive – but something had gone wrong for Manos, probably at embryo stage, and no one had bothered to correct it. Consequently she stayed out of the sun and clung to the shadows whenever she could.

'Homer is in the kitchen preparing you some food.'

I was too weak to be surprised but I know I felt a rush of pleasure.

'The Commissioner is going to visit you soon, so you had better eat to be strong. That man tests anyone's strength at the best of times.'

She left the room with the ease and familiarity of one who felt at home. It suddenly struck me how little I knew of her family, although I was aware she had sons and daughters.

I relaxed against the pillows, overwhelmed by a sudden thirst. I began to try to get out of bed, but my legs felt as though weights had been attached to them.

'Don't move.' The voice was quiet yet authoritative. It was Homer entering the room with a large jug of water and a glass. I didn't bother with the glass, but grabbed the jug and raised it to my lips. Homer watched with his arms crossed and an amused smile on his lips.

'More?'

I declined. 'A moment ago I would have done anything for a drink. I can see how thirst turns you mad. How did people manage in the days before water production?'

'I don't think they did. Millions died of dehydration, though you can be sure the Directors and their managers didn't go without.'

I was a little shocked by his blatant anti-Company comments. Even away from the village, one had to be careful what one said to others, especially if they were strangers. I decided not to respond and watched in silence as he placed a steaming bowl of soup before me and bade me eat. But the effort of drinking had left me weak and I was unable to lift the spoon, so Homer fed me. It was difficult to control my mouth and I was embarrassed by the drips that rolled down my chin. Homer wiped them away gently, implying a new intimacy between us that I struggled to ignore. I tried not to notice the strength in his shoulders and the dark hair that curled over the neck of his shirt.

'Who is Mariam?' Homer asked quietly.

I was suddenly jolted out of my relaxed state.

'Who? I don't know anyone called Mariam. It's not a name from this area, is it?'

'I don't know. But you kept calling for her enough times when you were delirious. I thought she might be a friend of yours. Or perhaps it was a call from an ancestor.'

So Homer had been watching over me. Why?

21

The Commissioner sat on the end of my bed looking flushed. In place of his usual cassock he wore a freshly laundered white tunic which hung over a black and gold sarong. His perfumed hair had been arranged over his ears and his fringe had been curled. It did his face no justice, but from the way he proudly posed his profile to catch his reflection in the mirror, he clearly thought otherwise. I was eager for news, but the Commissioner seemed distracted. He began to stroke my foot hidden beneath the sheet. I kicked his hand away.

I could not put off asking after my parents. He said he had escorted them to the main Company office at the port, where they had spent two nights before being taken to Olin in the south-east, the place from where most of the home-grown olives were exported.

'I know that your father has been given a laboratory to continue his work. It's much finer than the one he has here. Your mother has been tasked with several projects, which the Company admits are far too simple for a woman of her intelligence, but I think you will find she is grateful for even the easiest task that will keep her mind occupied. Of course, they are still grieving for your sister, and spoke of nothing else during our journey to the port.

Although they were much comforted when the Company President offered his condolences.'

I gasped. 'But that's impossible. No one meets the President!'

'You underestimate both the President and your parents, Jephzat. He occasionally likes to meet those who make a valuable contribution to the well-being of the Company. He has followed closely your father's work in the survival of the olive in alien atmospheres. It's of special interest to him, along with your mother's own work in the genetic field.'

He reached into a pocket inside his tunic and handed me a tiny parcel which I quickly unwrapped. It was a sound valve – hardly the size of a small button – which could be placed in the ear.

'It's a message from your parents. You can listen to it when I am gone.'

The valve was transparent and enclosed a minute disc, which had begun to vibrate in my hand. I placed it in my ear. I heard my father's recorded voice, stilted and formal.

'Hello, Jephzat, your mother and I are both safe and well. The journey was a little uncomfortable. There was so much dust on that road. The Water soldiers had already gone, but when we got to the port we were told that some of them had been lingering in the hills waiting to ambush lone travellers, so as you can imagine we had a lucky escape.

'We are now in one of the domestic units in Olin town. There are all the usual mod cons and we are managing to keep ourselves occupied with work the Company has given us. My laboratory is state of the art and now my notes have finally arrived I can start work in earnest. How is my little workplace bearing up?

'We miss you and your sister more than you can know. We keep thinking that Hephzibah will be waiting for us when we return. Did you get Sengita to sort out the fire crystals? I hope it wasn't too upsetting for you. Your mother gets very depressed and wants to return as soon as possible. She wants a word with you, so I'll say good-bye, Jephzat. Don't worry about us. We are fine. Make sure you eat properly. Goodbye, lovely, goodbye.'

There were kissing noises and then I could hear Dolores coughing. 'Hello, Jephzat. Hello.' Her voice sounded tired and she spoke as if she had rehearsed the lines many times. 'It's very hot here. The unit is nice with plenty of room for us both. It's a real town, not like the village, and there's a lot of traffic with air buggies going over all the time. Will you put the fire crystals in a window overlooking the sea? I don't know when we will be coming back. I hope the village has calmed down a bit and that you are safe.'

Her voice trailed off and there was some shuffling in the background before the valve closed down to silence. I was frustrated because they had told me very little. They merely confirmed the few details that the Commissioner had already given me. Frustrated and angry, I hurled the valve across the room. I doubted that their return would come soon; and with foreboding I realized that they were effectively prisoners of the Company.

The window was open and a breeze ruffled my hair. I could smell the estuary. I leaped out of bed, suddenly

nothing left that could be saved. The fire would burn itself out eventually. We both gazed at the ashes lying scattered in the area that had once contained the laboratory. There was very little that was visible to feed the fire now, yet its flames continued to rise high into the sky. The woman indicated with her head for me to watch the jet of water which was being pumped up from the estuary. She shouted for the valve to be turned on full, and aimed the nozzle into the heart of the fire. The water merely hissed, then crackled as if it were dried wood, and evaporated into a thin, iridescent mist that hung in the air for a few seconds before disappearing.

The fire raged for six hours and it was dark by the time it had burnt itself out totally. Most of the villagers had walked up to the house to watch the spectacle. Manos and I found ourselves running backwards and forwards from the house with trays of drinks, while Sengita, a late arrival, fussed around everyone with her potions, pills and sprays. Joachim stayed in the house, fearful of the strange green light which hung like gauze above the horizon. Homer sat on the veranda with the old men, saying nothing.

The villagers ruminated over the cause of such a spectacular fire, the like of which had not been seen since one of the Company's administrative offices in the port blew up. At their most intense the flames could be seen fifty miles away. Afterwards, the Company announced the cause as 'excessive solar energy', but this meant nothing, and only fuelled rumours that it had been an act of sabotage.

We expected the Company to send a platoon of

workers, along with a team of scientists to investigate while the fire was still burning, but not even the Commissioner had shown up.

The villagers hung around for some time, lying on the grass or taking it in turns to sit on the house steps. Others sat in the kitchen coughing, believing that by being indoors they would be protected from contaminated air. They were friendly towards me, but I noticed that they cast their eyes down whenever they spoke to me, a custom usually reserved for strangers.

Sengita sat down heavily beside me. She rested her arms with relief on the battered old medicine bag that lay across her lap. Her feet were swollen and she licked at the sweat that beaded her top lip. We stared across at the charred stumps of vegetation that now surrounded the laboratory.

'Normally I would advise shovelling up the ashes and putting them on the garden – the potash is wonderful, especially for tomatoes. But this lot should be dredged up and put somewhere miles away from anything living. Goodness knows what it will do to us,' she muttered.

I sighed and then coughed, bringing up a black tarry liquid. Sengita quickly tilted back my head and sprayed something cooling into my mouth and nostrils. I shivered uncontrollably as it made its icy path down my throat and into my lungs. She placed her large hands flat on my shoulders and rested them there for several moments before putting them on the front of my neck and chest. She instructed me to take a deep breath and I did so, this time without coughing.

'Does your father know yet?' she asked, her gaze focused on the green haze.

'I don't know. I have no way of reaching him,' I lied. Sengita did not know about my mother's bunker. 'I expect the Company will contact him, but the laboratory was such a huge part of his life that he will sense something is up. Father is like that.'

Manos threaded her way carefully through the sprawling crowd of villagers to join us. She was stern when she said, 'The fire has burnt itself out and people should leave.'

I said nothing. I was enjoying the bustle, having people around me again. Sengita rose from the ground with difficulty and we had to help her.

'Let's tell them to leave, Manos. This girl is tired and needs her sleep. No doubt the Company will be around in the morning waking her up.' Manos took Sengita's bag, and the two women set off slowly to disperse the gathering. I knew that Manos would not want to be here while the Company carried out its inevitable investigations.

I had resolved to return to the bunker when I heard a noise behind me. I swung round to find Homer facing me.

'Why are you still here?'

'Because someone needs to look after you.'

'I don't need looking after.'

'I think you do. I'm not leaving.'

I was too tired to persuade him otherwise. He led me into the house.

'Don't worry about having to deal with the Company in the morning. I'll do that for you.'

'But they'll want to question me about what happened. Someone had broken into the laboratory and probably caused the explosion.'

'We'll talk about this tomorrow – now is not the time, Jephzat.'

He watched me as I climbed slowly up the stairs to my room. I knew he would find somewhere comfortable to sleep – after all, he knew the house better than anyone.

23

It was dark when I slipped out into the garden and took the path that led to the bunker. The smell of burnt foliage mixed with a chemical pungency still hung in the air, but fortunately the fire had not touched the area near the bunker. Checking that no one was watching me, I removed the lid and eased myself into the tiny space, replacing the cover carefully before activating minimal light, which would enable me to find the tiny pressure points in the wall. The screen eased itself out of the compacted earth. I knew what to do and watched my reflection on the screen as I pressed my thumb against the wall of the bunker to activate the equipment. It was so quiet and still in the bunker that I could hear myself breathing.

There was a faint sound like pebbles falling on sand followed by Dolores's voice.

'We are fine,' she whispered, peering down into the palms of her hands that lay face up in her lap. I could not tell if she was holding anything. 'Don't worry about us. The Company is looking after us well. It says we will be able to return soon once things have calmed down, but I get the impression that all is not as resolved as the Company would have us believe.'

My father appeared on the screen beside Dolores, sitting in a wire chair with thick red cushions. His skin reflected the yellow of the wall behind him and made him look ill. He peered over into my mother's upturned palms.

'Are you all right? Tell us what is happening. No one gives us any news of home. Have you been looking after the lab?'

I couldn't put it off any longer. I told him about the fire and even in the bunker's poor light I could see the devastation in his face.

'Was nothing saved?' he asked sadly.

I shook my head. 'The cylinders burst open.'

He looked surprised. 'They were designed to be protected from extreme heat. This should not have happened.'

'The contents were released. They smelled strange and there was a weird green vapour that settled over the sea. It was luminous. People were ill breathing it all in. I want to know what the long-term effects of it could be. There was a funny sound as well, very low-pitched and painful to the ear.'

Father shook his head.

'I don't know. It is difficult working with materials that are new to the planet. Some of the experiments were designed to measure levels of toxicity. We won't ever have the answers now.'

He asked me how the fire had started and I said I thought the laboratory had been broken into and the fire set deliberately. The Company was sending a team tomorrow to sift through what remained, I told him.

'What shall I say to them?'

'They'll know what has been going on. Just tell them what you found, but take away the cylinders and hide them in the house. Tell them they disappeared in the fire. Salvage anything you can that might have escaped the flames,' he pressed. 'With luck we shall be home soon. The Company is keeping us both busy with data brought back from the last Federation space mission. It helps us to survive the days here away from you. But we worry about you all alone in that big house.'

I told them how Sengita visited regularly and that Manos was returning to the house. But I did not mention Homer.

The picture of them was beginning to break up and I wondered if the Company was intercepting. Their faces faded and I was left in the semi-darkness, feeling more alone than ever. I sat there for some time, straining to hear any sound that might indicate someone approaching and then climbed out. I carefully replaced the lid and headed for the ruins of the laboratory to retrieve the cylinders. They were heavy, but one by one I managed to place them in the bunker. When the final cylinder had been hidden, I replaced the lid and adjusted the camouflage, but stopped when I heard a noise in the undergrowth nearby. I turned to leave and heard it again: the sound of dry undergrowth cracking under weight and leaves being moved, brushing against something which I am sure was moving towards me.

I began to run towards the house but a hand clamped over my mouth and pulled me backwards. I knew instantly without looking that it was Homer.

'Don't make a noise,' he commanded and released his hand.

I swung round and stared at him angrily. 'What are you doing, following me like that?'

He stared down at his feet sheepishly. 'I had to make sure you were safe. These are dangerous times.'

'What do you mean, dangerous? What the hell's going on, Homer? I was feeling restless and needed to go outside for a stroll. You're making me feel like a prisoner in my own home.'

He gripped my arms and shook me as if trying to wake me. 'You are a prisoner, Jephzat. We are all prisoners. We cannot go where we choose, and if we try to the Company is tracking our every move. It could be listening in to this very conversation. Who is free, Jephzat? Who is free?'

A million questions exploded in my head. 'Tell me, who are you, Homer? Tell me what's going on.'

He remained silent for a long time before gently guiding me towards the summerhouse. The moon glowed passively above the mouth of the estuary and the water shone. He slipped a reassuring arm around my waist and I did not move away.

A faint smell of oranges lingered and we sat close together on the bench. I was trembling.

'Are you cold?' he murmured, drawing me closer to him. We sat like this for a long time, listening to the sounds of the night.

I did not resist when he kissed my cheek, and could not stop myself offering my mouth to him. A hunger was taking over my body, and his probing tongue did nothing to stop it. I felt myself clinging to him as if my life could be saved by his kiss.

He began to undress me very slowly and covered each part of my exposed skin with a torrent of exquisite kisses until I was naked, and my skin moist from his tongue.

We were locked for a long time in a passion that rocked and danced to its own rhythms. His tongue and breath in turn burned, cooled and blew on my skin with a fierceness that was at times unbearable. I rode him with a driven force that seemed to feed into me from his tongue and fingers. He followed in a sweet madness which turned his face into a stranger's that did not seem to recognize me, until he cried my name and bit my neck as if trying to anchor himself to me for ever.

The sun was sliding slowly above the horizon when we walked back to the house. I was conscious of my hips swaying beneath his hand and felt the fullness of my breasts moving against my dress. The air seemed brighter, clearer, and I felt new, whole and reckless.

Once inside the house, I returned to my bed, disappointed that Homer would not come with me.

'When you awake, say my name and I'll be there,' he promised.

24

I did not need to call Homer's name when I awoke, for there he was standing beside my bed, a broad smile on his face. He kissed me full on the lips and I held him close for more, but he broke free and, laughing, pulled me out of bed. Reluctantly I followed him through the door.

'Where are you taking me?' I asked, trying to keep in step with him. 'There isn't anything about this house I don't know, so don't think you can surprise me.'

We walked along the corridor that led away from the south wing. I was aware that he was watching me slyly from the corner of his eye, his head turned just enough to gauge my reaction to his withdrawal, which had heightened my need for his closeness. Refusing to show Homer how much I wanted him – this would only make me more vulnerable – I simply smiled as warmly as I could. He drew me to him and held my shoulders as we walked through the endless winding corridors, while I tried hard not to feel grateful for his touch.

We were heading for the centre of the house; a high, windowless, octagonal room, with concrete walls clad in light panels, which were activated by approaching steps. I knew the room well. Hephzibah and I had often sought it out for its coolness and the intricate mosaic floor that we enjoyed dancing upon. We liked the room's grandeur and its delicate acoustics, for the ceiling rose up into a large cupola. We would open the door on the far side of the room and climb the stairs to the top of the adjoining high tower. From a narrow balcony jutting high over the cupola, we enjoyed a panorama of remote hills and the estuary bleeding like a huge artery into the sea . . .

Disconcertingly, we now passed the room's heavy wooden door. I expected Homer to stop at one of the adjoining rooms, but he carried on walking round the octagon, his eyes fixed steadily ahead, guided only by the thin pins of light, which fell like stars from the ceiling on to the doors. He stopped suddenly at one of the corners of the octagonal chamber. He blew on the wall and it began to move outward into the corridor like a door, revealing an iron beam that supported part of the tower. As soon as it had opened wide enough to let us in, Homer pulled me through and the wall closed behind us.

A familiar smell hit my nostrils and I inhaled its intense pungency with surprised pleasure. We had stepped into another narrow corridor which would be invisible to anyone either inside the room or in the outer corridor. I looked around me in amazement; a thin veneer of light revealed the spines of thousands of books pressed together on countless rows of wooden shelves. They coiled around the circular walls of the corridor like the ribbed back of a serpent, and were stacked on both sides, from the floor upwards to the very top of the leaning arch of the cupola.

Incredulity robbed me of my voice. I ran my hand along a line of leatherbound books as if they were notes on a keyboard and shuddered. Each one was a death sentence. But at that moment I didn't care.

'Welcome to the library,' Homer said, a ring of triumph in his voice.

I walked away from him, wordless in a word-full sea. I stared along the shelves, overwhelmed by a new hunger that came from a famine I did not even know I had endured. I ran my fingers along the shelves, not knowing which book to open, overwhelmed by a desire to feast on every one simultaneously. I wanted to gorge myself on syntax, lick words curling from the page into my mouth, nibble daintily on alphabets as if they were sweets.

I picked out a book at random, handsized, the edges of its covers frayed, and gently turned its gauze-thin pages. Each page of print reflected its other side, like bone through skin. The script was strange to me and ran amok upon the paper, a tumult of dots and dashes and curlicues. Unable to decipher a single word, I leaned back against the shelves, weighed down by words whose meanings were withheld from me.

I returned the book and peered at its companions' titles – most of them also written in Old World scripts. My eyes revelled in the shapes of the various letters. Some had the square solidity of furniture, others were tortile, fancifully scrolled or whorled. There were those that lurched forward or backward as if blown by a wind, and some printed so tightly together I wished to unravel them. I closed my eyes to shut them out. It was as if all the books in the library were suddenly clamouring, 'Read me! Read me!' because only the casting of an eye upon their pages gave them life.

'Many of the books you see here are in English, the

old language of the American empire,' Homer explained, pulling out one of the books and another one beside it. 'Some people have become secretly skilled in book-binding, and have made exact copies here in Federese. But most books have translations handwritten into notebooks which are all kept in another part of the library. Smaller books tend to have their translations loose-leaved and placed between the pages. Over eighty languages have been translated so far, but there's so much still to do.'

He shook his head, and I gazed at him, wondering why everything he did seemed to have the significance of a miracle.

With the excitement and apprehension of a traveller setting off for the unknown, I pulled out another book at random and opened it carefully. I lowered my head to inhale the perfume of its ink and heavy, ageing paper. Looking up at Homer I asked, 'Do my parents know about the library?'

'We decided not to tell them in case they were put under pressure by the Company. The library has been here for a long time. Books have been stored in this house since before the Company moved in.'

'But my parents have books of their own. They're hidden away and when I was a little girl they would bring them out on special occasions, like on Federation Day. Each time I was read to, I was left feeling restless and unsettled. Now I realize that the books had unlocked doors inside me, but only to rooms that were empty and which I could not fill.

'We were told never to tell anyone else about them, on pain of our parents' arrest. In hindsight, it was a mon-strous responsibility for two small children.'

'These are monstrous times,' Homer whispered, taking my hand and walking me past the towering shelves. He stopped before several rows of battered volumes, all bound in faded maroon leather.

Again I couldn't read the script. The letters were strange to me, their shapes curved and looped like marine knots. I buried my head in Homer's neck and then whispered in his ear, 'Read me the titles. Let me hear you read. Blaspheme for me.'

I wanted to be a book that lay in his hands, bound in leather so soft that he slept upon it, its creamy vellum harbouring stories for his delight only.

'Fiction,' he said suddenly, moving away from me, as if afraid I would arouse him again. 'I think we're in S, so here we have a book in English, *Pygmalion* by George Bernard Shaw, a real visionary of his time. An advocate of equality. Imagine!' He flipped a smile into my eyes. 'Look at these. We have a rather nice collection of plays, probably one of the best in the Federation.

'William Shakespeare,' he announced, carefully sliding one of the leatherbound books off its shelf. 'He was – is – one of the world's greatest writers. A favourite of mine. I found him difficult at first, but well worth the effort. He lived nearly seven hundred years ago, but his plays were banned in the last days of the empire and haven't seen the light of day since. His works aren't anything like the turgid plays and performances the Company treats us to.'

He gently smoothed his hands over the pages. 'This man addresses what really matters – man's humanity to man and the condition of the human spirit – concepts so utterly alien to us that you probably don't even know what I'm talking about.'

'I can't read this script,' I mumbled, ashamed of my ignorance.

'There are translations,' he said, returning the volume to the shelf. He reached for a frayed and faded book: *As You Like It* by William Shakespeare was printed in Federese on its cover. He explained how over countless years all Shakespeare's works had been translated in secret by people who had spent a lifetime learning the Old World languages.

'It was hard at first – like deciphering difficult codes – but thankfully there had been renegade bureaucrats commissioned to stamp out the old languages who had hidden as many books as they could. Years later, old dictionaries and grammar books were found, which helped the Translators. The problem with Shakespeare and others, of course, is that the English spoken in his day is unlike the English that was spoken when the new Federation language was being created.'

I took the book from him and opened it at random.

Sweet are the uses of adversity
Which, like the toad, ugly and venomous,
Wears yet a precious jewel in his head:
And this our life, exempt from public haunt,
Finds tongues in trees, books in the running brooks,
Sermons in stones, and good in everything.

'Books in the running brooks,' I repeated. 'How lovely and how strange.'

Homer watched me intently as I spoke, and stroked my hair. We stood in silence for a long time. I closed my eyes, imagining a young man dipping his pen into ink and writing upon beams of incandescent light that became his messengers, posting words into the mouths of actors, delivering his art to spellbound audiences.

'The books keep coming. People are finding them all over the place. One man walked for three days to bring us two books he had found in a cave. He worked out his route via underground tunnels, some of which hadn't been navigated since the old empire when people moved underground to escape the pollution. When he arrived he did not want to part with them, and wept as he handed them over. He was caught on his return journey, and his cinders were deposited on his doorstep. He risked his life because he knew how rare the books were and wanted to make sure they would be forever safe.'

Homer walked over to a large metal desk tucked into an alcove. He opened a drawer and pulled out a large book. He opened it to reveal pages full of names. 'Martyrs,' he said fiercely. 'All these people have been executed for being caught in possession of books. They will not be forgotten.'

He returned the names to the drawer and slammed it shut. 'We are running out of space and will have to find a new place for another library. It's not just the books. We have thousands of texts stored on bits of old technology, and are trying to interpret them. Some of us had been thinking of building another library underground. But if everything goes to plan we might not need to.'

I gazed around the shelves surrounding the desk, attracted to a long row of scruffy hardbacks, full of scraps of paper. Curious, I picked one out, its cover decorated with a child's drawings. It was a photographic record of a baby's first year. A translation had been scrawled across the cover: 'Jaimin Patel, beloved son of

Arjun and Vaishali Patel, brother to Amisha, born July 2nd, 1952. The Patel family, residents of New Jersey, United States of America.'

Little Jaimin had been photographed with every member of the Patel family, his small fat face held up to the camera. The Patels seemed happy until towards the end of the album, when I noticed dark circles under Arjun's eyes and Vaishali had become so thin that her bracelets hung over her knuckles. Sadly I closed the album as I wondered why.

'Look at these,' Homer continued enthusiastically, indicating higher shelves. 'I think this is one of the most interesting sections of the library.'

He stood on tiptoe and stretched to pull out a thick, handmade notebook, with thin olive-wood covers and rough leaves of paper inside them. The print was crude but intelligible and the text was dense, occasionally trespassing the margins. The title of the book, *The Separation of Similars*, was in Federese and had been carved into the wood.

'This is our literature, from our time,' Homer said proudly. 'The story of a family riven apart by the Company. Both parents died in work camps.'

I looked up, feeling giddy. The shelves seemed to go upward for ever and I felt them leaning over me as if ready to topple. I saw books flying off the shelves, their pages spread open like birds' wings, and rushing towards me in dark cawing flocks. Words tumbled from the pages and showered me like sparks from an explosion. I shut my eyes and felt myself disappearing in a blast of fragments of script, which were forcing themselves into my mouth like feathers. Disembodied words that I could not read glowed red with heat and attached themselves to my skin as if branding me. I was turning into a book I could not read. The story was illegible and I did not know how it would end. Somehow I knew that I was not the story-teller, I was the story.

25

We returned from the secret library only minutes before the Company officials arrived. Six figures leaped from their streamlined vehicles and ignored us as they brought out phials of labelled liquids, powders and tiny machines which they linked together like building blocks. They wore protective clothing; in addition, fine mesh hid their faces and their eyes lurked behind close-fitting glasses. When one of them came over to greet us I expected the voice to be muffled, but it came clearly from somewhere beneath the woman's neck.

'Show us where the fire started,' she demanded without formal introduction.

I led her over to where the laboratory had once stood. Now only a blackened circle of charred debris remained.

'What happened to your father's work?' she asked sharply.

'I don't know. There was no sign of the canisters containing some of the experiments.' I spoke hesitantly, suddenly afraid that they might find the small cylinders Father had asked me to hide.

Then I recounted what had happened and mentioned the strange smell and green light that had come as a result of the fire. I knew I was being recorded and that my words would later be replayed.

When I had finished she turned to Homer.

'Why are you here?'

'I was bringing Jephzat some food. She has been ill, but when I arrived the fire had already started. I stayed to help her, and the villagers came too. They saw the smoke and were curious.'

I sensed that she was scrutinizing us carefully from behind the mesh.

'He stayed with me because the smoke made me feel worse. He was worried.'

Saying nothing, she beckoned to her companions and they began to sift through the debris. Carefully taking samples with their gloved hands, they placed them in small containers and poured combinations of the liquids onto them before sealing the contents. I offered them refreshments but they refused.

'We want to get away as soon as possible,' one of them said.

A faint humming came from beyond the hills and we turned our heads. A tiny black dot appeared in the distance below a small cluster of clouds. The humming grew louder and as it flew towards us I realized it was a Company air buggy. Air buggies were seldom seen this far away from the main towns. They moved quickly and turned with all the precision of a bird in flight, giving a dangerous sense of unpredictability. Suddenly it was swooping over our heads; bright and glinting like a small hard sun. It hovered above the house and then flew so low over our heads that we had to duck. For a moment I was afraid it would fall directly upon us.

Instead, it landed carefully beside the summerhouse, clearing most of the vegetation as it did so. The Company officials had resumed their work, but Homer and I stood transfixed, fearing the worst; air buggies were made available to only the most important Company members.

We watched as the door was raised and a figure in protective clothing jumped out. He was followed by another, who climbed with difficulty out of the buggy and turned directly to me. My heart began to beat faster and the palms of my hands grew clammy. I could not recognize the face under the mesh, but the bent back and the slow, loping walk of the figure coming towards me were familiar. He stood before me and his voice came out from below the mesh with a curious echo.

'Jephzat. It's me. Your father.'

I pulled him to me and held him close, biting back the questions I longed to ask him. Underneath the thickness of the protective clothing he felt frail, and I stared at him long and hard to make out his features beneath the face guard.

I reluctantly released him to a Company official and watched as he was escorted to where the laboratory had stood. He gazed at the scene of destruction for a long time before turning to talk at some length to one of the officials. Then he was led back to the air buggy. He turned and waved at me before stepping inside. With difficulty, I restrained my emotions rather than reveal them to Company strangers.

'Will I see my father again?' I asked the woman.

I could not see the expression on her face, and her voice gave nothing away.

'If the Company says you will then you will. It always has its employees' best interests at heart.'

The buggy shot up into the air and stayed motionless

for a second before swooping over the estuary to head for the port. I saw fishermen in their boats look up to the sky and heard them call fearfully to one another.

'We've finished now,' an official said ten minutes later, packing up the boxes and bags. The group returned to their vehicles without acknowledging us. I was surprised they had not questioned me further or searched the house. I turned to Homer but he merely gave me a look that silenced me.

'Be grateful they found nothing,' was all he said after they'd gone.

Homer seemed in no hurry to go anywhere, and stayed for a few days. The pleasure of awakening and finding him curled next to me was better than being woken by the sun streaming through the window. Manos came into the room once, without knocking, but did not seem surprised to see him there. She merely gave a sly smile and handed me a herb tea prepared by Sengita to clear away the lingering effects of the fire. I was so consumed by Homer that I forgot to drink it and I wondered if it had been like this for Hephzibah with her soldiers.

One morning, as if reading my thoughts, he asked me what it was that I missed most about her.

'Her smile, her needing me, telling her stories. Her laugh and her wicked humour, her unpredictable generosity. I suppose I miss her selfishness too.'

'How can you miss selfishness?'

'When you love someone who is selfish and you want to stay close to them, you always end up trying to please them and that determines how you spend much of your day – even your life. That's all gone now and I feel lost without her demands. It's the same with the laboratory. I knew each day would involve spending time helping Father in his work, and now he's gone and the laboratory's gone I don't know what to do any more. I keep hoping the Company will give me new instructions to keep me busy and absorbed, but I wouldn't want to be sent anywhere else. I want to be here for when my parents return.'

I did not tell him that I also wanted to stay in case Hephzibah came back with her child. I knew it was unlikely, but hope, like light, will always find a chink in a shuttered room.

Later, in the kitchen, Manos asked me if I was eating properly.

'Homer feeds me,' I said airily.

'I'm sure, but he feeds you only with love, and a stomach cannot feed on love alone. The heart, yes, but not the stomach. You have to eat.' And she gestured with her fingers at her opened mouth, as if I was still a child.

Homer came in. He had oiled his hair, and his sarong clung to his thighs. He stroked my arm and kissed my cheek affectionately. Manos looked on with brazen interest.

'It's good that you are here for Jephzat. Goodness knows how she would be if she did not have you. She would've gone mad by now.'

I didn't acknowledge her words, but flushed instead, knowing them to be true.

We sat on the veranda. I rarely saw Manos relaxing

in this way and thought how she had changed since my parents had left. She was less subservient, less busy, less anxious to return home. A tall woman, she now seemed taller.

We said nothing, our eyes focusing on a pair of parakeets playing in the bougainvillea, but each deep in our own thoughts. It was Homer who broke the long silence.

'The Company wants a big increase in the olive harvest next year. It does not say why, but it's already planning to bring in more workers. I don't know how they will get the trees to produce more than they already have. The young trees are not matured and won't fruit for a long time yet.'

'It's up to something,' Manos said.

'Yes, but what? And why does it want more people here? It's worrying.'

'Perhaps they've discovered another use for the olives, although I can't imagine what that could be. We are already scrambling to meet a huge demand from the rest of the Federation and working to full capacity. Even with all the scientific knowledge the Company has at its disposal, it can't just make an olive tree produce more than it's able to. Or can it?'

Manos sighed deeply and stood to leave.

'I've cooked for you and tidied around a bit. Don't forget to take Sengita's tea. Homer, you should have some too.' We kissed her fondly and she strode down the driveway, a parakeet flying behind her like a tiny bright jewel.

*

Desire overwhelmed me once she had gone. But it was not a desire for Homer. I had to return to the library. I could already smell the books' muskiness and in my mind turned over pages with as many differing textures as a forest; pages that were brittle and fragile which had to be coaxed to turn; pages that were soft and scented, presenting their words as if they were a gift in the palm of a hand, and pages that fell open heavily of their own accord as if weighted by the importance of their message. But more than anything else I was compelled by their mystery, by all the stories they had yet to tell me.

'I have to go to the library, Homer. I have to be with the books.'

He understood and accompanied me to remind me of the secret entrance. Then he left, promising to return in the evening, and kissed me gently on my forehead. I watched as he slipped through the wall like a shadow. I stood alone among the towering shelves, savouring my solitude, thrilled by what the books would soon reveal to me.

I stared at the shelves and waited. Where to begin? I strolled slowly past the rows of books, my eyes darting over the titles and names of authors. I paused beside a set of encyclopaedias, and randomly pulled one out. I could not understand the text, but gazed curiously at the black and white illustrations. Engrossed in studying a map of the Old World, I relaxed against the shelves. There was a sudden noise, and I recognized the sigh of the door as it opened automatically. I knew instinctively that it was not Homer. I hurriedly returned the book, and in a panic looked for somewhere to hide. Heart hammering, I crept further along the shelves until I saw a large cupboard beside a desk, which I quickly hid behind. With dismay I realized that the visitor would know someone was already in the library because of the lights. Then I heard footsteps heading towards me. I peered below the cupboard to see the hem of a familiar skirt sweeping past. I shifted myself for a better view. She had stopped and was climbing one of the ladders to a high shelf. She reached for a book and, placing it in one of her waistcoat pockets, began her descent. I was waiting for her at the bottom of the ladder. Sengita did not seem at all surprised to see me, and greeted me as if the circumstances were not unusual.

'I wondered how long it would take for you to find this place,' she said, and proceeded to congratulate me. 'The day you first come here is the most wonderful and important day of your life. We must celebrate another time, because now that you have found the books you will have very little opportunity to do anything but read. You will have thoughts for little else. You will be like a woman who has spent her best years sharing a bed with a useless lover, and in middle age discovers true passion for the first time.'

'I was thinking more of someone dying from thirst who finds a well,' I said.

'But you can die from drinking too much,' Sengita answered softly. 'You can never die from too much love, or too much knowledge.'

Suddenly I didn't feel so sure. 'You exaggerate the importance of these books, Sengita. It is surely dangerous to set such store by them. They're probably as full of lies as the Company messages we are given. They could even be planted here by the Federation – another one of its tricks.'

'Then why are you here?' she spat.

'I felt I had to come. I couldn't resist. I don't know why.'

Sengita took me by my shoulders and shook me furiously. 'Nothing, Jephzat, is ever going to be the same for you again. After today your life will change more than you could possibly dream. You have just had sex with a man and think you have been awakened to all the possibilities of life. It was so sweet, you can't imagine sweeter than that.'

I tried to push her away, but she would not let go of me and her eyes blazed with a frightening intensity.

'Little girl, listen! One night spent with these books, just one night, will turn your life upside down in a way that a lover never ever can. I promise you.'

We were both shaking when she loosened her grip. Her expression softened.

'I'm sorry, Jephzat, but these books are all we have left to tell us who we are and what has been taken from us. Sometimes you need only be in their presence to be touched by the words. You don't need to turn the pages, they speak to you from the shelves, and sometimes it jangles my nerves and I find it hard to be reasonable. I am just trying to warn you that some things are more powerful than we could possibly imagine. That is why the Federation has always wanted to destroy all this.' She swept an arm along the spines of a row of books. 'Words can empower, words can destroy, and words can resurrect.'

'But I don't know where to start,' I said miserably.

'I will show you. Everyone who comes here starts by finding out what has happened since the dark days began.

Not by reading the Federation's version but how it was recorded at the time. It will shock and disturb you, but don't stop reading until you understand how it really was.'

Sengita disappeared and returned with her arms full of books. She placed them on the desk and pulled up a chair for me. I started to read. And my new life began.

Book III

*I don't know where I
am going. You're the road and
the knower of roads, more
than maps, more than love.*

RUMI

Book III

CHRISTINE AZIZ

26

The sun was nudging the moon from the sky when I returned to my room. Homer lay asleep, his arms flung across the pillows. I breathed in the warmth and scent of his body, but could not sleep. My head was full of a new, unsettling learning. Could it all be true? If it was, how could we continue as we were, knowing that the Federation had taken everything, including our past, from our lives? It had created a lie for us to live by and in so doing had taken life itself away from us, leaving us stumbling in the dark with nothing more than an instinct for survival. To be a Company worker meant never considering the possibility of another way of living. I tried to comprehend the enormity of what I had discovered – I finally had a choice.

I realized there were others who already knew that the old maps had been destroyed. Not purposely, we were told; but the means to preserve them had been 'lost'. I also knew from my parents that borders had been redrawn around ownership of natural resources and centres of production. But until I began to read the books, I did not know that vast tracts of land had also 'disappeared', ignored by the authorities. Cartography soon became an art of deception.

The Old Countries had disappeared a long time ago,

their names and languages forbidden, their peoples and histories suddenly non-existent. Thousands of men, women and children were secretly sent out to space to form new colonies, but none survived. Countless others disappeared and were never accounted for, although rumours circulated that they had been sent to work camps to be retrained as the world re-created itself. Nationalities melted away, although some individuals managed to salvage tiny fragments of their old languages and their customs, drawing on a distant memory of oral histories and the subversively foraged books. Individuals were stripped of any sense of belonging, and torn from their communities and families at whim. There were mass transportations of people to camps where minds were altered, memories stripped and bodies trained to obey.

The lucky ones were the few who stayed put, or who had people around them who were not afraid to remember. People who had forgotten where the mountains were found them again, guided by water. But many did not know how to survive. There were those who did not know there was desert until strangers who had lost their way told tales of extraordinary heat, oceans of sand and animals with humped backs that travelled for days without water. People nourished by thick forests found themselves having to adapt to open savannas. People marvelled and wondered what else there was to discover. But it was already too late.

And the root cause of all this? When the climate changed, it transformed our earth for ever: flowers began to bloom through what had once been harsh winters; entire towns were made uninhabitable by flooding; slowly, the sea's tides consumed great swathes of coast, and ozone protection from the sun began to fail. You already know the beginnings of that story. Like an imploding star, your empire was no longer able to sustain itself. Then a growing shortage of potable water in most regions of the world destabilized it even further. Increasingly dependent on mega-corporations, governments did not see the writing on the wall . . .

Homer drew me to him, aroused. But I was distracted, distant.

'What's wrong, little goddess?'

'I read things last night that perhaps I shouldn't have. Sengita gave the books to me. There's nothing that woman doesn't know. It's as if she's everywhere at once.'

Homer sat up and stared down at me. I stroked his moustache and ran my fingers around his lips, but he pushed me away gently.

'Sengita loves you. She wouldn't do anything to hurt you. If she was in the library while you were there, it was because she was there to help you. You must trust her.'

'I trust Sengita more than I trust anyone outside my family. But the Federation makes trust a dangerous game. Trust the wrong person and you're dead. There aren't any books which teach us how to trust someone.'

'You have read only a tiny part of the truth. And remember, even in the old days facts were doctored.'

'But some things can't be suppressed for ever. The suffering that went into the creation of this Federation must have been enormous. All those people who disappeared. What happened to them? Massacred? But why? Because they weren't of any use to the Federation? Or born with imperfections the Federation couldn't be bothered to correct? Whole histories, languages, countries wiped out. No wonder the Federation made so much effort to erase memories, create a new world and shift huge populations around until no one knew where they belonged any more. It could not have survived otherwise. It makes me sad and angry at the same time.'

'How angry?'

'Angry enough to want things to change.'

Homer drew his face close to mine.

'You mean, angry enough to help overthrow the Federation?'

I did not dare answer. I had already said more than I should have to a man I barely knew. If Homer was a Federation agent, an answer in the affirmative could mean execution, no questions asked. I remained silent.

'You can trust me,' he said, reading my thoughts.

'I can't take that risk. You could be anyone. You appeared from nowhere. You might be using me to trap other people who use the library.'

'Come outside,' he said. 'I will tell you everything.'

We took coffee, bread and fruit down to the estuary banks and sat on a large rock while the water lapped around us. The dawning sun was already warm and there was a light breeze that ruffled the water. Should I have been surprised by what Homer told me? I wasn't. It was as if I already knew . . .

He explained that I could visit the library as often as I needed to, that the more I read the better it would be for me. Knowledge is power, he said, and I was thrilled. If I wished, Sengita would advise me on what further books to read, but I was also free to read randomly as much and as often as I desired. I must be careful not to neglect my physical well-being; he warned me of the dangers of 'book fever'. Books could become an obsession, which was dangerous because the Company would notice. There were people called Book Guards, he explained, who volunteered to check the library at regular intervals to make sure its visitors were only there for three or four hours at a stretch, and never during Company time. I had been allowed to stay longer because of who I was. This puzzled me, but before I could question him, he placed a finger over my lips.

He warned me I would recognize other visitors to the library, but it was best that we didn't acknowledge each other.

Then he told me about the Readers; an organization of people dedicated not only to the recovery, restoration and preservation of books and other forms of information from the Old Countries, but to the destruction of the Federation. He fell silent and watched me carefully for a few moments.

'You don't seem surprised,' he then said.

'It all makes sense,' I replied. 'I can understand that reading alone is not enough. You want to do something with the knowledge and the anger it causes. But it's futile. Nothing can destroy the Federation. Through the Company it has a stranglehold on us. I'm surprised you've been able to get away with what you've already done.'

'There are people in high places who are part of our organization and – how shall I put it? – manage to perpetrate acts of subtle sabotage that are to our benefit. The Federation too, don't forget, is corrupt and inefficient, burdened by its own top-heavy bureaucracy. It makes many mistakes in our favour. This doesn't make our work any less dangerous, but we need people like you to join. You would be a real asset to us.'

A wave slapped against the rocks and sent up a cold spray that lightly hit our faces. I instantly thought of my parents. How could I jeopardize their lives by joining a clandestine organization?

'I can't, Homer,' I said. 'It's too dangerous. I can't see it working. Small groups of people who are trying to save a few books are also aiming to overthrow a Federation that rules the world. It's crazy.'

He pleaded with me. 'Sacrifices have to be made. Think how it will be once the Federation has gone. The libraries will be thrown open to everyone and people will reclaim their past. They will be able to map the planet again, they will have the freedom to explore, and resources will be shared collectively, not owned by a corrupted minority. Workers will choose where they want to work. The Companies stole our basic rights centuries ago, then stole our very identities. Now it's time to reclaim our rights and our selves. Education will not be the rote learning of Company rules and a fabricated history as it is now, but will be about the truth. There will be discussion and dissent and no one will disappear or be executed as a result. We will be able to express ourselves creatively.' He seized my hands. 'Jephzat, we will be free!'

I sighed, struggling to understand some of the words he was using. 'It all sounds good, but so foreign, like those languages in the library. Things will not change overnight. We have lived like this for so long that most of us accept it. We can't imagine anything else.'

'But once you read the books you'll see other possibilities. You know that already. You'll realize that once there were times when our ancestors lived with choices, and that our rights have always had to be fought for. Those in power never give us our rights, they slowly erode them until there is nothing left. Unless we fight. Look at what Maya did for the world. Through her inspiration people were able to reverse catastrophic climatic damage. Why? Because she inspired collective effort. The Federation knows what can happen when people are empowered by knowledge; that's why they keep us apart, forbid us to collect in small groups, break us up if we are seen too often together, ship us off to sterile planets to die. Maya wasn't perfect and she made mistakes. But the people were ready for her. The Federation still adheres to her Green Scriptures, but has banished her name from the records *because they don't want people to realize they have the power to change things.*'

'I don't know much about Maya, Homer. I'm sorry. I don't know if I care, either. Things are as they are, and that's it. That's all I know.'

'You disappoint me, Jephzat. You, and millions of others like you, are a living example of how good the Company is at its job.'

He placed a restraining hand upon my shoulder as I moved to leave.

'I beg you, Jephzat. The Readers need you. We have needed you for a long time, but the time was never right. Now it is, and you are ready. You must join us.'

'And if I don't?'

'Then we are all lost.'

27

The sun was hot as we stretched out over the rock and stared up at a cloudless sky. I felt the warm roughness of the rock scrape against my skin as I moved towards Homer and gathered him into my arms. He gazed up at the sun.

'There were times when people couldn't do this. They had to cover themselves from head to foot,' he said, turning his body so that he lay on top of me. 'There was no protection from the sun's rays because of the pollution.'

'That's nothing new. It's one of the few things the Federation tells us about the past.'

'It's one of the few things it tells us that's *true*. They know we can't afford to get complacent, and it frightens us enough to follow the environmental rules. But I have read it too in the old books. We have to be constantly reminded how the planet will turn against us again if we don't look after it. Not everything about the Old Countries was good. We have to learn from their mistakes and move forward.'

'You're beginning to sound like the Commissioner.'

We both laughed.

We couldn't make love on the rock in case anyone was watching us. I glanced uneasily towards the house.

'I feel as if we are being spied on all the time,' I said.

'The Company's always trying to watch us. You just have to be cleverer than them, that's all.'

We made our way to the summerhouse and hid in its shadows. We lay on the cool floor and I twined my legs around Homer's body, gripping him as though without him I might fall into an abyss. He made love to me with his fingers and I came in the palm of his hand. He stroked my breasts and neck. 'Don't wash it away,' he said. 'I want to be able to smell you tonight.'

The Commissioner was waiting for us, staring thoughtfully out to the estuary from the veranda. I had never seen him look so relaxed, but he snapped into action when he saw us approaching him.

'You spend enough time here,' he observed curtly to Homer in greeting.

'Jephzat's been badly affected by the fire. With her family gone, she needs looking after.'

'The Company can do that. It's time you returned home. There's work to be done. Some of the vats need to be repaired. You should have been in the office when I called round. I need to collect some quotas there.'

Homer said nothing, but nodded tersely and disappeared into the house to gather his belongings.

'Manos and Sengita can come to see you're all right,' the Commissioner said when we were alone, his face redder than normal. 'The Company has work for you to do. Your father thinks some of his research notes are missing and he wants you to see if you can find them.'

'Is this urgent?'

'You know where he was at with his experiments when the accident happened—'

At that moment Homer reappeared. He was no longer the relaxed, soft-faced lover who had lain in my arms only a few minutes before.

'Are you sure you'll be all right?' he asked quietly, before turning to leave with the commissioner. There would be no opportunity now for a private farewell.

I smiled weakly, too scared to speak in case my voice cracked and gave my emotions away. The smell of sex rose up from my neck and Homer's touch still vibrated between my legs. It was with sadness that I watched the two figures turn the bend and disappear. I felt vulnerable and lonely. But I forced myself to remain watching the empty horizon for a few minutes when all I wanted to do was return to the library.

28

I ran all the way. Sengita was already there when I arrived, curled up on a divan reading a large book. She tried to look surprised, but I knew she had been waiting for me. She smiled in welcome.

'I knew you would come the moment you could. How could you not?'

I sat beside her and glanced at the pages of her book. She pushed back the hair from my forehead.

'You look wonderful,' she marvelled. 'You're glowing like a little sun. Is this Homer's doing?'

'You know it is,' I mumbled, embarrassed.

Her chest heaved and she gave a great sigh, her little bells tinkling. 'It is wonderful to be in love. There is no medicine like it. But make the most of it, Jephzat. It does not last for ever. If it did it would make madwomen of us all.'

I did not know how much I should say to Sengita about Homer, even though I was longing to share my new-found happiness with her. I wanted to ask her if it was normal to want to spend so much time with one person, to have my thoughts consumed by him and to recall his every word and gesture countless times, until my head whirled.

But before I could speak she led me round to a far

corner of the library that I had not yet seen. Vases of flowers and brightly coloured triangles of cloth had been placed amongst the books.

'These shelves are all devoted to Maya and the time in which she lived. There are many more books about her in other secret libraries elsewhere, and it would be impossible to read all of them, even in a lifetime.'

She made room for me on the divan and I lay beside her. She handed me a book and I began to read.

I became so engrossed in its pages that I did not notice Sengita leave, nor did I notice the arrival of a Book Guard, until I felt someone standing beside me. I looked up and recognized Miran, one of the old villagers. According to Homer's instructions I did not greet him, but smiled as he picked up one of the books and kissed it.

'Maya, Maya,' he whispered reverentially, and placed a chair beside the divan. He began to read very slowly, his index finger pointing the way.

'Isn't this wonderful?' he said after some time, taking my hand as if greeting a familiar friend. His palms and fingers were indelibly stained with years of picking and crushing olives and felt like shoe leather.

Miran had always lived in the village with a wife who constantly cursed him for his continual absence. He spent most of his time with the olive trees that grew two kilometres away on terraces overlooking the village. He tended them jealously, and the villagers, knowing his love for this family of trees, left him alone. He did not talk to his wife, but spoke only to his trees. Hephzibah and I had heard him many times on our walks. Once, as children, we had laid low behind bushes and watched him as he embraced the trunk of each tree in turn before standing amongst them and singing to them, praising them for their beauty, their generosity and friendship.

'He has no children,' Manos had said to us when we reached home and told her what we had seen. 'The trees are his family and he loves them like sons and daughters. You may laugh at him but he grows the finest olives and their oil is the only one that is seen on the Company tables and is sold for a fortune throughout the Federation. Not that poor Miran sees the money.'

Now he was holding the book up to me. I read *The History of the Olive* on its spine.

'My trees could be as old as a thousand years,' he said excitedly. 'If they could speak, what tales they would tell! They've seen empires rise and fall, survived floods and devastation. The people that planted them have long gone and they must have been heartbroken to leave their trees behind. It would have been a kind of dying for them.'

His rheumy eyes blinked.

'I am sure they found other olive trees to tend,' I tried to reassure him.

'It wouldn't have been the same. Every tree has its own character. Some like to be pruned, some don't. Some like their branches shaken, some don't. Some love the spring and the sprinkling of fertilizer around their roots, others love the hot bright sun of summer, and others suffer badly in the frost and need to be coaxed into fruiting.'

I could see how Miran now looked like the trees he had tended for a lifetime: the veins in the backs of his hands were raised and knotted like the tangle of olive roots; his fingers had grown gnarled and thick like their trunks, and his kindly eyes were like ripe black fruits. Even when he cleared his throat, which he did often, the noise reminded me of the rustle of leaves.

Miran returned to his book and I turned to go, touching him lightly on his arm as I did so.

'I don't come here often just to read any more,' he said suddenly. 'Only when I need to check up on something for my trees. At first I was here as much as my work allowed, but I just looked at pictures and maps because I couldn't read. I was interested in history, stories from the Old World and stuff like that, but the texts had to be read to me until I mastered the old scripts. There are secret classes, you know, if you want to learn to read in the original languages.'

'How long did it take you to be able to read the originals?'

'A few years. I wanted to read all the old books on olives and olive oil production. I wanted to learn as much as I could about the olive. I wanted to become an olive master.'

'And are you?'

I waited until he finished laughing.

'Ask my trees and they would say yes. Ask the Company and it would say there are no masters, just workers doing its bidding.'

I disobeyed Homer's instructions and asked Miran if he was a Reader. I was surprised when he answered immediately.

'I am, and proud of it. We're going to fight to return to the old ways. We shall all have a say in the running of our lives. There will be choices. We will return to our homes and the knowledge that has passed down through the ages will be available to us all again. We will be free to roam the world at our will. The village will own the terraces, not the Company, and will sell olives to whom it chooses. But first we must weaken the Federation and bring about its collapse. You must help us.

'You are already one of us, but don't yet know it,' he continued. 'Come to our next meeting. Homer will bring you. Come and I'll give you my first bottle of oil from the presses!'

Miran had inspired me. I smiled as I returned to my book. It fell open at a page of photographs. One was of a young woman standing in front of a dark blue wooden door with a coloured glass panel. Her arms were spread out so that each hand clasped the door frame. She was barefooted and her right foot crossed her left ankle. Her flared short skirt was yellow and revealed long legs that were bare and tanned like her arms. Her hair was pulled back off her face, highlighting eyebrows that were dark and thick, giving her face a fierce intensity that was offset by her wide, happy smile. She must have been no more than eighteen years old. Another photograph showed the same woman, but several years older. She was seated among several other men and women around a large table – clearly attending a meeting of some kind. This time her expression was stern and intense and her eyebrows met above her long, straight nose like a collision of scimitars. Her eyes, which could have been light brown or hazel, gazed intently at the camera, setting her apart from the others who were distracted by one another. Her lips were full but looked tense and she appeared to be clenching her jaw. Her dark hair had been styled and hung over her shoulders in the fashion of that day, which to me looked absurd, with its large sculpted curls and heavy fringe. Her hands lay clasped on what must have been a portable computer placed in front of her. Her apparent stillness in a room of movement heightened her authority. The caption read *Maya at the ratification of the Green Charter by the first World Environmental Mission, Helsinki, May 2102.*

So this is what Maya had looked like. There was something strikingly familiar about her, but I could not see precisely what it was. I felt as if I had seen her before, but could not remember where. When I finally left the library and lay in the darkness of my room I could not rid myself of her image: somehow she was already familar to me. It was as if I already knew her.

29

The days and weeks began to take on a rhythm of their own. I would wake with Homer and we would make love, or simply lie together listening to the sounds of the morning. We always waited until we were outside together eating breakfast before discussing what we had most recently read. Somehow our conversations in the house felt stilted, as we held back the excitement of new ideas and understandings.

After breakfast Homer would return to the village, and I worked on repairing the damage the fire had caused. Villagers had brought several olive trees and a young sapling I later identified in the library as a cypress. They planted them for me, saying little, but graciously accepting the food and wine I gave them. One of the women who had been very aggressive towards me in the crowd after Hephzibah's disappearance knocked on the door one day. She was holding a small rose bush. She said nothing but smiled as she handed the plant over to me. Gradually the villagers were becoming my friends again.

For several days I occupied myself with sorting my parents' bedroom. I wanted to restore some order to it before they returned. Dolores, like Hephzibah, was untidy, and I arranged her cosmetics and perfumes neatly on the dresser. I changed the bed sheets, swept the floor, and put Father's shoes away in his wardrobe. I saw the thin cotton tops he liked to wear hanging together in a line of vivid colour, his sarongs neatly folded over hangers, and his heavy linen suits tucked close together as if embracing. I buried my head in the hanging cloth and inhaled the familiar scent of cloves and lemon.

I picked out the outfit he had worn when Hephzibah was born and pulled it out of the wardrobe. There were tiny flakes of alabaster still clinging to it. As I began to brush them off, I felt something in one of the jacket pockets. I pulled out a creased piece of paper, and curious, unfolded it. It was a photograph that had been torn from a book, showing a group of people clearly enjoying themselves. I recognized the woman in the centre as Maya, seated and looking bright and confident, holding a glass of wine up to the photographer and smiling.

Several men surrounded her. They were standing and bending slightly over her, and could have been jostling one another to get into the picture. I looked intently at each of their faces but stopped when I noticed the man seated beside Maya, his hand resting on her left shoulder. I was surprised that I recognized him.

I peered closer, perplexed. Without a doubt, I told myself incredulously, this was Father as a young man. Or someone who shared the same genes. Would Father have been alive then? He looked about nineteen years old, but age had become deceptive, particularly as some people had access in the past to life-lengthening technology. If this was Father, then he must be far older than he claimed.

I knew him mainly as a serious man, a scientist who dedicated himself to his laboratory. The photograph revealed a man I did not know; jaunty, with a nonchalant grin and wide, laughing eyes. He seemed to be flirting with the camera, and the hand on Maya's shoulder was there in a familiar and tender gesture.

I sat down on the bed, deeply shaken and disturbed by a growing sense of betrayal. Maya's name had never even been mentioned in our house. This was a part of Father's life he had kept secret from us. But why? He had let us believe that he had lived in Ferat until he'd met our mother, and then had moved to the Olive Country with her. I had not considered him ever being with any other woman before.

Of course there was no reason why he should tell us everything of his past. But this meant that he was much older than I thought, that he probably did not have many more years to live. With a stab of sorrow, I recalled how frail he had suddenly become after I told him of Hephzibah's death, and how thin he had felt when I had held him the last time. I felt anger too; Father had taken a great risk by keeping the photograph. Its discovery would have meant certain death for him, and possibly the rest of his family. It was a selfish secret, as secrets often are, but whatever it was that the photograph still meant to him, it was stronger than any fear of execution.

Suddenly, I did not know what to do with myself, my mood at odds with the distant revellers in the photograph. I gazed intently at Maya's face, hoping that she might provide a solution to my dilemma. I wanted to keep the photograph, but knew it would be dangerous. I stood to leave and suddenly ripped the paper up into small pieces, ready for burning. Before shutting the door I looked back inside; the room now looked empty and forsaken, waiting only for the familiarity of disorder.

I decided to tell Homer nothing for the time being. I was confused by a thickening cloud of fact and emotion that made no sense. I hadn't sorted things out in my own mind yet. Sometimes I sat in the bunker, hoping to connect with my parents, but nothing came through. Several times I even visited the Commissioner to find out if he had any news from them. I also tried to find out what, if anything, the Company wished me to do whilst in my current limbo. Each time he would just wave me away, saying he was expecting news and that I wasn't to worry. As far as my work was concerned, this was a relief – I was happy spending as much time as I could with Homer, or reading alone in the library.

One time I was there Sengita came to me distraught: Joachim had disappeared. It was so unlike him, she said, shaking her shirts and lifting them up as if he might tumble from them.

We walked the mile and a half from the house to the village, searching the ditches that ran alongside the lane and the pathways that ran off to the olive trees. We walked around the allotments outside the village, peering into sheds and running through the orchards. Fearing he might have drowned, we walked along the estuary shores until we met the banks of the river. We did not call his name, as we did not want to attract the Commissioner's attention, but Sengita shook her bells and occasionally blew on a whistle hanging around her neck. We combed the terraces that surrounded the village, asking anyone we saw whether they had seen a small man-child. One woman pointed behind her, and said she thought she had seen a small creature scuttle up the hills beyond the furthermost olive terraces.

'Let's go back and search the grounds of the house,' Sengita suggested, partly because in the growing heat she was not able to walk far, and also because she did not think Joachim had the stamina or the physique to climb.

I raked through the vegetation that spread around the house, and searched through the citrus groves while Sengita rested and sat on the veranda shouting instructions. We finally found him in the summerhouse, curled up on the floor like a little mouse, hugging the bloodstained cushion. Sengita knelt down beside him, took his little body in her arms, and smothered him with kisses. He awoke grinning and chattering, unaware of the worry he had caused. I bent down to take the cushion from him, but Joachim refused to let go of it and snarled at me, like a wild cat defending its young.

30

During this period I had many dreams of Hephzibah. They were so clear, it was as if she had walked into my life again. Sometimes she was coquettish and sometimes depressed, or said she missed me. Each time she appeared I remarked a change in her; a slight haughtiness, a new sophistication. She used words that revealed a wider learning than the Companies would ever have allowed us and sometimes she made references to a past found only in the Readers' libraries. But her dream appearances were always fleeting. It was as if she was just visiting, opening a door, peeping through it and saying, 'Remember me?'

I was in the middle of one such precious dream when I felt Homer shaking me from sleep.

'What are you doing?' I was annoyed. 'You've woken me. I've been with Hephzibah.'

'Don't worry about her, she'll come back. This is much more important. We must leave now.'

It was a while before we reached the top of the hill whose crown overlooked the village, the estuary and beyond to the sea's horizon. We had had to move slowly and quietly, keeping our bodies low below the bushes or close to the ground to avoid being seen. Halfway up the hill we were met by the same woman who had given me the rose bush. Homer introduced her as Lilith. She nodded at me but did not smile, and turned to lead us up the rocky side of the hill that was hidden from the village. She and Homer frightened off a family of goats.

'It's a pity they don't have caves here,' she said.

'Where do you come from?' I asked, as we struggled through some thorny undergrowth.

'I don't know where my family's origins are, but I grew up in a place not far from the Surveillance Country. They took me when I was a child and trained me there in quantum mechanics and surveillance techniques.'

She noticed me staring at her clothes, a loose, plain-coloured shift and trousers that covered her totally. 'I wear similar clothes to those I was wearing when I was taken as a child. I've always made new versions of it to fit me as I grow. It reminds me of where I come from and tells people that I'm not one of those Company cretins in their fancy outfits.'

'Are you allowed?' I asked, incredulous, noting her pigtails.

'Why not? My skills are highly valued. I'm a good, loyal worker. I do what the Company says, and I don't argue. Which is what it likes.'

Homer winked at me. 'Shows you how easily the corporations can be fooled.'

'Yes, but if Lilith works in the Surveillance Country, how is it that she's living in the village? Doesn't make sense to me.'

Instinctively, I had addressed the question to Homer, but it was Lilith who answered, her voice flattening to a harsh whisper.

'I'm a Company intelligence agent . . . allegedly. It sent me to the village to keep an eye on you all, especially your family, Jephzat, and the Commissioner. They don't think much of him, by the way. I think he might be "disappeared" soon. The Company thinks I'm loyal, and trusts me. But I send back reports that lie only by omission and I cover my tracks. I'm cleverer than most of those witless Company operatives in their state-of-the-art Operations Centre. And don't worry, I haven't been watching you in your home. I don't know anything about your domestic arrangements. It was only the laboratory that the Company was interested in.'

Her words did not come as a surprise, but still felt like a physical slap. 'How do we know you can be trusted?' I asked, turning to Homer for support.

'She's a Reader, and it's not been easy for her, Jephzat.' Homer's voice was suddenly stern. 'To convince the Company that she could be trusted, she's had to betray several of our members, including one of her own family.'

I looked at Lilith's hands. They were pale and delicate, not like the hands of the villagers, which were callused and thick-skinned. I could tell she was not used to being in the outdoors from the way she pushed awkwardly through the undergrowth. It annoyed me that Homer often tried to make the way easy for her, while I made my own way up several paces behind them. I found myself wondering if Homer found her attractive. I answered for myself: she had the nose of a parrot and her teeth were too small. Her only redeeming feature was the shape of her face – like a heart with a dimpled, resolute chin.

By the time I had reached the top, the two of them were pulling back turf and lifting a small round wooden cover. I had not climbed the hill often before, preferring to be closer to water, but had sometimes walked here with Father. We must have stood on this very spot. Lilith descended first, backwards, followed by Homer. We climbed down a long steel ladder until we reached a dark corridor cut from the inside of the hill. Lights went on as soon as Lilith's feet touched the floor. She led the way, and as we walked on the lights went out behind us, so that when I turned back I saw only darkness.

We walked for several minutes along the corridor until it opened into a large room lined from floor to ceiling with metal drawers. It lit up as soon as Lilith entered.

She remained in the room as Homer escorted me into a side chamber with curved walls and a low domed ceiling. There were several rows of wooden chairs in front of a large screen. Homer led me to a seat at the front; to my relief, Lilith did not join us.

The lights went down and then the music started. It settled around us like mist, and I turned my head to look for the musicians. But there was no one else in the room. I was inexplicably moved and as the images appeared on the screen I settled back to watch. Homer took my hand in his.

People walked across the screen from another time, perhaps yours. They streamed down long streets shadowed by tall thin buildings and crammed full of vehicles belching smoke. They disappeared into entrances and were taken down into the ground by moving stairs, where they boarded long thin trains. They sat close together, not talking, some with heads bent over books or shuffling pieces of paper. I looked at Homer. Where did they get all those books from? Some women had fair hair, like gold, and wore skirts that were short. Some wore long black trousers that were tight around their waists and hips, and shoes with high, thin heels. They looked like the birds who waded on long legs into the estuary silt. The men wore suits, similar to Father's but stiffer, the material thick like wadding.

'This was before the multinationals took over the empire,' Homer whispered in my ear. 'This was how the workers travelled in the big cities. But it wasn't like this everywhere.'

I squeezed his hand. 'I know,' I said, 'I've read about it.'

Then there were images of where these people lived, in small houses with tiny gardens, or in rooms built on top of one another. Even then the difference between the workers and the corporate elite was obvious. The large houses with glittering interiors and the ostentatious vehicles parked outside were obviously not the homes of ordinary workers. We cut suddenly to a fleeting glimpse of young people in a library wandering around the aisles of books and recorded music with the nonchalance of those who have never been deprived.

Our own texts were standard and related only to the Federation. Its formulaic and unsubtle Company Stories only served the ideals of profit, submission and brand loyalty. Stories of the imagination, or those thought to be influenced by any aspect of the past, were banned. Those of us still blessed with the ability to imagine, created secret inner worlds which we shared only with those we trusted. We were all very much alone.

'The clips are going to go by very fast, so don't blink!' Homer's voice startled me out of my reverie. I looked up at the screen again, fearful of what I was about to see next. I leaned my head back, and suddenly found myself flying over what looked like huge hills of rock, covered with what I knew to be snow. It shone a cruel, pristine white and the peaks were deserted.

'Mountains,' Homer whispered.

Where were these mountains, so cold, so harsh, so beautiful?

I flew for what seemed like miles over towering peaks that struck blue skies like knuckles, and then spun down towards icy chasms. I skimmed jagged ridges, flew with birds and over high forests, glinting waterfalls and glaciers. I was dizzy at the speed of my flight, and was unprepared for the sudden switch to another image, this time of a narrow street captured in black and white. People were moving quickly, their bodies jerking in a comical way. I began to laugh. Apart from the strange movements, these people looked more like us than the others had done; the women wore skirts that skimmed their ankles and although their hair was long, they dressed it in such a way that the napes of their necks were visible, but without any sign of tattoos. The children wore long smocks or, if they played in the streets, a mixture of rags. I saw a woman drinking from a beautiful, tiny cup, and a man in a glass room like a garden occasionally turned to us and smiled, as if sharing a joke.

Then I saw many things that filled me with horror. But the images were fleeting and I became merely a shocked observer, letting the collage of events rain down on me like a storm of small sharpened stones.

I witnessed nearly three hundred years of history in what could have been only three minutes and saw areas of our planet and its inhabitants I had never known existed. I witnessed terrors that had been excised from the truth. I saw the wars of your time, and noted the primitive weapons – how could a man kill another while looking him in the eyes?

Soldiers marched before me, engulfing a bus of women and children with fire; bodies like sculpted charcoal screamed from burnt-out vehicles; an explosion sent torn limbs flying towards me; somewhere men and women with marked armbands burned books in the streets. I watched hopeless, haggard faces contemplating vast desolate plains; emaciated children, staring at me with swollen, crusted eyes and begging for water; huge waves rising over towns like claws and raking their inhabitants into the sea; vast tracts of forest turning into dust bowls; uncontrollable, devouring fires. Thousands of people queued for food outside government buildings and then turned on each other, until some fed off the dead, cooking limbs over braziers.

The homes I had seen in earlier footage changed to sealed complexes of underground dwellings as people took protection from the sun and pollution. A woman, her head and eyebrows shaved, explained a programme of genetic modification for children to help their bodies survive the toxic atmosphere.

Then I recognized Maya addressing a gathering of thousands in an enormous air-tight tensile structure above ground. She spoke in a low, authoritative voice of the possibility of reversing the effects of two hundred years of pollution.

As Maya pointed out, the new toxic environment was good for business; the worse the daily environment, the more gadgetry people had to buy to protect themselves from it. Big business was afraid of Maya and the backlash had begun. Populations began to emerge from their underground labyrinths, and expose their natural skin. People swam in rivers and in the sea and reclaimed the once deserted streets. All around them were posters proclaiming Maya their saviour.

My eyes were beginning to hurt, and my head ached. I craned my head forward to read the Federese that flashed before me. I knew the rest of the story already: Maya's disappearance and the massacre of her followers. The end of the empire as you knew it.

I saw men, women and children fleeing from their homes and incinerated to ash by lasers directed from the heavens. I heard the screams of small children being torn from their parents and the wailing of naked women wandering, as if blind, through deserted streets. Thousands of people were being herded into work camps, waiting for mass transportation to other areas of this new, divided empire. Emaciated and with the same blank stare as the children, they stood motionless, imprisoned not by the high steel walls, but by the theft of their lives, their names and a murdered memory. The screen lit up with scenes of fire; great pyres of books and papers, whose smoke darkened the sky. A multi-storey incinerator was being fed all kinds of items from the Old World, destroying valuable information in a matter of seconds. I watched what was left of your world burn and melt, leaving us nothing to remember you by. Except, of course, the remnants salvaged by those willing to die for what had once been yours.

31

I do not remember how I returned home. Maybe Lilith and Homer carried me, or perhaps I walked. Perhaps there was daylight, or maybe it was still night. I know Homer undressed me and put me to bed, because it was while I was lying there that I first began to be aware of my surroundings again, and heard the familiar sounds of the house calling me awake.

Homer sat beside the bed, watching me anxiously. He rose and came towards me, but I gestured at him to stay away. I did not want to be touched by anyone, not even him. But before I could speak and explain my feelings to him Sengita stepped into the room, as if she had been standing outside for some time listening for any sign of life. I could see Joachim's eyes glinting through a crack in the door.

She fussed over my bed, straightening the sheets and plumping the pillows. 'What you saw up there was just a tiny drop in the ocean. There's lots more you can see if you want.'

I tried to speak again, but nothing came: only a faint squeaking escaped.

'So we have a little mouse amongst us!' she joked, but I didn't find her comment funny.

'We'll soon sort this out,' she soothed. 'I'm sure I've

something which will do the trick. In the meantime, don't attempt to say anything at all. Just rest and think about what you've seen and what it all means.'

For several days, I rose from my bed in the morning by rote. I then dressed and wandered downstairs, silent and restless. I spent hours sitting motionless at the kitchen table before moving to the veranda, where I stood, arms clasped across my chest, watching the birds for what may have been entire afternoons. Occasionally I walked to the summerhouse, where I sat staring across to the towers and domes of the house, or at the spot where Mariam had lain. Sometimes I walked through the endless rooms of the house, visiting places that had been childhood favourites. It was to be over a week before I could summon up enough courage to take refuge in the library again.

Once there, I took books from their shelves, turned their pages and did not read their texts. Instead I read the calligraphy of larvae: the splashes of liquid that stained some of the pages like a new wayward grammar, the sepia maps of tea, the tracks of a tear perhaps, droplets of wine, or perhaps blood? Dried flowers or crusty insects sometimes fell from the pages, their petals and wings desiccated. Tickets from the transport systems of America and its colonies hid between leaves, and once the bloodied finger of a white silk glove fell from a cookery book.

Unable to concentrate, I took to wandering through the labyrinth that was the library. The shelves seemed unending; whenever I thought I had explored most sections, I would discover another. One section had its own specially allocated Book Guard – a man I recognized from the village who had chastised me during the war for keeping company with the soldiers. Here all the books were chained to the shelves and could only be looked at no more than an arm's length away. The books on the higher shelves had to be reached – and read – on a ladder. These were the oldest and considered to be the most precious books of all. Some were older than the oldest olive trees and written in languages which had been dead for centuries, and which even the old empire had not used. Under the watchful eye of the guard, I took one from the shelf, attracted by its black leather cover embossed with gold. The chain, thin but strong, with the evidence of repair, clanked as I opened it. I took a deep breath, inhaling the intoxicating scent that arose from the pages. It was the smell of time and a craft so ancient it has been forgotten. The elaborately tooled calfskin cover was worn, and portions of the spine had already turned to dust. I held it with the same fear and delight with which I had once held my newborn sister. It had a cross engraved in gold on its cover.

I stood for a long time with my nose in its pages, not reading, but inhaling its particular smell, which evoked images of the book's scribe, sitting alone, staring at the creamy new sheaves of parchment before him and, in the candlelight of that time, writing into the future with words of black ink. The Book Guard had been standing a discreet distance away, but approached me as I began to turn the pages. He coughed and peered over my shoulder.

'Lovely, isn't she?'

I smelled rancid oil, and stepped away from him.

'This book's special,' he continued. 'The parchment is made from the skin of a stillborn goat. It's so precious that it was used again and again and you can still see the old text, lingering like shadows, in the background.'

I wondered how I could tell him that I could not speak, but he didn't wait for a response, and launched into details of his precious charges in the chained library.

'Look at this, how lovely she is. She's been around since the ninth century. Can you imagine that? Even the Company chiefs can't live that long.' He chuckled and opened the book, which when closed was no larger than his hand. He took a deep breath. 'Did you know that a three-hundred-page book usually took a hundred and fifty skins, and the ink was made from oak apples, and the scribes wrote with quills that were made from goose or swan feathers? Amazing, isn't it? Such simple tools, and all to hand, but when combined they produced something as lovely as this. A scribe would write the words, and an illuminator drew the pictures. Sometimes they copied, and sometimes they created something original, like this. This one's what they call a psalter. It's got stuff in about their gods. Don't know much about their old habits and beliefs, but it's how they illustrated them that's the marvel. Look at her. Staggering, absolutely staggering!'

We both gazed down at a hand-painted illustration covering half the page. The colours were luminous and lustrous, as if newly applied, and showed a man in strange costume, with several animals I had never seen before, some with wings and long tongues that curled, or serrated jaws that breathed fire. Trees were painted in vibrant green and the sky was dressed with clouds that curled like waves.

'Look at that gold leaf! Marvellous. Finer than a fish scale. And speaking of fish, they used gum with the pigments made from the sturgeon's bladder. Who would have thought it! This blue, have you ever seen such blue? It's lapis lazuli, a semi-precious stone that was ground down to powder. Well, so they say, and you'd think that the red was blood from the artist himself.'

He turned to another page, where scribbled in a margin in Federese I could read the words, 'In the beginning God created the heavens and the earth. Now the earth was formless and empty, and darkness was over the deep, and God's spirit was hovering over the surface of the waters. And God said, "Let there be light," and there was light.' They were such beautiful words, I thought.

Homer left me alone, although I was sometimes aware that he followed me, making sure I came to no harm. I was not annoyed, but comforted by his presence. Sometimes I also thought I heard Sengita's bells, or caught Manos's shadow leaving the kitchen.

It was a relief not to speak. If I could, I would have to discuss, perhaps describe, what I had seen, and I couldn't bear to hear it. I grew used to having notes passed to me and writing replies. Sengita's focused on my health, and she would give me little pills. Manos asked about food, and she would slyly place sweetmeats by my bed that melted in my mouth. Homer passed me slips of paper which said, 'Please let me hold you,' but I wasn't ready.

Once when I came down alone, someone had left a note which said the Commissioner had paid a visit and would call again. It looked like Sengita's writing, and I knew she would not have allowed him to linger in the kitchen. I was getting suspicious of the Company's apparent neglect of me, and there was still no news of my parents. The only person who could provide news was the Commissioner, so I was disappointed that I had missed him.

Usually I went to bed early, but that day I wanted to stay downstairs until late. The house was empty and I sat in the kitchen, missing my family. The collage of images that seemed to have burned themselves into my brain, and the guilt of Mariam's death weighed heavily upon me still. And now I knew I'd have to cope alone.

I stared at the patterns in the table's wood. Unable to speak, I realized that my sight had begun to compensate by picking out details and colours I would otherwise not have noticed. The grain of the kitchen table was dark, indicating it had been cut from an old tree. I traced Hephzibah's initials, which she had gouged into the wood once when she had lost her temper. There were whorls of russet red in the grain which, if stared at long enough, began to look like glowing faces. I stared deeper into the wood, lost in its eddy and whorl, and heard a woman's voice singing softly from inside the house. I stood up to find out where it was coming from. It was a voice I did not recognize, and it sang in one of the 'library languages'. The timbre was husky and deep, and although I did not understand the words, I knew she was singing of desire and longing, and I was suddenly transported away from all the thoughts that were depressing me. I felt as though I was following a beautiful bird and having to leave the Earth to do so. Her voice swooped, and I swooped too from sadness to a place of promise that called me from somewhere close by. I walked slowly towards the room where my parents often sat when they needed privacy; the door was closed but I could hear the woman's voice rising, this time with a chorus of male voices that seemed to beckon. I reached for the handle and turned it. The room was dark and as I entered, a shower of blue-green sparks exploded before me and I felt insects brush against my face. I let out a scream which shocked me after days of silence. My eyes grew accustomed to the dark, and I saw a figure standing before me. A man's voice sang along with the music, and I drew closer.

Homer held out his arms to me as I approached him. Tiny lights floated above us as he pulled me to him. I put my arms around his waist and buried my face in his neck, overwhelmed by relief. I didn't realize how much I had missed him.

'Glow-worms,' he whispered, holding me and beginning to sway his hips. 'Aren't they beautiful?'

My voice, albeit husky and broken, surprised us both. 'Where did you get them from? I've never seen them before.'

I began to move with him.

'This isn't their natural habitat. They prefer a more humid climate, but a friend managed to get them for me. I took music from the library without anyone knowing. I know you like a man full of surprises.'

We moved together around the room in time to the music.

'Why did you shut me out like that?' he whispered, his hips pressing against mine.

'It wasn't intentional, Homer. I didn't mean to hurt you. I just couldn't cope with anything other than my thoughts and trying to come to terms with the terrible things you and Lilith showed me.'

He ran his hands through my hair, and kissed the crown of my head.

'There's a lot worse, little one, but we decided to spare you. You already know a lot from your reading. I don't know anyone who can read as fast as you.'

'I don't think I can read any more. I just look at the pictures now, and smell the scent of the paper.'

A silence settled between us. I knew what he was going to say next. It was the one question I had been dreading.

'Will you join us?' he asked quietly.

32

'Listen to me, Jephzat. This is our only chance. The Commissioner was lying about the peace treaty. The Water Country is threatening to stop our water supply, or flood the whole country. You know what that means. The olive trees will be destroyed, along with us all.'

I thought of the old man who loved his trees as if they were his own children. He wouldn't be able to survive their death.

'We're having a meeting in a few days' time,' Homer urged me on. 'It's an important one. Crucial, in fact. Things are moving fast. You have to come.'

I pulled away. The singer's voice rose to a climax with crashing percussion.

'I don't have to do anything. You sound just like Hephzibah; she was always telling me what to do.'

I tried to feel angry, but instead felt my breath constricting as the woman began a new melody, its pace faster, the chorus impatient. The singer had become a woman in a hurry, calling to her lover. I was beginning to catch her mood.

'What's she saying?' I asked, trying to buy time.

'Come, come. I know I spurned you, but now I see how mistaken I was. The wheel is turning, and I am opening for you like a flower.'

I punched him gently in his side. 'You're making that up!'

He broke into laughter and began to twirl me round the room, faster and faster, until the light of the glowworms became a circle of turquoise and aquamarine light, like a crown above us. The strength of his arms, his breath on my face, the smell of his sweat mingled with his perfume seemed suddenly to purge me of all my misery and hopelessness. But I knew, too, that it was only a temporary reprieve . . .

Manos gathered the entrails of the fish into her hands, walked across to the veranda and threw them onto the grass.

'Don't do that, we'll have every cat for miles scratching at the door,' I chided. 'Not to mention the smell.'

Manos just pushed her nose up in the air, as she usually did, when hearing something she preferred not to.

'Where's that man of yours?'

'Don't ask.'

'Then don't tell me what to do with the fish!'

We were both being childish and we knew it, but the tedium of the house and the endless wait for news were wearing us down.

'If your parents were here . . .' She stopped short when she saw the expression on my face. I kicked the door post and leaned heavily against it.

It was as if I had lost one family and acquired another. Manos, Sengita and Homer paid regular visits to the house, bringing food and cooking it, removing dirty clothes and returning them washed, cleaning for me and – I felt – watching my every move.

'You're worse than the Company, spying on me all the time.'

'And if we did not come, what would you do?'

'I'd live. I'm not a child.'

'True, but you'd be lonely and we care about you.'

I walked over to her and put my arms around her. I knew I'd hurt her feelings. 'Sorry, Manos. I'm just a bit tense. I can't stand this waiting.'

'Waiting for what?' she asked, vigorously scraping the scales off the fish, their dead eyes tiny bowls of protruding light.

'News from my parents, news from the Company. I'm in limbo.'

'Anything else?'

I wondered what she might be referring to. Was she, like Homer, waiting for me to decide whether or not to join the Readers, or did she know that Hephzibah was still alive, and that I was waiting hopelessly for her return? I decided she was trying to gauge my true feelings for Homer, but resolved not to reply.

Manos guessed my mood and smiled sympathetically. 'Why don't you go and sit outside? It's a lovely afternoon. You can smell the blossom out there now. It'll relax you. I'll bring you some tea.'

There were several chairs on the veranda, but I chose the one that Father always sat in during the early evenings, sipping his home-made lemonade. I plumped the cushions and as I did so a slip of paper fell to the floor. I picked it up and unfolded it, thinking it might be one of Homer's notes left over from when I could not speak. But I did not recognize the writing. 'Go to the bunker,' it read.

I tore the paper into tiny pieces and walked across the grass until I was amongst the lemon trees and could not be seen from the house. I buried the message there before walking towards the bunker.

I was now certain that the note must have come from the Commissioner; he had missed me when he last visited. But I was puzzled by the curtness of it, and the hand-writing was that of someone who had not been through a Company school – it was irregular and badly spaced.

Inside the bunker I pressed the compacted earth wall and the screen appeared. To my delight I saw my parents sitting side by side. They could see me as they looked directly into my eyes when they smiled. They looked well, and I thought Dolores had put on weight. We all started to speak at the same time and then laughed.

'I'll start,' Father said. 'The Company says we can come home soon, but first we have to work a little more on our project.'

I knew I couldn't ask anything about this project in case the Company was eavesdropping on our clandestine communication.

'How are you?' Dolores asked. 'You look brighter and your skin is radiant. What are you up to?'

'Nothing.' I laughed. 'Just plenty of fresh air and Sengita's tea.'

I told them I was fine, that I was being looked after by Sengita and Manos. I did not mention Homer. I asked if Father wanted me to do anything for him, although with the laboratory ruined there was very little I could do

– I had even been unable to examine the cylinders' contents.

I heard my voice break as I told them I had tidied their room, and that I had placed Hephzibah's crystals in a window overlooking the sea as instructed. Father shook his head and for a moment I thought he would burst into tears.

Dolores rubbed her face abruptly as she told me they had met up with some old friends. Her voice sounded strained.

'We have something to show you,' Father said, bending down so I could see the crown of his head.

With some difficulty he placed a large bronze bowl in his lap. It had a handle on either side and I could see that its appeal lay in its simplicity. Father turned the bowl so that I could see inside it, revealing a smooth rounded basin.

'It's called a singing fountain bowl. It comes from a place once called China, and dates from the eighth century.' The bowl was even older than the book I had last admired in the chained library.

'Just watch, Jephzat,' Father instructed as he reached behind him. From a jug he poured water into the bowl so that it was almost three-quarters full. He spat into his palms and began rhythmically to rub the two handles with his wetted palms.

A deep, resonant note began to rise from the bowl's depths. Its droning filled the bunker and as the bowl sang, Father lowered it so I could see the ripples forming on the water's surface at four equidistant points. Slowly the water began to look as if it was boiling and droplets splashed in the air. As the droning continued the water sent up spouts of water from the four points; they rose to become a fountain of water so high above the bowl that it obscured Father's face.

'The vibrations are believed to generate the precise frequencies needed to produce standing waves,' Dolores explained. Father stopped rubbing the handles and the fountain subsided like quickly melting ice.

He started to say something, but there was interference. The sound began to crackle and their faces fragmented. I banged the wall but it only made matters worse. The screen became a blur and fell silent. We hadn't even been able to say goodbye.

I was about to close everything down when I heard the faint murmur of a voice. I stared at the screen and made out a shape that was becoming sharper – there seemed to be one person now, not two. I felt myself turn cold at the thought that one of my parents had been taken away – that the bowl had been an illegal possession and they had been discovered. The image sharpened and I saw a woman staring back at me; not my mother, but a young face, the hair pulled sharply back, the forehead and cheekbones high, and a wry smile on a mouth with a vein of a scar rising from the top lip. I caught my breath in excitement as a calm, familiar voice addressed me . . .

I felt a sudden fear that I was being tricked and that the image would disappear as suddenly as it had manifested itself. I moved my face closer to the screen. Hephzibah had changed, and acquired a maturity that revealed itself not in her skin, but in the expression of her eyes and the set of her mouth.

It's strange how, at significant times, silly, irrelevant questions pop into the mind.

'Have you cut your hair?' I asked.

'Don't ask me such questions, Jephzat, ' she said sharply, making me feel stupid. 'We don't have time—'

'Are you all right?' I broke in. 'You're being held prisoner, are you?'

I watched a faint smile of amusement undermine her seriousness. 'I'm fine, Jephzat. In fact I've never been happier. I have a beautiful daughter. But listen, I want you to come and visit me and meet your little niece. It's all been arranged. There will be no problem with the Federation. Even the transport has been organized. You will be contacted later with the details.'

I touched the screen, as if to feel her flesh.

'Don't go yet. Tell me what has happened since you left. It seems such a long time now. I miss you, Hephzibah. You know Dolores and Father have gone. They say the Water Country is going to hold back our water supply, or even flood us. Have you—'

She interrupted and I saw movement behind her. Her face began to fade as she blew a kiss.

'Got to go now. See you soon. Don't forget. It's all been arranged.'

I sat in the semi-darkness, my face buried in my hands.

33

The house was empty when I returned. A small light burned on the veranda even though dusk had not yet descended. I knew Manos had placed it there, fearing I would otherwise return to a dark house. I sat outside for a while, breathing in the scent of the blossom, and watching the bats skim the tops of the trees. A cup of cold tea and a small bowl of olives were placed near the chair and I could smell baked fish. But I couldn't eat. The thrill of seeing Hephzibah again had left me too excited, and fearful. How had she sent the note to me?

I was oblivious of time, as I contemplated events in an attempt to find the answers that eluded me. Eventually I retired to bed, leaving the light burning on the veranda in case Homer returned during the night.

It was dawn when I awoke from a dreamless sleep. The house felt gloomy and still. I was hungry now but before eating I decided to open all the shutters. I had only been using the kitchen, the large sitting room and my bedroom, and when the morning sun burst through their windows, its light initiated the day's domestic rituals, and my mood lifted slightly. But when I opened the shutters in my parents' and Hephzibah's rooms, the sun tumbled in like a performer, who on discovering there was no audience became still.

I was disappointed that there was still no sign of Homer and returned to my room to wash and dress. I splashed rosewater over my body in case he did suddenly sneak up on me. In the kitchen I poked at the cooked fish, and decided it was too early to eat it. I filled a glass with water and drank it in one gulp before exploring the cupboards to find something else for breakfast. It was then that I noticed the pool of blood gathering on the floor close to where I stood. I watched in mounting horror as the dark stain grew bigger. The blood was seeping from beneath a cupboard door. I squatted down, and a sharp, metallic smell rose up from the floor. My hand was trembling as it reached for the handle. The door suddenly flew open and I fell back on my heels.

It is absurd how horror can embrace the mundane. At first I thought I was looking at a sculpted model, some-thing robbed from the past. I could not comprehend how Homer's bright blue eyes could be so lifelike. They had to be glass of some kind, but the skin looked so real. I reached out to touch the hair, crusted with clots of blood. His expression was peaceful, but there was a slight twist to his mouth – the seed of a scream perhaps. Wild, racking sobs assaulted my body like thieves, robbing me of all reason. I stood up, the ghastly apparition staring at my shins. I tore off my clothes and bent down again to push my hands into the blood pool and smear it over my skin and into my hair. I lifted the bloodied dish containing his head from the cupboard. It was so heavy; my arms could barely bear the weight. I stared into Homer's unseeing eyes and forced myself to kiss him for the last time. I placed the dish gently on the table. It was only then that I allowed myself to break down. Screaming, I ran out into the garden and continued running blindly, naked and bloodied. I did not know where I was going, but eventually found myself in the village, and then outside Sengita's door, where I stood banging my fists hysterically against its rough, unyielding wood.

'Sengita, Sengita,' I screamed, 'Homer's dead! Murdered. His head. S-s-s-severed from his body. The blood . . . there was so much blood . . .' My voice cracked with the weight of the words and I could not go on.

I did not know then that villagers had run out into the streets to help me, because Sengita opened the door and pulled me in before any of them could get close.

It was the only time I ever saw Sengita lost for words. She gathered me in her arms, took me inside and wrapped me in a blanket. She pulled me down onto a pile of cushions and held me, just hugging me tightly and rocking me, while I sobbed. We ignored the banging on the door. I don't know how long we stayed there, but at some point Sengita suggested I wash. I refused; Homer's blood was all I had left of him, and it meant he had not yet abandoned me.

I could not return home. For six days I lay half delirious in Sengita's house, listening to the coming and going of voices, and the receding steps of visitors. I heard one man whisper that the rest of Homer's body had been found, and I felt a deep relief. He was whole again. Sengita finally managed to wash me. I watched the blood run off and wept at the final departure of my lover as I stood naked before the mirror. It was as if a stranger stared back at me. I was thinner, but there had been another, more profound change that came from within. It was as if a part of me had been sponged away with Homer's blood, and I looked hollow and vulnerable. Nothing mattered to me any more.

It was the sea that saved me that time. For long hours I sat on the harbour wall, soothed by the movement of the tides and lulled by the salted light tumbling over driftwood and the curl of waves. I felt as if I had become invisible. The little of me that remained had flown far out to sea to settle on the horizon.

My only comfort was in knowing that Sengita would have given Homer's ending as much dignity as she could, and that he lay in that sweet-smelling room surrounded by the crystals. I knew, too, that she was lying on the cool earth floor beside him, listening to the sounds of his body turning to dust. I just could not be there with her.

34

I was unable to go anywhere near the kitchen, but Manos
marched straight in with the bags she had packed for her
stay. She shut the door behind her and I heard her banging
about, opening and shutting cupboard doors and moving
utensils around. After a few minutes she reappeared.

'It's been cleaned. There's no trace, no bloodstains,
nothing.'

'I'm sorry, Manos. I still can't bear it. I'm going for a
walk. But please stay. You can sleep in my parents' room.'

She shut the door again and I headed for the summerhouse. The sun was hot, and I was perspiring by the time
I arrived there. The floor had been swept and the cushions
removed. Thick, heady curtains of jasmine now hung over
the openings, blocking out the light. I sat in the middle of
the floor and buried my head in my knees. I closed my
eyes and in the darkness heard only the sound of my
breath. I raised my head and watched a large black spider
speed towards the door and disappear. I felt a pang of
envy. I wished I was also free to leave, perhaps travel to
visit Hephzibah. With her, I could slip into my old role as
her caretaker and pretend everything was as it always had
been. Homer's death had been a warning that someone
knew about the Readers and the library. I had a strong
sense that his killer, and the writer of the note, were the

same person. One had followed on so quickly from the other . . .

Suddenly I heard raised voices coming from the house. The Commissioner. I walked into the garden and quietly made my way back, hoping that he would not see me. He was standing on the veranda with Manos, and saw me through the trees. He waved, but I did not return the greeting. I took a deep breath as I walked towards them. Somehow I managed a smile as he spoke to me.

'I'm looking for Homer. Have you seen him?'

I caught Manos glance at me, slightly shaking her head, as if instructing me to say nothing. I complied.

'No. Why?'

'I need to talk to him, that's all. If you see him, tell him to come and see me. It's nothing important. The Company is sending in more workers, and I need to discuss things with him.'

Manos and I remained silent. I could see he was expecting an invitation to tea, and when it was clear this was not forthcoming, he wiped the sweat from his greasy brow and turned to leave.

Manos escorted him down the path and watched him as he walked away towards the village. She returned, clearing her throat, her pale skin mottled from its brief exposure to the sun.

'More workers. Where are they going to put them all?'

'There's plenty of room in the house.'

'That'll be a problem,' Manos said, looking agitated.

We both lapsed into silence again, considering the grave implications of strangers searching through the rooms.

'I'm not eating, Manos. I'm going to disappear for a while.'

I didn't want to mention the books, but she knew where I meant to go, and gave me a sympathetic look.

I walked along the corridor that led towards the library and remembered the first time Homer took me. I imagined his arm around me, and the smell of his skin. I felt my throat catch and held back a sob. He had wanted me to join the Readers, and I had disappointed him by prevaricating. Now it was too late.

Someone was sitting in a corner, busy scribbling, a book in front of them. As I drew closer I saw it was Lilith. Her top lip rose over her tiny teeth.

'I'm learning the language of the old empire – English,' she said, 'so I can read some of the books which haven't been translated. Then I might be able to translate some of them myself.'

I shifted uneasily before her. I didn't know if she had heard about Homer.

'I'm sorry,' she said quietly. 'He was a good man, and committed. His death is a great loss to the Readers. He wanted you to join us, you know.'

'He loved the books. Sometimes I thought he'd read all of them, he seemed to know so much.' I could feel the memories threatening to rise up and overwhelm me.

'He told you about the meeting?'

'Yes, I told him I would think about attending.'

'And will you?'

'I might,' I said ambiguously.

'It's been brought forward. We have to hurry now.

There's talk the Water Company is going to flood us or stop our water supply completely. And in addition there are the new workers to consider; they'll be coming to the village and we can't trust them. There's also a possible traitor who must be in regular contact with the Company. It will soon know about Homer, and then we'll all be in trouble.' She ran a shuddering hand across her throat, and looked up at me. 'I know you don't like me, but I want you to know that I think you'll be a real asset to us. Now that Homer has gone, we need someone like you. You have an important contact who could be very useful. And if you want to know who it is, come to the meeting and find out.'

I was getting impatient with her cryptic comments and moved away. She returned to her book, mouthing words quietly to herself that I could not yet understand.

I made my way to the Mayad section, and took down one of the larger volumes. I opened it and Maya's face stared back at me. She was smiling wearily and there were lines around her eyes suggesting this was a portrait taken when she was older, already confronting the corporate takeover of a dying empire. She had been a remarkable woman, with a huge following and global influence. She and her followers had resuscitated our planet, but they had been unable to prevent the mega-corporations from creating the world in which we now lived. How had we come to this, I wondered, looking into her troubled eyes. Homer was merely another victim of a savage jig danced through the centuries and his death should not have been a surprise to me; our planet had long been turned into a charnel house. I had read enough history to know I was oversimplifying, but anger is a vicious scalpel, soon cutting to the bare bones of injustice.

'It has to be stopped.' I found myself addressing Maya's picture. The light dimmed and I saw Homer standing before me. I stepped towards him, my heart constricting, suddenly believing his death to have been a dream. He held out his hand and pointed above me to a shelf. Then he disappeared. I slumped forlornly against the rows of books for a few moments, unable to believe what I had seen. Gathering my strength, I found a ladder and climbed up to the shelf he had indicated and saw that in this section, all the books concerned water. I pulled one out at random and sat on the ladder step, flicking through its pages. A picture caught my eye and I turned back the pages to a singing fountain bowl, similar to the one my parents had shown me. The caption was translated as Fish Washbasin Fountain, from the Ming Dynasty, China (1368–1644). What could the connection be?

So I headed for another part of the library and found a section on China. I read for several hours until my eyes hurt. China, I learned, used to be an ancient empire in the east, and had made many contributions to the world's early cultural development. It had, I noted, invented paper. It was also involved in the first of the Water Wars. In the early twenty-first century glaciers in the Himalayas had begun to melt and, towards the middle of the century, the plains which had once been watered by seven great rivers began to flood. I repeated the names of the rivers, fascinated by how they sounded: Ganges, Indus, Brahmaputra, Mekong, Thanlwin, Yangtze and Yellow. According to one book, the Himalayas used to contain the largest store of water outside what had been called the polar ice caps, and when they, too, began to melt, several countries, including China, experienced catastrophic floods as the rivers overflowed with the melted ice.

Then the opposite occurred. With nothing to replenish them the rivers ran dry. By the turn of the century, they were nothing more than miserable trickles, and the mountains, an impassable range of hot, bare rock. The squabbling between the various countries led to the first of the Water Wars, in which China and India seemed to be the most aggressive. In your time, wars had been fought over the old fossil fuels. It's strange how history repeats itself. The regions' inhabitants who were not killed in the wars died of thirst or hunger. No wonder the discovery of how to produce water was so crucial. It had effectively saved the planet.

Lilith's words were still ringing in my head when I returned. 'See you at the meeting,' was all she'd said when I had left the library. In my bedroom, I picked up one of Homer's shirts from the floor. I crushed it to my chest and then buried my head in it, breathing him in greedily as if he was still in my arms.

Had I imagined his presence in the library, or had it been a cruel trick, a stored image replayed solely for my benefit? He had directed me to the library's section on water, and my parents had shown me a bowl that produced water waves as if by magic. Did the singing fountain bowl indicate the direction their research was taking? I groaned as I rolled into bed. My simple, prescribed life had been till now a world safely shut off on all sides, but since Hephzibah's departure it had become a boundless place of fluid geometry. I no longer recognized myself in my new violated past, nor in my expanding future, which was unravelling faster than any omen.

Sobbing quietly, I heard Manos come into the room and check that I was asleep. I didn't open my eyes and breathed gently as if in a deep slumber. She came over to me and stroked my forehead before leaving. I lay still, as if healed by her touch, but it had pushed me deeper into grief and my bed shook with my sobs until the morning.

I found Sengita sitting in the summerhouse one afternoon later that week, staring at the vista of trees which led to the estuary. Her face wore an expression of grave melancholy. It could have been the heat which made her so still and pensive, but she was anchored by her thoughts and did not notice me.

'Hello, Sengita, are you all right?' She jumped at the sound of my voice but said nothing.

'If there's something worrying you, please tell me. Is it Homer?' I persisted.

'Yes, it's Homer and a lot of other things.'

'It's hard when you miss someone and know you're never going to see that person again.'

'I know, don't tell me, I know.'

I thought of her son, murdered by the Water soldiers.

'I've brought something for you.' She rummaged in one of her pockets, then held up a necklace of fire crystals, each one blazing like a miniature sun.

I held my breath as she placed it around my neck.

'They're Homer's crystals,' she said unnecessarily.

The crystals felt cool against my skin, and I clutched them as I leaned over and kissed her cheek.

'Don't be silly,' she said brusquely, pushing me away. 'Just be thankful you've something to remember him by.'

She swallowed hard – a fissure in her wall of contained mourning. I realized then that her grief for Homer was perhaps as profound as mine.

'What did you do with the dust?'

'I have the dust with me. I thought we could sprinkle it beneath the olive trees.'

We made our way slowly to the terraces and chose one of the oldest trees. We stood beside its rugose trunk and Sengita took out a small cloth bag and handed it to me. I held it to my chest and closed my eyes before opening it and shaking the fine powder into the air with an uplifted arm. As I did so, a light breeze shook the branches and caught the dust so that it drifted with the blossom as it fell. I began to sing – ' "Come, come. I know I spurned you, but now I see how mistaken I was. The wheel is turning, and I am opening for you like a flower." '

I did not stop singing until I arrived back at the house alone, the crystals like a cold hand clenched around my neck.

35

Sengita's silence was beginning to concern me. She had not visited the house for several days now, so I went to look for her in the village. I found her standing morosely by the harbour wall, staring out to sea. She greeted me, but said little else.

I returned to find Manos waiting for me in the garden with her umbrella open to protect her from the sun.

'You're worrying about Sengita, aren't you?'

'Yes. She's never been like this before. I didn't know she was so fond of Homer.'

'It isn't Homer.'

'Then what is it?'

Manos beckoned me into the house, and we sat in the room where Homer and I had last made love. I tried not to look at the threadbare carpet where we had lain together most of the night.

'Joachim is dead.'

I swallowed hard, unable to believe what she had told me.

'Another murder?'

'Sort of . . .'

'Then who . . .' I turned to see Manos's frightened expression.

'Only I and a couple of other Readers know about

this. You must not tell anyone, not your father, not your mother, and certainly not your sister.'

'But Hephzibah's gone,' I protested, and I slumped back into the chair, waiting for her to recount her story. She cleared her throat.

'We found the rest of Homer's body secreted around the kitchen in the cupboards on the lower shelves. It was as if the killer could not reach any higher. The moment Sengita realized this, she suspected Joachim. He had been behaving strangely for some time, disappearing and then locking himself in his room. She tried following him several times, but he always seemed to get ahead of her, which is odd, considering he usually had difficulty walking. Then two days ago, she searched his room, and found an item of Homer's clothing stiff with dried blood and a sound valve which, it seems, connected directly to your sister. She also found several items that belonged to your sister, items of clothing, intimate things.' Manos looked embarrassed. 'She also found one of your scarves, that blue one you liked to wear. It had been slashed. She put everything back as she had found it and said nothing to Joachim when he returned. She'd come to the terrible conclusion that not only had her grandson murdered Homer, but he had also been in love with Hephzibah for some time.'

I remembered how, panicked, Hephzibah had mentioned that Joachim had seen her with the soldiers in the summerhouse, and I wondered if he had also seen me there watching her suffocate Mariam. I said nothing of my suspicions and let Manos continue.

'That night when Joachim returned, Sengita prepared a drink for him that gave him a terrible fever. She let it be

216

known that he was ill, and the Commissioner came to visit, fearing it was the start of an epidemic. You know how nervous he is about sickness. But Sengita managed to reassure him, and when he had gone, she rubbed one of her ointments into Joachim's sleeping body to loosen his tongue. He woke up briefly, and garbled away in his usual incoherent fashion – incoherent, that is, to everyone except Sengita. He kept saying your sister's name, and how you had sent her away, and how you needed to be punished. He had been following you, and knew about the secret room of books in the house. He described how he had broken into the laboratory, and how the fire was an accident. According to Sengita, he didn't say why he did that, unless it was out of spite to get back at you. Then he fell asleep and never woke up. Sengita buried him at sea to join his father and mother. The village thinks he died of the fever.'

It pained me that Sengita had lost the last member of her family, and it shamed me that I did not share her loss as deeply as I felt I should. I had never felt comfortable in Joachim's presence, although he had been kind to me at times and had often climbed on to my lap when he was a small child. My discomfort was not due to his strange appearance, speech and habits. It was the way he would look at me with his gimlet eyes, then snarl. From what he'd said to Sengita in his last moments, he implied that he knew Hephzibah was still alive, and I would not be surprised if he had also planted the note. If so, he must have received instructions from Hephzibah, who told him about the bunker.

'Did Joachim say anything more about my sister?' I asked Manos quietly.

'If he did, Sengita didn't tell me. Fancy him being in love with her. I wonder how long that was going on for. He was a sly one, and no mistake.'

Manos's tone seemed to be implying that Hephzibah may have responded to Joachim's affections.

'I don't think my sister would have been at all interested in Joachim. He was little more than a child,' I responded indignantly. Manos burst into a loud laugh.

'Joachim was much more than a child. His cock was so big he had to strap it through his legs. What better for the village women than a large cock belonging to someone who spoke unintelligible nonsense? It would always be a secret. No one taking him as a lover need ever feel ashamed of themselves or afraid that they would be found out.'

Manos peered at me, but I was too tired to argue with her conviction that my sister had bedded Joachim. Perhaps she had and perhaps his subsequent jealousy had launched this armada of unexplained events. In my sadness for Sengita, my ache for Homer momentarily lessened. Joachim was all Sengita had left of her family, and she had sacrificed him for the security of the Readers – and for mine. I left the room with Manos, not wishing to remain there alone. I told her not to wait up for me, but didn't tell her I was going to visit a friend.

36

I had to bang long and loud on Sengita's door and my fists were bruised when she finally opened it and let me in. She looked pleased to see me, and ushered me into her kitchen. The shutters were closed against the daylight and the room felt cold. I shivered, hoping she would invite me onto the terrace outside, but she merely stood against the sink, her arms folded, staring at me.

Her eyes were swollen from crying and I could smell camphor.

I told her that Manos had recounted what had happened, and how sorry I was. I chastised her for not sharing her suspicions with me and I apologized for having been so caught up in my own grief that I had not noticed hers.

At the end of my speech, she remained silent for some moments, but continued to stare at me until I could no longer meet her gaze.

'Sometimes, Jephzat, we have to make sacrifices for causes that are greater than our own. We have to take our history into account and make sure some things are never repeated.'

'We have no history,' I scoffed.

'According to the Companies we have none, except for what they tell us. The world we inhabit is nothing more than a Company fiction. But we are Readers, and we know better than that.'

I noticed that she had included me as a Reader now. She was right. I was a reader; I read anything and everything I could get my hands on, but that didn't make me an active member of the organization.

'As far as I can tell, history, whoever tells it, is the story of the subjugation of one people by another, or of attempts by the subjugated to free themselves.' My new-found knowledge had made me cynical.

'Exactly,' cried Sengita, slapping her thighs delightedly. She encouraged me to continue by gesticulating with her hands, as if pushing me, but I didn't want to discuss history now.

'Did Joachim really . . .?' I began, but she quickly stopped me.

'Don't ever mention his name again. It upsets me too much. He's at peace in the sea where he belongs, with his father and his mother, and that's the end of it.'

I glanced at a cloth tied around a pile of objects in a corner near the door.

'They're going, too. Nothing of him will remain,' she said sharply, her eyes watering suddenly. She moved away from the sink and pulled open a drawer.

'There's a lot to be done,' she said, taking out a piece of paper. 'Neither of us can afford to stand around weeping and wailing all day.'

She handed me a picture of Maya. Unlike the one I had recently looked at in the library, this was a picture of a much younger woman, with long hair and a stubborn, square jaw that was more pronounced than in other pictures I had seen.

With a surprised gasp, I realized that this time her youth, her hair and her expression made it clear that I was looking at a reflection of myself in a mirror. I looked at Sengita, my hands shaking.

'I know, you don't have to say anything,' she said, taking the picture from me and scrutinizing it. 'You're so alike, it's as if you are sisters, not mother and daughter.'

My legs felt weak, and Sengita helped me on to the terrace and sat me in a chair.

The sun blinded my eyes, and as I closed them, an image of Dolores emerged from within the darkness.

'I already have a mother. Maya can't possibly be my mother. The resemblance is uncanny, but I can't see how she could be my mother, unless of course . . .'

My voice trailed into silence as I considered the biological possibilities. Many women in those days had had their ova extracted and frozen. Later the eggs were taken directly from newborns. The eggs often survived their donors, and some had remained protected in 'ova sanctuaries' for over a century. I'd read of experiments occurring just before and after Maya's death, where human ova were used to create clones immune to toxins and disease. They worked effectively in the expanding production centres, and I suspected many of the dead in space had been the result of such experimentation, made expendable by their flaws.

The eggs were also a vital component of the 'flesh farms' where organs and body parts were grown for body enhancement. Embryos developed from the eggs had even wider applications beyond eradicating old diseases, which seemed always to be replaced by more virulent ones. They also provided genetic material for a variety of uses, particularly in the old 'built to last' programmes which gave the privileged a useful lifespan of well over a hundred years. Inevitably, by the time Maya had died, genetic technology had long outstripped our wisdom in applying it.

Sengita sat with her back to the sea, telling me the story of my birth.

'Fortunately for you, the Company which had been entrusted with Maya's eggs, and was charged with their disposal, was careless. A young scientist, who had known Maya very well, managed to rescue them, and at great risk to himself kept them out of harm's way. The young man grew older and harboured dreams of resurrecting the Mayad movement, and thought that perhaps a child of Maya would help reignite the momentum of the past. He fertilized several of the eggs with his sperm, but only one survived full term, and you were born to your surrogate mother and biological father.

'He and his wife were living in Ferat at the time, and luckily the Company did not suspect your genetic inheritance. In those days permission was always required from what was called the Fecundity and Labour Enhancement Programme, but your parents had registered the conception as natural and requested a biological birth that did not involve your premature removal from the womb and the usual genetic fingerprinting. This also meant that it was easier for them to sidestep the genetic copyright law, which, as you know, enables the Federation to own the genetic make-up of each individual. I think at that time, the Company was preoccupied with a little subversion in the north, and some of its technology had been sabotaged. Its bureaucracy suffered as a result.' She gave a satisfied smile. 'One of the Readers' earlier blows to the Federation, of course. Naturally, it was covered up, and there were reprisal killings, but it shook them for a while.

'You were, by all reports, a lovely child, although your mother was said to be somewhat distant with you. Your father doted on you, but being the man he is soon gave up on his plans to create a new movement. It was as if, for him, your arrival robbed him of his revolutionary zeal, and I think this was due to your uncanny resemblance to Maya. It was as if that connection was enough, and he needed to do nothing more to invoke her energy and memory.

'It was shortly after your birth that I heard the rumour that Maya had had a posthumous daughter. At first I refused to believe it. It seemed incredibly sad that such a long time after her death she could be a mother for the first time. Maya and I had worked on the Green Revolution together, and there was nothing that we didn't share, even our men. We were like sisters, real sisters – the old kind who looked out for each other. There was nothing I did not know about her, and she about me. It was hard losing her, harder even than losing a son and a grandson.

'So when I heard she had a daughter somewhere, I set about finding you. By that time I was a Reader. I'd been one of the first gatherers of books and had organized places to hide them, initially in the old underground dwellings. Over the years I've rescued thousands of books, recordings of music and discs from the old technology, mostly from right under the noses of the Companies.

'I knew your father when Maya was alive, not well,

but a friend told me he'd had a child who looked like Maya, so I went to find out for myself. At that time I was also earning a good reputation with my healing. The Federation never agreed with my methods, but the Company presidents and their minions have all benefited from them, so it was easy for me to get the requisite permits to travel around.

'I saw you coming out of a large building in Ferat, one of those still standing from the days of the old American empire. You were holding your father's hand tightly, and you turned to me as you passed, your little Maya face smiling. I caught my breath and for a moment was dizzy. You were about two years old then.

'Later I contacted your father. He was annoyed that I'd discovered his little secret Mayad treasure, but what could he do? I think he was relieved when he was sent to the Olive Country to work with Dolores. He thought he could shake me off then, but I followed – legally, of course. I came to keep an eye on you. And I've watched you grow up, becoming more like Maya every day.

'I've wanted you to join the Readers from the start, but I have had to wait. I couldn't show you the library when you were small. Children can't keep secrets and I didn't want your father and Dolores to know. They work quite closely with Company officials sometimes and I didn't want to put them in any danger. Having chosen to build the library in the house they subsequently lived in wasn't exactly keeping them out of harm's way, was it? But we'd had to put it somewhere, and it had seemed such a good option. The books would be dry, well hidden, we could regulate the temperature, and we had easy access, via a tunnel running up from the village to your house.

Your parents rarely left their quarters, and there were just you and Hephzibah exploring the place – two small children who would never have been able to find us. I have to confess, I prayed that you would discover the books eventually. Not with Hephzibah, just you alone, so that I could have taken you by the hand and read you stories, even played a little music for us to dance to. It was something I never did with Joachim. Sometimes we have to trust our own instincts, although I had persuaded myself that I did not want to put him in danger. Life is strange, eh, Jephzat? Finally it was he who jeopardized our security. Perhaps it was Hephzibah's departure that turned him from pitied child to jealous man.

'So I watched you grow up and I waited. Eventually, some of the Readers in the Olive Country learned of your birthright. They were delighted to have you amongst them. We were all looking out for you as you grew up alongside that wretched sister of yours. I used to laugh to myself, watching that proud little madam. Ha! You were the one closer to being a queen. My only regret in life is that I helped Dolores give birth to her, and not to you.'

I listened with full attention. I had never heard Sengita speak for so long and choose her words so carefully. Her face was flushed and there was a new animation in her voice. I was moved by her story and lightly touched the crystals around my neck.

'I am sorry about Homer, Jephzat. There was nothing anyone could do. We always knew we were at risk, but not in this way. Not like this. No one deserves to die like that. Believe it or not, in its assassinations, the Company's techniques show more mercy.

'Homer was a good man. We do not have a leader,

we make democratic decisions, but if we were to have need of one, he would have been appointed. Not me, I am too old now, and have seen too much. They say experience brings wisdom, but more often than not it clouds one's mind, makes one dither fatally as one weighs up one sorrow against another. Experience dwells too long on irrelevant memories.'

Sengita seemed to slump then, as if it was all too much. I stroked her hand, encouraging her to go on.

'Homer was a young man when he came to us, sent by the Company for his strength and knowledge of the virulent diseases that now affected the trees. Despite the new hybrids and genetic modification, some of the younger trees were suffering. That's why he managed to keep out of the way of the village and the Commissioner; he lived out amongst the more recently planted groves with a small portable laboratory from which he was able to feed his findings to the Company. Needless to say, as a Reader, he also used it for our benefit.'

'He never told me any of this,' I whispered.

'He wouldn't, would he? You'd refused to join the Readers, and as far as we were all concerned you could have been a security risk. You're Maya's daughter, but you still have a mind of your own. One that doesn't think sometimes! His mission for the organization was to get you to join us.'

I felt as if someone from a great distance had hurled a spear into my chest. I struggled for breath as if under violent attack, while Sengita poured water into a glass and offered it to me.

When I could speak, I asked bitterly, 'Does that mean we were lovers only because we had to be? He had to seduce me to have a better chance of getting me to join the Readers. Was I really just "his mission"?'

'No, Jephzat. How he went about persuading you was nothing to do with us. That was his free choice, and he wanted to be with you in that way. He didn't seduce you just to try to get you to become a Reader. He was only intending to reveal the library to you, and leave you to read until you discovered the truth and could not refuse to join. Jephzat, any fool could see he was totally smitten with you, and in fact, we were all worried by it. People can lose their reason when – in the words of the old empire – when they fall in love.'

'You think he was in love with me,' I whispered.

'For sure. And you with him. You know – deep inside yourself – that he wanted to be with you from choice, apart from the times you refused to join us. That upset him. He couldn't understand how after the last days, after all you had seen and read, you were still asking for more time to decide. Frankly, I was disappointed too. Maybe I was being unfair on you, expecting too much of you as Maya's daughter, but you didn't seem to have the same hunger, the same desire for change, for revolution and the freedom it will bring. Imagine being free! Jephzat, we need you. We need you to bring us together. With you, we can attract the support of the Mayads, and bring some history and hope into the movement. It's been tough going these last few years. Some of our best embedded members, high up in the Company hierarchy, have been picked off. People will have faith in you, they'll trust you as their forebears trusted Maya.'

*

There was still a dull ache in my chest as I rose to leave. Sengita remained where she was, and did not escort me through the house. I passed the room where Mariam had once lain, and wondered if she too had been a Reader. One day I would allow myself to grieve for Homer in the same way as those who loved Mariam would grieve. It was, as Father said, a universal law.

I walked slowly along the harbour, watching the twilight settle on the horizon. A kingdom of clouds rested on a sheet of mercury. Suddenly I heard a whisper. It seemed to come out of the harbour wall and gather around me, like a mist. At first I could hardly hear it, and then it became a voice, like a child's. 'The meeting will be held a week from tomorrow at three a.m. in the library. Do not bring anything, and do not greet anyone by name.'

I looked around me, but saw no one. Sengita's door was shut, and the shutters closed. The boats that bobbed alongside the jetty were moored and empty.

37

When an acrobat lands precisely where she intended, she cannot explain exactly how she did so. As she somersaults and swiftly descends towards her destination, she is aware of a elegant arrangement of independent variables which will give her an accurate, safe landing. The one thing she cannot identify is exactly how they occurred and in what order. Where and how she lands depend on how she travels: a slight turn of a wrist or ankle will affect the precision of the outcome. But to the onlooker her spinning contortions are nothing more than an act of instinctive agility, rhythm and grace.

I cannot recall the exact moment when I decided to become a Reader.

This is unusual because I am normally precise about beginnings. I wish I could have told Homer when he was alive that I would join him in his fight to overthrow the Federation. I wanted to tell him I no longer wished to be a conduit for Federation greed, nor did I wish to hide any longer from history's hideous truths. I was no longer able to stand back and watch people risk execution every time they turned a page in a clandestine library. What held me back – my fears for the safety of my parents and sister –

had suddenly dissipated and I no longer considered sacrifice a self-indulgence. Silently I sent him a message, 'I've joined. I'm a Reader at last!' and imagined the smile on his face.

Then I reminded myself that to think of Homer all the time as if he were still alive was now a dangerous distraction. He was a gentle fool to have been tricked by Joachim and his blade, but in my mind I could hear his deep voice asking me, 'Do you want life at any price?'

I would tell no one I had agreed to join the Readers until the meeting. The fact of my arrival would inform them. I did not want Manos or Sengita to think I had made the decision because of the revelation about my biological mother. Maya remained as remote to me as a distant galaxy and there was no sentiment for me in shared genes. So I said nothing to Manos or Sengita and spent most of my time in the library, occasionally visiting the bunker. Manos complained that I was being careless. Homer's death and the revelations about Joachim meant we all had to be more vigilant. So I began to restrict my visits to the bunker to the early hours of the morning when it was still dark. I never stayed long, but waited hopefully for signs of life on the screen, although nothing ever appeared.

Once, I climbed down into the cramped space and found myself brushing against an intruder. There were no lights – whoever it was had felt my vibrations through the earth and switched them off. Someone swore in the darkness and immediately I recognized the voice.

'Lilith, what on earth are you doing here?'

'I've been waiting for you,' she snapped as I squeezed

in next to her. She had a tiny object in her hand and was holding it in front of the screen. There was a faint buzzing.

'I have a right to be here,' I said. 'It's private. You're trespassing.'

'Nothing is private any more. We have to try to get your sister to contact you. I've been sending a small signal which should be picked up at her end. Don't worry, you're safe.'

The screen began to lighten. Lilith turned, moved quickly up the rungs and disappeared. As she replaced the lid, she whispered urgently, 'Everything will be explained to you later.'

The screen's light grew more intense and I saw Hephzibah trying to arrange herself, as if she did not know I was watching her. Someone was smoothing down her hair, and another pair of hands massaged oil into her cheeks until they shone.

'Hephzibah,' I called, 'what's going on? What are those people doing to you?'

She remained poised and glanced up at me as if I had just walked into her room.

'You know how vain I've always been, Jephzat. I like to look my best, even for you. Have you heard from our parents?'

'Not since we last spoke.'

'Is there any other news?'

'None,' I said. Whether it was because of recent events, or because I was now a Reader, I was reluctant to give Hephzibah any dangerous or incriminating information.

'Well, you're in a chatty mood today. Cheer up, dear sister. You'll be able to meet your little niece soon. I'll let you know when. But don't try to contact me again. I'll get in touch with you.'

She blew a kiss and her image faded. She had not asked how I was, or noticed my new necklace.

I decided not to visit the bunker for a while, and spent more time in the library instead. I read all night and then slept for most of the day. I did not often sleep in my own bed – I kept reaching over for Homer. Manos would search for me, peering into the rooms closest to the kitchen. She sometimes found me lying on the veranda, uncovered and shivering, or curled up in a blanket on the summerhouse floor. I continued to avoid the kitchen, and ate with Manos and Sengita at a table set on the veranda. Their anxious and concerned looks irritated me as much as the insects that hovered over our food. I would often leave the meal unfinished and walk through the lemon groves, or climb the terraces overlooking the estuary, considering for hours whether it was possible to love and remain unmarked and whether the dead found other homes to go to.

I took a notebook with me on my visits to the library and made copious notes as I read. One evening I found the Book Guard who had once shown me the chained section and I asked him to find me more ancient texts on the Earth's creation. He was delighted and watched me as I moved from one shelf to another with the ladder, pulling out his recommendations with gloved hands. Some were not translated, but the next time I visited he produced handwritten translations of some of the shorter texts. One that particularly interested me was included in a remnant of an ancient book. All that remained were several sheaves of thin parchment, which smelled faintly of spice. I did not know if it was an original scripture or an interpretation by a sage of that time, but this was not important. It was the idea it conveyed that intrigued me. 'Brahma created this world with the sound of the . . . [here was a word that could not be translated], and this sound is not destroyed even during a great deluge. [Here the text had been made illegible by the appetite of an insect] . . . it begins to move within itself, setting up the initial vibrations of the evolving universe. These initial sounds of creation can . . . [here the text was torn badly].' I turned the page over gently, and read via the translation, 'Out of the Primeval Sound became manifest all creation composed of the five elements, namely: space, air, fire, earth and water.'

I closed the book carefully, satisfied finally with the direction my research was taking me in.

38

One week and one day after Sengita's revelations, Manos came into my room at two-thirty in the morning and was surprised to see me fully dressed.

'You're coming then?'

'Yes,' I said nonchalantly, although I had planned to go unescorted to surprise them. 'I think it's about time, don't you?'

She grinned widely and held out a hand to me. We walked arm-in-arm in the dark to the library.

I could see people already slipping through the door, and we followed. The figures disappeared around the curving shelves and I could hear the murmur of many voices. As we turned the corner we were confronted by the sight of over one hundred people, most of whom were balancing on the rungs of ladders, leaning back against the books. They lined both sides of the library, like flocks of birds clinging to a rock face. Everyone was looking at a small group of people standing in the centre, who seemed to be waiting for us. There was silence as we approached the group.

'Welcome to the Olive Readers,' someone called from above me, and there was clapping.

Sengita, who was standing amongst the group, stepped

towards me and bade me sit in one of a line of old wicker chairs. Manos remained standing.

Sengita pulled out a piece of paper from one of her pockets – so she had guessed my decision – and began to read from it.

'We wish to welcome Jephzat to the Readers. It is a welcome that is long overdue, but I am sure, as we can all appreciate, it has not been an easy journey for her to join the organization.'

'Nor for anyone,' someone interjected.

Sengita ignored the comment, and continued. 'Jephzat is a particularly important addition to our ranks, not only because of her many strengths, but also because she is a direct descendant of Maya.' People began to fidget and exchange glances. I wondered if some might not fall off their ladders. 'She is, as a few of you are already aware, the daughter of Maya herself.'

There was a stunned silence and everyone scrutinized my face and then, as if satisfied by what they had seen, they burst into more clapping, which grew in strength and confidence. Some banged their feet on the rungs of the ladders. Many of the faces were familiar to me, including those I had seen in the library either as Readers or Book Guards. Others I had known from childhood, and had been fellow students at the Company school outside the village. They smiled when I caught their eye. I even recognized some faces that had been part of the hostile crowd who had surrounded me in the village, and they, too, smiled, but sheepishly, as if ashamed. There were others who were strangers who must have travelled from other parts of the Olive Country and risked their lives in so doing. One man saluted me as my gaze passed over him. I noticed Lilith perched opposite me, several shelves up from the floor.

Eventually Sengita called for silence. 'We must, as usual, be quick with our business, although this meeting may be a little longer than usual.' Everyone looked at me and I lowered my head, feeling awkward.

'But first, I would like us to devote a moment to our much beloved and courageous colleague-in-arms, Homer, who was recently murdered and who will now be remembered as a martyr to the cause.' Several Readers wiped their eyes, and a group of women sighed in unison. A slow, steady rhythm filled the library, joined by a low chanting of Homer's name which became louder. His name was repeated, each time on a single out-take of breath, and became a hypnotic refrain. People began to sway, and some nudged books off the shelves, so that they came crashing down onto the floor. Finally, Sengita blew her whistle and silence descended again.

Then an old man waved a cloth from the Mayad section. 'We have heard the Company is sending more workers. Will we have to dismantle the library before they arrive? And whoever murdered Homer was probably a Company agent. How can we be sure that it does not already know of our plans?'

Heads nodded and tongues clicked as he spoke. A large woman, who lived on the outskirts of the village with two men and several children, clapped her hands loudly to get Sengita's attention.

'What about this rumour that the Water Country's stopping our water supply? I've also heard it might try to flood us. How true is this, and what is the Company going to do about it?'

'Forget about the Company. They are probably spreading the rumour to frighten us into supporting another war so that the Water Country will be distracted,' said one impatient voice. I turned to see a tall young man, little more than Lomez's age. He wore gold earrings, the mark of a fisherman.

I rose from my seat, and the young man moved aside to make way for me. I wanted to stand beside Sengita for reassurance. She was frowning when she raised her hand to speak.

'My fellow Readers, I was the first among your ranks, and since becoming a Reader I have decided that I have always to tell you the truth. To build a foundation on courage and loyalty, there has to be truth. My grandson, last living of my family, was the agent of which you speak, but not I think, of the Company – simply of his heart. He killed for a misguided love.'

She then proceeded to tell her audience how she had ended Joachim's life – and why. People leaned forward, shocked into silence.

Then a tall woman stood up on her ladder and, balancing precariously, addressed the audience.

'Let us salute the courage of our dear sister. She could have said nothing, let him live, and hidden him in the hills.'

'It was not for her to avenge Homer's death,' Lilith retorted loudly, her voice ringing like a harsh bell. 'It should have been a collective decision. It should have been discussed with the Olive Readers. If we make decisions individually instead of collectively, then we become no better than the Company elite, who make decisions without heed to anyone or anything except their bank accounts. If we are to bring change, then we have to live it, together.'

Approximately half of the Readers present clapped and cheered, but stopped abruptly when Sengita began to speak again.

'I apologize for what I did. It was not easy, as you can appreciate, but I knew that time was of the essence. I have it on good authority from Readers in the Water Country that Hephzibah does not know that her sister has become involved with us. This is, after all, her first meeting, and Joachim is now dead. But soon enough Joachim would have informed Hephzibah, and Jephzat would have walked straight into a trap.'

Then there was a rustling sound, like mice scampering in straw, as women raised their hems to wipe their eyes. Sengita's stricken face revealed how much it had cost her to make her confession here, so I decided to deflect the crowd's attention.

'I know from good authority that the Company, along with other members of the Federation, wish to discover the water formula for themselves,' I began, sounding more confident than I felt. I looked around the crowded shelves. 'I know that my parents, for example, have been working on it for some time.' I paused as the Readers began to talk excitedly among themselves.

Sengita shouted at them to be quiet. 'We shall be here all night if you keep wagging your tongues every time some-one addresses you.'

The chattering subsided and all eyes were fixed upon me as if I were about to perform a miracle.

'I am Maya's daughter, this is true, and I know that you expect a lot of me because of it. But I am not my mother, and I don't want you to assume that whatever I do is going to succeed, or that whatever I suggest is the right thing to do. I want you to make up your own minds and if you feel I am running in the wrong direction, I trust you will tell me. But I am prepared to do anything you ask of me.'

Heads began to nod, as if understanding what I was trying to say.

'I have my own ideas on water production. Homer led me to the right place. I think I could discover how it is done.'

'We don't want to dismiss your idea,' said a small woman, stepping forward. Her hair was short, and her skirts long and full. I did not recognize her. Her light brown eyes scanned the shelves. 'But we do not have the time. For many years, ever since we learned the truth of our past, we, the Readers, have been organizing to over-throw the Federation. Our intelligence sources are excellent, and we have been gathering weapons, some of them old, but still effective. However, we have to strike now. The Water Company has become greedier than ever, and threatens the entire planet. Its plans to colonize space exclusively are already well under way, and once they seize the Federation's Space Defence and Military Com-munications System we shall all be held to ransom. We already know of this plan, which according to reliable intelligence sources will take place in a matter of weeks. But we have our plans, too.'

The woman acknowledged Sengita, then resumed her place, and as she turned I noticed the tattoo on the back of her neck.

Sengita followed on from the woman. 'Thank you,

Ruth. You are right of course. For a long time we have been trying to find a way to get hold of the water formula. If the Readers are able to find it, we will have the Federation eating out of our hands. It will be the end of oppression, and the birth of freedom from slavery.'

A Book Guard shouted angrily from high up in the reference section, 'We know what it will be the end of. We want to know how and when we are going to do it, so that we can begin our life of freedom.'

Sengita looked annoyed, and wiped the sweat from her brow with her sleeves. 'If you let me get to my point, I wanted to say that an unforeseen turn of events is offering us an open door into the Water Country. As a result we are sending someone there immediately to acquire the water formula and lead the sabotage of the water production centres. This person has contacts in high places which will make it easier for them to get access to the information we require.'

I looked at the old man, wondering if he was the Reader with the important Water connections. He stared back at me, along with Manos and Sengita, and several of the others standing around me. I felt the gaze of the assembled audience burn into me. Then I realized the implication of their looks.

'You can't possibly mean—' I said, laughing.

'Yes, daughter of Maya, you,' Sengita said quietly and with huge dignity.

'I can't. I don't know anyone in the Water Country. I didn't have anything to do with the soldiers when they came.'

'*You* didn't,' a woman said. 'But your sister did.'

It was Lilith, and I turned round to face her.

'What do you mean?'

She jumped down from her perch, her pigtails flapping like little wings. 'Contrary to what you wanted everyone to believe, the body discovered by poor Lomez was not your sister's. That was someone else, and her death enabled your sister to escape with the Water soldiers. By aiding and abetting her in murder you thought you were doing your sister a favour, but in fact it's the Readers who are going to benefit. Fortunately for you. It'll help with any guilt you may be feeling.' She thrust her face into mine. 'Did you really think Sengita was that stupid not to recognize the body?' She gave me a contemptuous look. 'Good try, Sister.'

Sengita stepped in front of me and pushed Lilith aside.

'That's all in the past now, let's deal with the present. Hephzibah is living with the son of the Water Country President. He was one of the officers she met here and is the father of her child, natural born too, which makes the child more precious. Among the Water people she is considered genetically pure. Hephzibah has become a very powerful woman, and she is the key to the formula. You are her sister, and she will take you straight to the heart of the Water Country. It has been very difficult for our Readers to gain access because security is so tight. But you, Jephzat, will be given the access that even the Federation agents only dream of.'

I could see that Lilith was relishing my shock.

'We already have it planned,' she said, addressing the Readers. 'Homer worked it all out before he died. I have his instructions, and we all have a part to play. Everyone must know what to do, and it must not be discussed once we leave here. Readers from all over the Federation will be involved in this last push. If it fails, we are all finished.'

I took a deep breath and felt my heart race, surprised by my eagerness to embrace the plan, even though I did not know what it entailed. I confessed that Hephzibah had already been in contact with me, although I did not say how.

'She has arranged for you to visit her,' Sengita said. 'We know about this, and your visit is planned for the next few days. We don't know when exactly, but the Commissioner will receive the information from Olive Company headquarters and will come and tell you. The Company has agreed to her request, which came through the auspices of the Water President. It doesn't want to upset the Water Country at this point, and its surveillance department will ask you to spy for them. You will agree, and they will give you the necessary equipment. The Water Country will send its own transport for you, and you will meet your sister in a restaurant. She will then take you to her home in the main city. From the moment you leave this village your life will be in constant danger. You will, however, be protected by Readers along the way. Not all of them will be Olive Readers; some will be from other parts of the Federation. There are also Water Readers – some are present at this meeting. If you recognize one of them while you are there, do not show it, and do not expect your sister to have your best interests at heart. Her reasons for wanting to see you are duplicitous. Do not trust her, or anyone close to her. Do not be distracted from finding the water formula. You will have only four days.'

I had to raise my voice to ask my question. 'If I fail, will the insurrection still go ahead?' I was shaking.

Instead of answering, Sengita took my arm and embraced me warmly. Then she explained how, at the end of each meeting, a Reader was selected to choose a favourite book and read a short extract from it. I was the chosen one that night.

I had to push through people to find the book I had chosen. A young girl moved aside as I reached for it. I held the volume tenderly in my hands and returned to my place. I found the page and handed it to Lilith, asking her to read it first in English. She bowed her head slightly to me, as if honoured, and cleared her throat.

'Sweet are the uses of adversity
which, like the toad, ugly and venomous,
Wears yet a precious jewel on his head:
And this our life, exempt from public haunt,
Finds tongues in trees, books in the running brooks,
Sermons in stones, and good in everything.'

Those who understood the language of the old empire burst into applause. Lilith handed the book back to me, but need not have bothered, as I knew the text in Federese by heart. I closed my eyes. There was silence when I finished. Then I felt a hand touch my necklace, and then another, and another. People were paying their last respects to Homer. Some hugged me and kissed me on the cheek, while others held my hand and kissed it. I felt uncomfortable, but Sengita comforted me. 'Don't get big-headed,' she whispered in my ear. 'This adulation is for Maya, not for you. You're the closest they will ever get to her, you and her books.'

I stood for what seemed a long time receiving salutations for the mother I had never known, and the lover I had not known long enough. Finally everyone dispersed to different parts of the library to receive their instructions. Their faces were expressionless and still as they listened, knowing that what they were being told to do could lead to their annihilation. Lilith took me to one side and gave me mine. She made me repeat them many times, to be sure. Like the others, I did not flinch at what she told me, nor did I question. What I was being asked to do would lead to unimaginable change, and would, I was convinced, finally bring those killed by the wars to a place of eternal rest.

39

It was as Sengita had said it would be; the Commissioner came to the house with instructions and the necessary permits for my journey to the Water Country. I was already in my room preparing to leave when I heard his voice below my window.

He had lost weight, so that the skin hung loose from his neck, and his eyes looked large and swollen. He also seemed nervous, and kept pulling at the lobe of his right ear. He announced the fact of my impending journey solemnly, his protruding eyes scrutinizing my reaction. I feigned shock and surprise, and attempted to look disconsolate. I did not want to leave the house that had been my home for most of my life, I said. He argued that I had been lucky to live for so long in one place and that I wasn't being banished to a work camp. It was, he said, a privilege afforded only to those who worked well for the Company.

'And, by the way,' he added, 'your parents are very well. I spoke to them this morning, and they send you their deep affection. It is hoped they will return soon.'

I did not believe him. He had been instructed by the Company to tell me this and there was nothing in the message that gave me hope. I asked how long I was expected to stay in the Water Country.

'No longer than two weeks. Someone has requested your visit, I don't know who. The Company doesn't tell me these things, but I suspect it must be connected to the work you have been doing with your parents.' He placed a hand on the nape of my neck and I flinched. 'You are clever, beautiful and loyal to the Federation – it is not surprising that you should be in demand.'

He pulled at the lobe of his ear again and lowered his voice. 'I have been instructed by the Company that it has important work for you to do in the Water Country.' I felt his hand grip my elbow tightly as he propelled me away from the house. 'The Company considers you to be one of its most highly valued workers,' he whispered earnestly into my ear.

'This is sudden and surprising news,' I said sarcastically.

He squeezed my elbow so hard that I winced. 'When the Company needs you, you can't question. You will be very useful to us when you arrive in the Water Country, you will be able to feed us all sorts of useful information.'

'What do you want to know?'

'We want to know exactly how the source of the water-creation project can be accessed. As far as we are aware, there is only one location where the world's entire supply of artificial water is produced. The water is fed through pipes to its numerous customers, including us. We want to know the exact water supply route from its source within the Water Company to the Olive Country, so we can move to protect the source and route before we are threatened again.'

'And if I say no?'

The Commissioner loosened his grip and smiled, as if

it pleased him to say that I would probably not see my parents again if I refused. Then he pulled out a filament of silver wire, no longer than a fingernail and hardly thicker than a strand of hair.

'Hold out your left arm,' he ordered

I obeyed, and flinched as he pushed the filament carefully under the skin above my elbow.

'What will this do?'

'It enables the Company to know exactly where you are at any time, and gives precise information on each location. For instance, at this moment it will know exactly the number of trees surrounding us, their classification, their height, the composition of the soil we are standing on, what we are wearing . . . even the number of flakes of dead skin as they fall off us.'

'Can the Company hear what we are saying through this implant?'

'Not at the moment, but when you meet up with your counterpart in the Water Country, and the equipment is adjusted, everything you say will be listened to.'

We walked back towards the house while he persisted in talking. 'Good luck,' he said bending towards me. 'You're going to need it in that place. From what I hear it's nothing more than a vast reservoir supporting a few floating towns. Sounds damp and cold to me.'

I leaned back when I saw he was going to kiss me, and turned my head so that he toppled forward. I did not attempt to catch him and watched as, wrong-footed, he stumbled and fell face down onto the grass. I stifled a laugh.

Manos came running out of the house, and giving me a stern look, tried to lift him up. He brushed off the dirt clinging to his cassock, glared at me, and turned on his heels to walk quickly towards the village.

Manos turned to me, a smile on her lips. 'You must be careful how you treat the Commissioner. It doesn't do to make an enemy of him.'

'I'm leaving in a couple of hours' time – when I return he and his kind will no longer be here.'

'Now, that's the sort of thing I like to hear,' Manos said bravely, turning her face away from the sun.

I decided to take some personal things with me for Hephzibah, such as her hair set, perfume bottles and several embroidered scarves. I gave Mariam's crystals to Manos, instructing her to place them on a window overlooking the sea in Sengita's house. I then took a short walk up towards the olive trees. I stood beneath the old tree around which I had scattered Homer's dust, and gazed up through the gnarled branches to a cobalt sky. I did not know if I would return; I felt as if I had already left, and that if and when I returned, it would be like visiting a new, strange place. I walked quickly back to the house, stumbling over terrain that suddenly seemed unfamiliar to me.

Manos came into my room with me, carrying a small package. We unwrapped it and she held out a membrane as fine as gossamer. I stepped into it, and peeled it up over my body so that it covered me like a second skin. It was lighter than my own skin, and became one with it.

'I hope Lilith and her friends are right about this,' Manos said, and recited some of the skin's properties as if reassuring herself: its protection against decompression in a vacuum, radiation and toxins, its air-tightness, and insulating capabilities against extreme temperatures and electric voltage. I knew, too, that the skin's malleable micro-texture allowed for underwater swimming and had what Lilith called 'fish capacities', letting the wearer breathe in deep water. This was just as well, I had told her, as I was not a strong swimmer.

I draped a grey scarf loosely around my shoulders, and smoothed down the lilac skirt that skimmed my ankles. Manos brushed my hair, letting it hang loose behind me, while we stood on the veranda watching the air buggy swoop down towards us like a falling star. The sun hit its metallic cover as it hovered over the olive terraces and then landed on the burnt-out expanse of soil where the laboratory had once been.

I took my bag and turned to Manos, who held me close to her.

'Be careful, and do not let anyone take or watch you unpack your bag. Remember, you are the sister of the most powerful woman in the Water Country. Your kinship is your protection – for a while at least.'

'I love you, Manos,' I said in English, and she laughed. I turned away.

Alone in the tiny cabin, I stared ahead through the window which formed the entire front of the air buggy and part of its floor. I clasped the rail beside me as the buggy rose effortlessly into the still air. It hovered over the house, revealing the topography of the land below me. I looked down and saw Manos, a tiny figure still waving at me. The village streets lay like minute arteries between the houses, and I saw people look up, shielding their eyes from the sun, until we were skimming the water and flying out towards the open sea. I kept looking back until I could no longer see the village. But the house reached up defiantly above the trees like a salute.

Book IV

Revolution is not a bed of roses.
Revolution is a bitter battle fought to the
death between the past and the future.

FIDEL CASTRO

40

Apart from the two years I spent in Ferat as a child, I had never travelled beyond the village before. Nor had I wanted to, unlike Hephzibah, who had always yearned to see what lay beyond its borders. Now I was leaving home, propelled by forces outside my control.

The air buggy turned over the sea and headed back towards land and the port of Olea. Its urban tentacles clutched at the water's edge, a chaos of tall buildings, old villas and small, flat-roofed houses. The huge vats of lye, where the harvested olives were soaked to rid them of their bitterness, gaped like fledgling mouths, and here and there I saw empty squares of green. I hung onto my seat as the air buggy swooped down as if to give me a closer view. Teams of people moved from between the vast low buildings that housed the various machines that processed the olives, and the oil. I could smell the strange mix of solvent and pomace hanging over the city and, as we flew further away, the faint scent of freshly pressed olive oil. I marvelled at the vast stretch of olive groves, some still feathered with blossom. Reservoirs of water, which fed the pipes linked to the trees, glinted like moist eyes.

It was some time before the landscape changed and I was rising over high rocky hills that appeared to be unin-habited. It was hot in the air buggy and I began to feel sleepy. I must have dozed off for a short while because when I woke up I was flying over a sparsely vegetated plain, dotted with what I assumed to be Federation buildings, mostly crowded, high-walled compounds, and shocks of forest and empty roads leading to abandoned towns of orange dust and broken roofs. In the distance, arms of broken rusted pipes embraced vast tracts of sand. I looked back and saw no sign of the sea, only rocky outcrops rising behind us. We climbed higher until we were above the clouds and I could no longer see the Earth below us. I fell asleep again and dreamed of the library, silent and dark, bats settling on its empty shelves.

When I awoke the interior of the air buggy was lit up and the window was no longer clear. At first I thought it was night, but in fact the glass had darkened to a deep blue as a defence against the piercing sun.

I shivered with cold in the air-conditioned interior, and stared at my face reflected in the dark glass before me. I went over Lilith's instructions in my head, and tried to imagine how it would be when I finally met Hephzibah again. I felt my stomach knot in apprehension.

It was some time before a voice warned me to prepare for landing and, my insides churning, I felt the air buggy begin its descent. The glass cleared and I craned forward to take in the metropolis that spread before me. It was evening now and the sun was setting against a spectacular dusk sky. Before me lay a city that looked as if it was created from fire crystals. It was only later that I realized the translucent buildings were reflecting the final flare of the evening sun as it descended with me.

I closed my eyes as the buggy began to plummet down towards a crop of towers that rose from the centre of a large lake whose banks were fringed with green and purple vegetation. When I opened them, I was hovering over the flat top of one of the towers. The automated voice instructed me to prepare for landing. As I drew nearer, I saw that the tower appeared to encase a fountain that rose up through its middle and roared upwards towards the roof, which lay like a crystal lid over its top floor, and upon which I suddenly realized the buggy would land. I was grateful for the harness that held me as we dropped towards the tower roof at what seemed a great speed. When we landed, I still felt a sensation of falling as the capsule opened and the harness released itself.

I held on to my bag as two figures helped me out. They stood before me, tall, angular and motionless, as I tried to compose myself. I looked down at my feet and saw what appeared to be sprays of water hitting the floor beneath me. A faint breeze ruffled my hair as my gaze drifted across to a stellate city spread below us preparing for the night.

I glanced up at the face of one of the two watching figures and did not know if I was looking at a man or a woman; the person's hair was short, dark and greasy and flattened against the skull, and the eyebrows were finely plucked. The skin blushed cochineal, as if it too was reflecting the sky's flame. The other's skin was paler and I noticed that the hands were puffy and the fingers long and fat. Because the clothes they both wore were very tight – a high-buttoned jacket and trousers that fitted against their skin – it was difficult to tell if either of them had breasts. They stared back at me, fascinated it seemed by the movement of my hair and skirt in the wind. One of them kept glancing at my necklace and I raised a protective hand to it, before handing them the required entry documents. They both looked through them carefully.

It was only when one of them spoke that I realized she was a woman.

'Welcome to the Water Country. I hope your journey was comfortable.'

'Thank you,' I said, attempting a smile. 'It was very pleasant.'

'Follow us, please,' the other said in a voice equally feminine and formal. They spoke Federese with a lilting accent unlike anything I'd heard in the Olive Country.

As we descended down stairs and into the tower, the faces of my escorts lost their colour, and gleamed instead like transparent pools of water. It was not until that moment, when I stepped down into the light of the building, that I felt my real journey had truly begun.

The stairs were made of a soft material that rebounded when we stepped upon it, and the suggestion that they went on for ever into the earth brought back a distant memory of deep stairwells in tall buildings. The walls were like frosted glass but warm to the touch, reflecting shadows and ripples, giving the impression that the building stood under a waterfall. Once inside, there was no sign of the fountain I had seen rising up through the centre of the building. The banisters were ornately carved with figures of marine life and exotic plants. This was the only fanciful part of the building – everything else was symmetrical and plain, and there was very little colour. The deeper we descended, the more I had a sense of moving through liquid, and as I stepped off the stairs to follow my escorts into a room I could feel my limbs moving slowly, as if through water. I stopped and shook my body furiously to rid myself of the sensation.

'That's better. I just felt a bit strange,' I said. 'Must have been the flight.' I stood still and smiled at them.

One of my escorts smiled back at me, a warm, wide smile that surprised me, revealing perfect teeth – except for one, which appeared to be painted in several colours.

'Excuse me,' I said as politely as I could, 'but do you have a decorated tooth?'

She proudly held up her upper lip so that I could see more clearly. I peered closely at the image painted on to the white enamel. Hephzibah stared back at me, a miniature portrait suspended from healthy pink gums.

'We are the personal bodyguards of your sister,' my escort explained. 'We are proud to serve her and we all carry a picture of her somewhere on our bodies. It indicates our loyalty and the importance of our position within the Company. Come, we've arrived at the checkpoint.'

I stood outside the room, hesitating for a few seconds. It was bare except for several wide cream seats that stretched around the walls. The floor was transparent, with turquoise water bubbling directly beneath it. I took my first step hesitantly, thinking that perhaps I might get my feet wet.

'We need to search your bag before you meet with your sister,' one of them said.

Terrified I tightened my grip around the bag's handle.

'I only have items for my visit, and gifts for Hephzibah, things that she treasured but could not take with her.' I was surprised by the authority in my voice. 'These are personal items, and I am sure she would be very annoyed if anyone else were to handle them.'

The couple looked at each other uncertainly.

'Of course,' I continued, 'I understand your need for security and it's entirely up to you, but I know that my sister is a very private person. This is something I am sure you have become aware of while in service to her. Take my advice: don't jeopardize your privileged position over such a trifle.'

My gamble soon paid off.

'She's right,' the one with the decorated tooth said. The other remained silent, then reluctantly turned towards the door.

They walked across to the door, their skins tinged faintly with blue light thrown up from the floor. I breathed a sigh of relief as we began to descend again. The building seemed empty – we never passed anyone coming up or going down, and the only sound was the soft tread of our feet upon the stairs.

We were no more than four flights down from where the buggy had landed when one of the women took my hand and led me on to a landing where two doors opened automatically, revealing a tiny, brightly lit space. Her companion entered and we followed. The doors closed and I had a sensation of dropping at great speed, although I felt no movement. Then the doors opened again and we stepped into a large room. It was furnished in a way that was strange to me, and the walls were no longer frosted, but painted with a wash of terracotta. Some of the furniture was rustic and wooden, and there were rusted wrought-iron chairs with cream cushions arranged artfully round the room. Floor-to-ceiling windows of clear glass looked out over a panorama of the city, now no longer fiery, but a galaxy of incandescent lights.

'This is where you will meet the Company Mother,' one of the women said, escorting me to a set of chairs in a corner by a window. 'It's one of our best restaurants. The food is very good.'

The two bodyguards left me sitting in the room alone, my precious bag beside my feet. One of them returned minutes later with a tray of hot, strong coffee, milk and sugar. She set it on the table in front of me, and giving an exaggerated smile, turned towards the doors. I poured myself some coffee and sat back, taking in my surroundings. Soon I was nervously scratching at the spot where the Commissioner had inserted the filament.

The coffee was cold by the time the doors parted and my sister entered the room.

41

I was relieved to see that she was alone and, my heart beating fast, I rose from the chair to greet her. Her step quickened until she stopped abruptly, and swept her eyes over me like searchlights. If she was shocked or disappointed, she did not show it. I watched her mouth slowly expand into a smile. Like a bright flare, it served as a signal for us both to fall quickly into each other's arms. We hugged each other tightly, and as I sobbed into her neck I smelled the faint scent of mimosa. She kept repeating my name and twined my hair through her hands before gripping my arms tightly and holding me away from her. We looked each other up and down, giggling delightedly.

'You've changed,' she said, animated. 'You've lost weight. It suits you.'

I spun her around so I could see the back of her, and exclaimed, 'You haven't cut your hair! I thought you had.'

She tugged gently at the mound of hair sculpted into the nape of her neck.

'The custom here is for women to wear their hair very short, but pressed close to the head; the men too. I refused to cut mine when I first came here, despite being nagged at by Riffa, my husband, and his father. I think they want me to blend in with the surroundings and people as much as I can. I've tried, but I'm not cutting my hair. I've always been the rebel, Jephzat, even though I can express that side of my character now only in small ways.'

She had indeed tried. Her eyebrows were finely plucked arcs above eyes which now seemed lighter and greener. She was bare-legged and wore a skirt that was cut off at her knees, reminding me of the exposed legs and high heels of some of the women from earlier times I had seen in the film. Her jacket was similar to those of her bodyguards, except the material shimmered silver as it caught the light. Her shoes were flat, tight-fitting and rose to her ankles. I remarked on the colour: red.

'A bit of colour stands out, doesn't it? Sometimes everything here seems pale, washed out, and when there is colour it mutates or fades.' She took my hand. 'You'll see what I mean when you've been here a little longer. Riffa thinks I'm rather gaudy, but I told him that I'm not used to this visual austerity; I need colour round me, our clothes, the textiles, the streets, the flowers climbing round the house, the lemons . . .' Her voice tailed off, as if she was saddened by the memories.

'Do you miss the Olive Country, Hephzibah?'

Ignoring my question, she removed her hands from my shoulders and came to stand beside me, linking an arm with mine.

'I think it's time to eat. There's a table for us by the window, so you can see how beautiful the city is at night.' I picked up my bag and she led me to a lower level of the room, walking lightly through furnished tables, all laid for a meal, but empty.

A waiter appeared from nowhere and moved the

chairs out from under our table, first for Hephzibah and then for me. He wore a severe black jacket over a white shirt. It looked strange to me, and his uniform, along with his high cheekbones and swollen eyes, reminded me of the soldiers from the Water Country. I winced as he bent over me to place a napkin on my lap. Hephzibah instructed him to bring the wine. She had always had a ring of command in her voice, even as a child. I watched the waiter move away from us, alert and inscrutable. She smiled across at me and toyed with a bowl of pale, delicate flowers that smelt of almonds.

'The war is over. Relax.'

She then told me she had already chosen the menu. 'I know what you like to eat, so the chef has created some dishes especially in your honour.'

The waiter poured white wine from a crystal decanter. We raised our glasses to each other.

'I hope you have a wonderful time here, Jephzat, and I'm sure you'll love Riffa and his father, Bolgez. I know they'll do everything they can to make you feel welcome.'

Suddenly she pressed her hands into her napkin as if it might fall and I asked why the restaurant was so empty.

'Because I'm here, Jephzat,' she answered simply.

'Stupid question,' I joked, unable to think of anything else to say.

As we waited for our food, I grew increasingly weary of doctoring the events that had occurred since she had left: Homer, the library and the books I had read, the horrors revealed to me, Sengita and Joachim. I had to keep reminding myself that I was in the Water Country as a Reader, and that my reunion with Hephzibah was a means to an end. I desperately wanted to share it all with her and felt trapped by the obligations of deceit and secrecy that came with my mission. I reminded myself that it should come easily to me; after all, this was no different from life under the Company. But now I was betraying Hephzibah, and longed to be alone so that I would no longer have to lie by omission to her, nor hear Sengita's warnings ringing loudly in my ears.

'What happened to you after you left us, Hephzibah?' I asked, and stared down at the dish being served to me. I remarked that it looked more like a bouquet of flowers than a meal. She thought this was funny, and I relished the sound of her laughter filling the room. We took up our cutlery and between mouthfuls she began to tell her story.

She had travelled for several days with the soldiers. They had been ambushed three times, and by the time they reached Olea, half of them had been killed.

I interrupted at this point to ask her the one question I needed to put to her.

'Was it the soldier's idea to kill Mariam? Or was it yours?'

'Mine, only mine. Remember how desperate I was, Jephzat.' She had answered as if owning up to a disarming trick in which something vanishes, and no one knows how.

'Riffa wouldn't hurt a fly. He doesn't know about it, so don't tell him.'

She continued her story, as animated as ever, confessing to me that Riffa's number had cropped up more often than the others, and she thought it likely that he was the father of her child. He had seemed pleased when she told him. He was due to end his tour of duty once they reached Olea, which by then was swarming with Water soldiers.

Riffa took care not to present Hephzibah as a prisoner-of-war, and groomed her before introducing her to his father. She was concerned that she was without the necessary Federation permits. Riffa assured her that this was not a problem. Of course, it would not have been – his father was the President. By then she had adapted to the Water way of dressing and some of its customs, as well as gaining weight around her midriff. She told me how nervous and excited she had been at the prospect of becoming a member of the Federation elite. She said she couldn't tell me everything because of security, although, she insisted, she trusted me more than anyone else. The President had said that he could not accept her into the household until tests were carried out to confirm that his son was the father of the expected child. This was, Hephzibah assured me, the only time she had been afraid. It was of course possible that he was not the father, although he was the man she had slept with the most often. She admitted to being both relieved and elated when the tests came back positive. Her new family was especially pleased because there had been no genetic modification for at least two generations. This gave the forthcoming child a much-valued purity.

'It could have been a very high-tech birth,' Hephzibah said, cutting into her fillet of fish. 'But I insisted on the natural way. It's never done here, and they had to bring in women from elsewhere especially to be with me. I thought of getting Sengita over, but she's so bad-tempered a lot of the time, I thought better of it.'

Then she began to reminisce and talk about our childhood with affection. We laughed together over shared memories. We made fun of the Commissioner, and she mimicked some of the villagers, including Sengita, raising her eyebrows and looking stern. It was as if we had never been separated, as if nothing had changed. I began to relax a little.

'Have you found a nice village boy yet?' she asked slyly.

I could not tell her that the very thought of being touched by any man other than Homer repulsed me.

I sliced a prawn neatly in two. 'No. And I'm not interested. I've been too busy looking after the house and worrying about you and our parents to care much about that sort of thing.'

'It's funny; you never were very interested in boys. I always had to do the flirting for you.

'Riffa has a very handsome older brother, Gabriel,' she continued. 'He's a bit lazy but he's a true Water patriot. When he does work, he works very hard but not consistently, and he loves the company of women. I think you would get on very well.'

'I'm not here for matchmaking,' I replied tersely. 'I've come to see you and meet my niece.'

Hephzibah sighed. 'I was only trying. I thought you just might be a bit lonely, that's all.'

'There's more to life than men,' I said with forced optimism.

'I know that you'll like Riffa,' she said, sensing my need to change direction. 'He doesn't say very much, but he's a deep thinker like you and can be lots of fun. I can't wait for you to meet him. And his father. He treats me like the daughter he never had.'

I asked her if she intended to stay in the Water Country. She looked surprised.

'Of course! You don't think I'd want to go back, do you? I couldn't bear it. The Olive Country is a backwater of the Federation. No one goes there unless they can help it, which is a good thing in one way – it meant we could do what we wanted, within reason. But here I can do what I like too. I'm in the inner sanctum, and can make or break rules as I like – as long as Bolgez doesn't mind.'

'He sounds very fond of you.'

She gave a low, suggestive laugh. 'You could say that.'

I averted my gaze and looked out across the city spread before us, luminous but delicate, as if it would crumble under the impact of a single hand. We were still very high up and from our window I could see that no other building was as tall as the tower. Lights outlined the grid of waterways that divided the city into blocks, but there were few boats moving on the water, although there were several air buggies travelling slowly through the sky. I sighed and thought of fire flies in a closed room. Hephzibah pointed her fork at me, determined suddenly to prime me with a few Water facts.

'The country is less than a quarter the size of the Olive Country, but look at that!' she said, proudly indicating the distant shimmering horizon. 'The entire city is built on water. It floats, but you wouldn't know it. It's moored to a tiny piece of land.'

Her eyes had become unnaturally bright and hard, but I decided to take my chance.

'Where are the water production centres?' I asked.

She waved her hand across the night outside our window. 'Oh, they're not in the centre of the city, and there's only one production centre. It's massive. If you're good, I'll take you there as part of our tour. I'm sure Bolgez will be agreeable. I warn you, though, security is very tight and he won't allow you beyond the visitors' point.' She leaned across the table and addressed me with all the pride and patriotism of a Water Country native. 'This is the capital of the most powerful country in the Federation and all because of water. We can do what we like because we are the only ones who know how to make water and this is why the rest of the Federation despises us. We can do anything we like!'

'Like what?'

'Flood the Olive Country, for example.'

My mouth became dry. 'All of it?'

'Yes. Why not?'

My voice rose in disbelief. 'Surely you must know the answer to that.'

Her lips tightened and I felt the tension palpable between us. I waited for an answer that did not come, and we lapsed into silence. I laid down my cutlery.

'I can't eat any more. I think I'm too tired.'

'Of course, it's been a long day. If you want to leave we can go now.'

I nodded, and she called over the waiter, who took our plates and returned to refill our glasses. We both declined and Hephzibah rose to leave. The waiter stepped back and followed us obsequiously to the doors. He offered to carry my bag, but I held on to it tightly, as if it were the only friend I had.

42

I was not used to travelling on water and felt sick by the time I reached Hephzibah's home. We had dropped in a second from close to the top of the tower to the ground floor. A sleek, low-hulled boat was waiting for us, and once again, pilotless and harnessed, I was speeding to an unknown destination. Hephzibah sat motionless beside me, occasionally indicating landmarks as we sped down straight canals of dark water, flanked by tall spires of light. It was only as we slowed down, heading for a high stone quay, that I noticed the flotilla of boats that had accompanied us. They drew alongside, ostentatiously armed, their occupants scrutinizing us as we were assisted up onto the quay. I took the hand of someone standing above me and looked up to find myself gazing into Pedro's deep brown eyes. He was Lomez's friend, a fellow fisherman, and an Olive Reader. I quickly lowered my head, not daring to look at him again, but felt instantly relieved, knowing that I was not alone. We were escorted by Hephzibah's bodyguards towards what appeared to be an island of buildings surrounded by a high wall and a moat full of foaming water.

'If you fall into that you'll melt!' Hephzibah whispered into my ear. Her voice seemed to echo in my brain and I shuddered as we passed over a bridge and entered the courtyard of what seemed to be an assembly of large-domed crystalline houses. I turned when I heard the bridge rise up and seal the wall. Uniformed security guards patrolled the grounds and slivers of laser light cut through the night.

I followed Hephzibah into the largest building of the Presidential complex and found myself in a vast, brightly lit hexagonal vestibule. The walls appeared to reflect a moving rainbow, and the floor was scattered with ancient carpets. Hephzibah beckoned me into another room, larger than the first, with a rounded ceiling that looked like a mass of bubbles and a floor that appeared to be a sheet of water. All around the effect of lambent moonlight flickered on the surfaces and cast shadows on our faces. Through the glass wall facing onto a garden, I could see vast illuminated urns of flowers and trailing plants. A man was lying on one of the many sofas scattered around the room. He sat up when he saw us enter, then rose to greet us.

'Meet Riffa,' Hephzibah said, throwing one of her dazzling smiles at him, which he rewarded with an affectionate embrace. He turned to acknowledge me with a slight bow and welcomed me effusively to his home and country.

I had recognized him instantly as the officer who had stayed with us and had stood beside Hephzibah, watching Mariam before I led her to the summerhouse. He had been a little shorter than his companions, and his shoulders and chest broader, but he had the same bloated skin. The puffiness of his face gave him an undefined chin, which contradicted the apparent strength of his physique. I remembered him as being very quiet, observing everything around him. Once, Father had caught him looking through some of Mother's personal belongings in a room she sometimes used as a study. He had been very polite and promised he would not do it again, saying that war made you do things that you would normally find abhorrent. Afterwards, Father said he felt quite sorry for the boy.

'We've met before, I believe,' I said curtly.

'Yes. But I saw little of you. You were locked in your room most of the time.'

He had spoken kindly, unlike my own defensive response. Hephzibah threw me an irritated look.

'Well, that's all in the past now,' she said emphatically. 'Riffa and I are proud to have you here. I've driven him mad talking about you all this time.'

He did not acknowledge her words, even though she looked at him for confirmation. Instead he began to take his leave from the room, bowing again to me as he did so, and beckoning Hephzibah to follow him.

'You must be very tired,' he said sympathetically. 'It's been a long day for you. The Water Country is very different from yours and it's a big change for you. There's a lot to take in. Tomorrow you'll see our beautiful daughter, but now you must sleep.'

My room reminded me of a boat deck, with its stretched awnings of old ship sails, their weathered sea stains patterning the canvas, and an uneven floor of antique timbers, probably once stripped from one of those old ships I had seen illustrated in books. The bed was a low-lying, simple structure and I flung myself onto it. I sank into its softness and as I lay there felt a slight movement. It was as if I was floating on the gentle waves of the sea and drifting off to another place. I began to feel my eyes closing, aware that my bag lay on the floor. Reluctantly I got up. There were things I needed to do before I could sleep.

As I opened the bag, a potpourri of scents rose like a rope pulling me back into the past: the musk of old parchment, the fragrance of mimosa, olive oil, lemons, the odour of Homer's sweat on the last sarong he had worn. I began to unpack some of the contents, desperately hoping that the Readers had done their work well and disabled any surveillance equipment planted in the room. According to Lilith, the Water agents would be watching nothing more than a virtual image of me 'behaving myself'.

I laid out my clothes and prepared myself for bed. I took out Hephzibah's possessions and arranged them on the small table beside the bed, and regretted that I had not brought a gift for my niece. I did not unpack everything, but kept the bag beside me under the blanket. Finally I wrapped Homer's sarong around me, and once more I was betrayed by a grief I could not banish.

I was almost asleep when I heard the door open. My heartbeat quickened as I heard the door shut, and then the sound of breathing and footsteps approaching the bed. I felt my body stiffen in panic and began to sweat. None of the Readers had told me how to deal with the immobilizing effects of terror. I did not open my eyes, even when I felt the covers lifting. It was only when I smelt the perfume of mimosa that I allowed myself to relax.

'Hephzibah!' I whispered. 'What's the matter?'

At home, she would only come to my bed when she was unhappy, or had had a nightmare. Still warm from another bed, she said nothing as she snuggled into my arms.

'I couldn't sleep,' she replied.

We lay in silence, enjoying the familiar comfort of each other. Her hair spilled loose and full onto the pillow.

'Do you like your room?' she asked.

She said she'd had it designed especially for me. She thought it would remind me of the harbour.

'That's a bit drastic,' I replied. 'I mean, for a guest who's only staying for a few days.'

She sat up abruptly, tears in her eyes.

'Oh, you're staying longer than that. I'm not going to let you go that soon. I want it to be how it used to be.'

I was disconcerted by how upset she was, and pulled her back onto the pillows and attempted to comfort her, as I had always done when we were children.

'Tell me the story of when I was born,' she said, drawing closer and twining her legs around mine.

I stared at her face, wondering how an adult could still look so much like a child. Afterwards as she lay sleeping I remained awake, looking up at the sails, waiting for a wind to blow through them, knowing that, no matter how much Hephzibah desired to salvage our past, it was already irretrievably lost.

43

When I awoke in the morning Hephzibah was gone. I heard voices beyond the door and rose to wash. Clothes had been hung over a chair. They were in the Water style, and looked expensive. I did not like the silver-grey outfit but wore it to please Hephzibah; although the fabric was soft and flexible, I was not used to its constricting tightness. It revealed my figure and I felt vulnerable, as if naked. I was, however, pleased with the shoes, which were soft, emerald-green and rose to my shins.

Anyone watching me lock my bag would not have noticed me take a minuscule item from it and embed it in the fingernail of the middle finger of my left hand. I stowed the bag beneath the bed, and gathered up Hephzibah's items into her scarf and tied it, just like we'd do on childhood picnics. Someone knocked on the door, and I stepped into the corridor self-consciously to find one of the bodyguards – the one with the painted tooth – waiting outside for me. She greeted me politely and announced she had been sent by Hephzibah to escort me to the dining room, where I would be served breakfast. As we walked she cast a sideways glance at my outfit.

'It suits you,' she said. 'You're a real Water person now.'

As we entered the dining room, Hephzibah seemed to

think so too, as she rushed towards me, her arms outstretched.

'You look gorgeous.'

She turned to Riffa, already busy eating his breakfast. 'I've been dying to get her out of those dreadful clothes ever since she arrived. Doesn't she look good, Riffa? Just like one of us!'

Riffa gave a brief, terse smile, so she turned to my escort. 'Kehmet, don't you agree?'

Kehmet nodded her head and stepped discreetly into a corner of the room. I handed the bulging scarf to Hephzibah.

She took it reluctantly and quickly untied the knot. She stared intently at her hair set, perfume bottles and the scarves but did not pick any of them up. She appeared displeased.

'Why did you bring me these?'

'I thought you might like to have reminders of home,' I replied, discomfited.

'I don't need to be reminded of home. I have you to do that.'

She summoned Kehmet and handed over the items, instructing her to take them away. Then, as if relenting, she turned to me and said, 'It was a lovely thought. Don't be offended. I was just surprised to see them. They seem out of place here, don't you think?'

No one seemed to notice my disappointment. Riffa turned to me and indicated the chair beside him. Hephzibah walked restlessly around the room, planning my day. The sun was pouring in through a transparent wall, highlighting the copper in her hair. She wore an outfit similar to the previous day's, but in a dark bronze material, with gold buttons. She looked older, more elegant in these clothes, but they restricted her natural athletic grace.

'When you've finished your breakfast, I'll take you to meet your niece. Bolgez sends his apologies that he can't breakfast with you. He has some business to attend to.'

Riffa grunted. 'Hephzibah, you know he never has breakfast.'

'I didn't want Jephzat to think that the President is ignoring her.'

Riffa looked up at her, smiled and squeezed her hand. 'You're always so busy thinking of everyone else, and organizing everything. I don't know how we managed life without you. Even Bolgez says you've made his life easier.'

He turned to me. 'She knows more about how this Company works than I do.'

'That's because you're not interested, Riffa. You just want to play with your space toys.'

He chuckled. 'Nothing wrong with that. Space is where the future is. You know that. But the difference between the two of us is that you want to invade it, and I want to explore it.' He began to drum his fingers nervously on the table. 'It's one thing ruling Planet Earth, but another to control the universe. We still don't know what's out there.'

'That's the fun of it,' Hephzibah said, determined to get the final word.

Silent figures served us, while my sister fussed over the table, giving orders and occasionally scolding. She appeared to dominate everyone, including Riffa, who seemed oblivious to his surroundings and lost in his own thoughts as he ate.

He still wasn't listening to Hephzibah as she addressed us both with her plans for the day.

'After you've met your niece, we shall go on a little tour of the city and in the evening Bolgez has organized a dinner party in your honour. I have chosen an outfit for you, and some jewellery.' She eyed my crystals disdainfully. 'You won't be wearing those.'

We walked along a wide corridor, then climbed up some sweeping stairs. I looked up at the tall ceilings, which were disconcerting at first; it was as if a clear stream of water was flowing above us, carrying with it brightly coloured objects which shone and sparkled like lights. Once we reached the floor above, I expected to be walking on the same swirling stream, but found my feet passing over calm water below.

Hephzibah stopped outside a door and, putting her fingers to her lips, gently opened it. The room was a surprise of vast, brightly coloured walls of pink and blue with a mural of a huge yellow bear dipping its paws into a jar of honey.

A woman walked towards us smiling, a baby in her arms. The colours of the walls reflected on her face as she moved. She was strangely yellow when she handed the small bundle over to me. I gazed at my niece's perfect little face, a rosebud mouth sucking on the air as if she was still feeding. Her bright green eyes looked up at me and she smelled faintly of fresh milk and mimosa. I hugged her close and placed a finger in her dimpled hands. I felt a lump rise in my throat as her delicate fingers squeezed mine.

Hephzibah laughed and the woman applauded.

'Oh, look! She's smiling at you. She loves her aunt already.'

The baby began to wriggle in my arms and a foot struggled out from the shawl. I went to tickle it and noticed the tiny folds of transparent skin between her toes, like webs. Hephzibah noticed my fascinated gaze and quickly covered her up again.

I walked towards the window that rose from the floor to the ceiling, and held my niece so that she could enjoy the view with me. We looked over a long garden, threaded with rivulets of water, and planted with trees and flowering bushes. I noticed several olive trees directly below, and watched three men sauntering down one of the paths. It was almost like home.

One of the men, shorter than his companions, turned round and looked up at the window as if I had called him. He smiled in a tight grimace, waved and then continued walking.

'Look at the olive trees, little one,' I said, waggling a finger at the green branches beneath us. 'Your mother and I used to climb trees like these when we were young, but they were bigger than these ones. When you're a little bit older, you can climb them too.'

I became aware of Hephzibah standing beside us. She took her baby and nuzzled her soft cheeks. Mother and daughter gazed greedily into each other's eyes. I had never seen Hephzibah behave so tenderly towards anyone. I had experienced her affection, as had Dolores, particularly when, as a child, she had embraced us or brought us gifts of stones, or olives wrapped in leaves, and posies tied with grass. I had seen her smile fondly at Riffa and lightly touch the nape of his neck, but this doting upon her child reminded me of the meaning the English dictionary had given for the word 'love'. Her baby was her treasure, and I could see that in this moment she was so absorbed by her daughter that her immediate environment no longer existed. I did not regret that I was childless – just as I had never desired to travel before, I did not yet desire to be a mother myself. So I do not know what provoked the sharp, jealous gnawing that overwhelmed like a sudden hunger. I turned to speak to my sister, aware that I had yet to ask my niece's name.

'I've called her Mariam,' Hephzibah replied, a cold triumph in her eyes. 'I've been waiting for the right time to tell you.' I felt a sickening dizziness as the confining mystery of my love for her gave way to the liberating logic of hatred.

44

The pilot navigated the covered boat into a wide, high-banked canal, and Hephzibah immediately turned her attention to her surroundings. In the morning light the city had the look of a face fresh from a spell of crying, purged of all passion. My hearing seemed particularly acute and I felt as if the sounds of the entire city were filling my ears. The boat nosed slowly into a wide avenue of water with lawned banks and rows of trees teased and manicured into spears. I gazed up at the tall, elegant buildings pushing their way up from the water's edge. Opaque spires and towers reflected a blue sky, and rose from low-storey buildings that swirled nearby like eddies of water.

We were soon joined by a flotilla of armed boats, their weapons discreetly aimed at the banks. Waves smacked the hulls, and I heard shouts from people gathering in knots along the water's edge. They spoke in Federese, but their words were partially drowned by the commotion surrounding us.

'What are they saying?' I asked.

'They're calling for me.'

'What on earth for?'

Hephzibah turned to stare at me. 'Because I'm the Company Mother. That's what they're calling. For some reason the Water people seem to have taken to me,' she went on airily. 'This, in part, is due to the handsome amount of public exposure that Bolgez awards me. For reasons I won't go into now, there hasn't been a female of note in the family for several generations; until I came along, that is.' I could see she relished telling me this. 'Bolgez makes sure I'm seen regularly on the Company screens. He thinks people can identify with me more than with Riffa, who's got his head stuck in the ozone layer.'

'Is it the same set-up here with the screens as it is back home?' I asked. 'Used not only to give out Company propaganda, but also to spy on workers in their homes?'

She signed at me to lower my voice, and looked nervously at the pilot, whose back was turned to us.

'Bolgez says that surveillance on that scale doesn't happen here. Everything in the Water Country is much more advanced. The programming is more entertaining. Unlike at home, the workers here actually watch the programmes.'

I was surprised by her apparent eagerness to believe anything Bolgez told her, and tried hard to conceal my sarcasm. 'So it's not all Company-speak?'

'Not really. They like to watch us. People love seeing us. You know, scenes of Riffa doing his research, me holding Mariam, Bolgez in his office, that sort of thing. I've suggested that you join us. You'd be very popular as the Company Mother's sister. I'll suggest it to Bolgez. Unlike the rest of the Federation, he's big on family.'

The flotilla gathered around us like a pack of dogs as the boat passed under a bridge. I heard the echoes of dripping water and the steps of people walking above us. What made my sister think I could be part of this world?

Hephzibah took my hand. 'Stop thinking too much. You'll get a headache. Just sit back and enjoy the city.'

She handed me a glass of chilled champagne which seemed to come from nowhere, and then turned to acknowledge the people now lining the avenue and waving Water Company flags at us. I heard the slop of water hitting the boat's hull and the sound of land vehicles, although I could not see them, the sighs of elevators travelling up and down buildings, and a wind moaning through the canyons between the tall towers, although the air around us was still. I stared out at the fantastic crystalline architecture of a city built to express the wealth and power of its corporate owners, and found myself longing for the small, simple houses of our village and the silver-green of the olive trees.

Hephzibah continued smiling and waving as she spoke. 'Here in the Water Country they've adapted Federese to suit themselves. They've only retained three words for colour, which approximate to green, red and blue. When the world is drained of colour, the hearing becomes more acute and sound becomes much more important. They've many words for different sounds; in fact, I'm still having trouble learning them all.' She cupped her hand to her ear. 'We've passed the bridge and it's a long way behind us, but can you still hear the echo of the water drops?'

I strained to listen, and sure enough, above the constant hum of the city, I could indeed hear the same regular dripping from the bridge, but fainter than before. I turned back, but could no longer see the bridge.

'The word they use for the sound of those drops conveys at once its frequency, amplitude and pitch, so it gets very complicated.'

As if on cue, the crowd on the banks let go another roar.

'Don't you get fed up with all this?' I asked.

'I love it. But this is nothing. You should see the adulation when I'm with Bolgez. At the moment I'm second-rate. You have to be President to get the real crowds.'

'It's very different from the Olive Country,' I reminded her. 'The Company President is hardly ever seen. I think it's better that way. Do you remember when the entire population of the village was transported to the city to make the crowds look bigger when he made one of his rare appearances? I couldn't see the point; no one saw him. He just whizzed by in a blur, surrounded by his bodyguards. Do you remember those flags they gave us, and when you cried because the guards wouldn't let us keep them? I don't think more olives grew on the trees afterwards.'

She ignored my sarcasm.

'Look, look,' she cried, pointing to a low-domed building set beside the water and heavily guarded. 'That's where Riffa spends most of his time.'

'What on earth does he do there?' I asked, imagining the serious Riffa scrutinizing the galaxies in much the same way as a child regards a stranger.

The crowds thinned out and Hephzibah stopped waving. We were clearly in a high-security section of the city that housed the main Company offices. 'At the moment he's researching gravitational lensing. You would know better than me what that means.'

'Are you asking me to tell you?'

She nodded her head slowly. 'I think I might be. I'm always too scared to ask Riffa in case he thinks I'm a backward Olive girl. If I could follow at least some of what he was talking about . . .' She drummed her fingers on the side of the boat while I struggled to recall whatever I had read on Riffa's favourite topic.

'For some time now identical galaxies have been recorded. They're believed to be the result of what is called gravitational lensing, which occurs when light, on its way to Earth and from a distant galaxy, passes close to another galaxy.' I paused to watch two of the armed boats break away from the flotilla and head for a jetty. 'The mass of the intervening galaxy distorts the path of the light, and produces multiple images of the distant galaxy which vary in brightness.'

'Something like a collaged mirage in space?' Hephzibah asked.

'Not quite, more like a reflection in water.'

'I can't see the value of this kind of information. Surely all we need to know is where the planets are, and the means to reach them.'

'But that's just the point. If you were travelling in space it would be crucial to know that what you were heading for was your real destination and not just a trick of light.'

The pilot swivelled round and raised a hand. Hephzibah then turned to me, looking slightly tense. 'This is the best bit of the tour,' she said. 'Just hold on tight.'

Hephzibah let out a cry of excitement as the boat juddered and was sucked underwater by a force beneath us. I hung on to her, and immediately regretted the champagne. Water bubbled around us and I noted in my panic that we were still attended by the flotilla, which now huddled more closely around our boat. Their proximity, which until now had annoyed me, became reassuring. Hephzibah held my waist. 'Not much further to go now,' she said, referring to our descent. The bubbles had cleared and we were drifting in clean, clear water through which sunlight filtered. At first there was silence and then came the muffled sound of what seemed to be beating drums. I turned to Hephzibah.

'Heartbeats,' she said, anticipating my question. 'It's the heartbeats of the workers.'

The pilot was now steering the boat alongside a series of buildings which appeared to be the lower storeys of those we had seen while sailing through the waterways above, although I could not be sure. I could see people walking inside the buildings and staring back at us. The sound of beating became louder and less muffled and I heard, too, the sound of the boats as they pushed through the water, and voices as if in a great hall. Tiny silver fish darted around us, and the floor around the buildings was strewn with rocks anchoring a variety of waterweed. We were drifting through what could have been a reflection of the city above, but was an underwater city in its own right. Figures in second skins like mine swam in and out of chutes that led into the buildings. Several of them had webs between their fingers, and these people moved faster through the water than the others. I could not see their faces, as they wore tight-fitting masks with tiny tubes running from their nostrils to the neck of their second skin. Their bodies were small and streamlined, fishlike almost, and they moved with a water-induced grace, exaggerated in motion. There was interaction between some of them as if they were conversing, but I could not see how they communicated. Several groups pulled at molluscs that clung to the foundations and rocks, and I saw divers swimming amongst them, carrying long vicious rods which they prodded and poked at the workers, causing them to curl up in the water as if in pain.

'Is it necessary to treat the workers like that?' I asked.

'Sometimes. You know how idle they can be.'

Hephzibah then tried to divert my attention to the other side of the cabin, and I reluctantly turned my head, sickened by what I had seen and saddened by her apparent tolerance of it. 'Look at these wonderful colours!' she exclaimed. 'I love coming down here. It's the only place you can see the true and full spectrum.' Unperturbed, she began to name every vibrant creature.

'Over there! An Ochre Star,' she said, pointing at a deeply hued starfish pinned to a rock crevice. An orange fish flipped past us. 'Great for eating – the Vermilion Rockfish. And that violet one is a younger version.' We gazed at a cluster of orange, white-spotted anemones, and a Onespot Fringehead poked its pop-eyed head out of a chipped ceramic pot. I wanted to ask my sister if she had acquired her knowledge of marine life from books of the Old World, but settled for admiring comments instead. Hephzibah had always preferred flattery, and this was not the occasion to question the legality of her knowledge.

The sounds became a muffled clamour as we sailed into darkness. Lights shone in our cabin and a beam of light fixed to the stern revealed fine wires coming up from the water bed and disappearing into the darkness above us. The temperature dropped as we wove through them and I shivered. Hephzibah looked at me and smiled sympathetically.

'Don't worry, the city is built on a series of floating platforms and we are just passing under the largest of them. The platforms are secured by these wires, but as you've just seen, some of the buildings have their foundations in the water bed.'

The claustrophobic darkness unnerved me, and I could feel myself sweating beneath my second skin despite the cold. I was relieved when I finally saw light breaking through the water above us. I heard the drumbeats again, resounding around the cabin, and realized it was our own rapid heartbeats. I found myself shouting above my own heart's chatter.

'Where are we going?' I asked, suddenly fearful, and moved closer to my sister.

'To the Water Production Centre. Bolgez agreed to your visit. But we have been restricted to no more than ten minutes. You're very lucky.'

I hoped that Hephzibah had not noticed the acceleration of my pulse as I began to sense our proximity to the very source of life.

45

I knew we were sea-bound when I saw the water bed beneath us turn to sediment. The water clouded momentarily and I felt the push of a tide against our side. On our left a rock escarpment, covered in swollen fronds of weed, suddenly dropped down into a pitch-black chasm. In the distance, mountainous rocks loomed ahead, and I gazed in wonder as all around us the waters suddenly broke into life. We nosed through blizzards of larvae, plankton and delicate sea gooseberries. Schools of brightly coloured fish broke through forests of tangled kelp and flirted with our vessel. Thousands of silver anchovies, coordinated into one swirling cloud, swooped above us before swimming away. Particles like disturbed dust rode the currents, and several sharks, three times the size of the boat, tailed us lazily.

Hephzibah pointed to a cluster of jellyfish. I had seen them washed up on the shores of the estuary like deflated balloons. In the water they drifted delicately, combing the water for prey with their dangling tentacles attached to ghostly pulsing bells. My sister pressed her nose to the boat's protective cover. 'Funny how the most beautiful creatures can have the most deadly sting,' she observed, and gave a quiet laugh, as if enjoying a private joke.

I calculated that we were no more than 300 feet below the surface of the sea, as light was still filtering through. It was some time before we plunged deeper. Hephzibah held me tightly as once again the cabin grew colder. The pilot turned his head to inform us we were moving over a deep sea canyon. I peered down to the sea floor, but saw nothing but darkness. I felt my second skin tighten around my body and felt constricted, although I had no difficulty breathing. Hephzibah rested her head on my shoulder and began to doze, while I remained alert and curious.

I nudged Hephzibah when I saw long tentacles reaching out around us as if about to tie us to the sea floor. They were lengths of cylindrical membrane like soft, flexible pipes that pulsed with the clear liquid flowing through them.

Hephzibah shook herself awake. 'Oh, these are the water pipes. Some of them are huge. They feed the water to the different Companies.' She tapped the pilot on the shoulder and instructed him to show us the Olive Country feed.

He turned the boat and we headed straight for another massive tangle of pipes that spread like roots around us. Fish swam easily among them, and the pipes swayed with the water. Sometimes the membrane bulged and I saw the force of a hand push from inside, or caught sight of shadows swimming through the pipes. Smaller pipes twined around their larger counterparts like capillaries.

'These are the pipes feeding in the water that keeps the olive business alive.'

'They look a bit vulnerable to me,' I said, wishing I could prod the membrane and feel its texture for myself.

'We've devised a material that can survive a meteorite hit. It won't burst, and it expands to take any amount of water.'

I was angered by the pride she displayed in her adopted Company's achievements. She seemed to find it so easy to switch her loyalty to those who intended harm against her home and village. My anger spurred me on to press her again on the one question that had been preying on my mind since she'd raised it at our dinner together.

'What about the rumours circulating in the Olive Country that there are plans to cut off our water, or flood us?' I said, studying her face carefully for a reaction.

Before she replied I heard the rapid movements of fish in the water, the popping of tiny bubbles and Hephzibah's deep-drawn sigh.

'As I said, there are plans to flood the Olive Country, yes,' she confirmed, turning to me, her eyes reflecting the water around us and its inhabitants.

'What on earth for, Hephzibah? What's the Olive Country done to the Water people?'

'Nothing, nothing at all, but that's not the point.'

'Then what *is* the point, Hephzibah?'

I scratched at the filament in my arm and held back my fury.

'Bolgez says that we now have to show the Federation who's boss. There has been too much backstabbing, and we don't trust the Federation any more. Its members are all after the water formula, and would do anything to get their greedy little hands on it. What's more, our space settlement programme is held up because of their ridiculous bureaucracy. We've even kept the price of water down, to make it more easily available to everyone. But now we intend to show all the Companies that they need us much more than we need them.'

'So this is Bolgez's idea! Drown a Company and put up your own Company flag?'

Nothing the Olive Readers had said, nor what had happened in my life before, could prepare me for her following words. Hephzibah raised her chin, and stiffened her back, as if ennobled by what she was about to say. 'It isn't Bolgez's idea. It's mine. I suggested it. He was reluctant at first, being a man of caution. But he could see the sense in it after I discussed it with him. He could appreciate how it would lead to greater things that would benefit everyone, everywhere.'

She arched her thread-thin eyebrows, and spoke with the same spiteful relish as she had when she revealed her intimacy with the soldiers to me all those long months ago. Once again I found myself tormented by the Hephzibah I had always loved, and could not recognize this merciless young woman who now addressed me.

'What use is land that has been effectively wiped out by a deluge or parched by drought?' I responded half-heartedly, knowing that, at this stage, logic would make no difference.

'Those old trees will never recover,' I pressed on. 'They would be lost for ever. More importantly, what about the people? What about Sengita and Manos? What if Father and Dolores are back in the house? Will you stand by and let them all be washed away to their deaths?'

'Sometimes sacrifices have to be made for the good of the world as a whole, and in any case, Father and Mother will be here with us soon. It will be just as it has always been, except we will be able to do what we like.' She swung round to face me. 'You know the Olive Country is keeping our parents as hostages, in case these "rumours", as you call them, become substantiated. That's why they were taken away. The Company will throw up its arms and say, "Don't flood us because we have Hephzibah's parents." Are they so stupid as to think that will make any difference to Bolgez? Once he has made up his mind he will go ahead regardless.'

Then she threw me a reassuring look. 'Don't worry, our parents will be here by the end of tomorrow. My threats have seen to that.'

I wished the relief I felt for my parents' imminent safety would overwhelm the feeling of icy foreboding that was beginning to dry my mouth.

'I can't stay with you, Hephzibah,' I said miserably. 'You know I can't. I have to return, and then you'll be sending me home to my death.'

There was a sudden furious light in her eyes. 'Don't believe for one minute that you are going back. You're staying here with me. You can help me with the Company. You have a better brain than I; all you lack is ambition. But once you experience the fruits of my vision, you'll change your mind.' She grabbed my arms. 'It'll be better than before, Jephzat. I have Mariam now and we can both build her a new future.'

I lowered my voice, mindful of the pilot. 'You can't buy me, Hephzibah, you can't. I won't be your prisoner.'

She remained silent for a while, staring back at her reflection in the cabin cover.

'You have no choice, Jephzat,' she said finally. 'You have no choice.'

We moved away from the tangle of water pipes into a still darkness, as if all the sea's inhabitants had fled. I could no longer hear our heartbeats, or the sound of our breath. I had the eerie sensation of floating in a vacuum. Then the vibrations started.

I wanted to hold on to Hephzibah, but could not bring myself to. To overcome my repulsion, I imagined her as the childhood playmate I had adored, and blanked out the beautiful woman sitting beside me, her shadowed face pale and thoughtful.

I began to feel lightheaded and calm. The water started to shimmer in waves as if responding to the oscillations that had begun to affect our cabin.

'We're getting close,' Hephzibah said, and took my hands. The water began to shimmer, as if responding with phosphorescent light to the vibrations. It was difficult to contain my excitement as the boat picked up speed and we dived deeper, pushing through underwater currents, until we were engulfed by the sea's own special night.

It was a while before I saw a pin of light ahead of us, fixed like a star in the blackness. The boat moved towards it until it became large and bright enough to illuminate one of the heavily guarded ports of the Water Production Centre. It was busy with water vehicles speeding in and out of the tunnelled entrance. Armed divers swarmed everywhere, weighted down by surveillance equipment. I was still aware of the vibrations passing through my body, and wondered if it was this that was making me feel suddenly energized.

'Is this show because the Company Mother has arrived with her sister?' I asked, indicating the activity outside.

'No, it's always like this. There isn't anywhere in the world as heavily fortified and guarded as the Water Production Centre. You're about to see some amazing things, Jephzat.'

The boat entered the tunnel and passed into a chamber that sealed behind us. We berthed at what was ostentatiously flagged 'The President's Arrival Point'. I sighed with relief as the cabin cover was flung back and my claustrophobia lifted. We were helped out of the boat on to the quay by a clamour of eager hands.

We were quickly ushered into a room lined with comfortable chairs and smelling of fresh coffee. Four men and one woman stepped forward to greet us. I was amused by how they bent their heads in deference to us. 'Welcome to the Company Mother's sister,' one of them said. Another placed garlands of flowers around our necks and I smiled graciously, instantly disliking the heavy scent that rose up from the fresh blooms.

All five continued bowing as I thanked them effusively. Hephzibah dug me in the ribs and I lapsed into silence. She introduced us to the Centre director – the man who had welcomed us. To be the director, he informed me, was a privileged position indeed, and one which carried a great deal of responsibility. The responsibility was so great, he warbled, because the planet's future depended upon the Centre's efficient working and protection, and sometimes at night he hardly slept, so anxious was he for the continued survival of humanity. He cast an admiring glance at Hephzibah and simpered. 'Of course, the Company Mother is an immense inspiration to us all. Water production has increased by eighteen per cent since her arrival, which I can tell you, is no coincidence.' Tiny beads of sweat broke out along his top lip, and he wiped his forehead. His breath smelt of composting sewage and I tried not to gag.

Hephzibah bent her head slightly in the man's direction and clapped her hands as if summoning an entourage of waiters. 'Marcel, my sister and I appreciate your kind welcome, and may I relay from the President himself his appreciation of the wonderful work you and your team are doing here.'

The quintet smiled, bowing and simpering simultaneously like windswept grass before stepping away from us. Hephzibah remained composed and still.

She drew me over to the chairs and we sat while sweetmeats and coffee were brought to us. I slung my garland to the floor, disturbed by the vibrations which had become stronger. Out of the water, my hearing was no longer as sensitive, and I could not be sure if I could hear a faint humming in the distance.

Marcel reappeared, hovering like a fly. 'There is only one source of water production at the moment,' he began. 'Once we are able to duplicate, we shall set up water production centres throughout the Federation.'

'And in space, too?' I queried.

'Naturally,' Hephzibah replied.

Marcel seemed nervous as he led us along a narrow white corridor, and began whispering to Hephzibah. We were joined by a large number of heavily armed bodyguards, all of whom were tall and wiry with eyes that bulged like fish eyes and skins that were rough and scaly as if diseased. We were escorted into a windowless room. In the middle was a table with a small-scale model of the Centre.

I could see that the building was composed mainly of a vast opaque dome, with several port outlets. I guessed that the water was probably pumped into the dome, but Marcel explained how the dome expanded as water was produced within it. I could see strings of the free-flowing pipes leading from beneath the dome to several inland reservoirs.

'The storage of our water is very important,' he said. 'We store our water in vast containers which cut out heat and light and maintain its freshness. The dome itself shuts out sunlight. For Water Country consumption only we like to combine the water with river water as this enriches it with minerals and trace elements.'

Marcel spoke of his water with an almost touching passion and watched eagerly as I sampled a glass. He laughed delightedly at my approval. It was different from the water we received in the Olive Country – sweeter and more refreshing, but somehow bland. 'This sample is what we call juvenile water. There are people who prefer water that has gone the full cycle from subterranean regions to the atmosphere and back again. It's an acquired taste, and expensive. For our own consumption we tend to mix the two, but what you've just drunk is straight from the source.'

He apologized that as a visitor I was unable to go beyond this room for security and safety reasons. 'Special precautions have to be taken before approaching the dome, otherwise the water in your body begins to reproduce itself, with fatal consequences. Pop!' He gave a high-pitched laugh.

I pointed to the model and asked which pipe fed the Olive Country supply. 'This one,' said Marcel. I stared in the direction of his finger, studying the details intently. I knew that my life, and that of others, would depend upon it.

'So how exactly is the water produced?' I asked as naively as I could.

There was a long silence as Marcel looked to Hephzibah for permission to respond. She gave a slight nod of her head, and he motioned at me to bend down close to the model, asking me what I saw there. It was only when I looked into the centre of the dome that I saw the tiny black orb revolving within it, suspended by the water.

'We call it the Sphinx. Someone came up with the name and we liked it. We were even thinking of changing from Water Company to Sphinx Company, but we don't know where the word comes from or what it means.'

'It's a lovely word. It's certainly not Federese.'

There was an uncomfortable silence then. I suspected that a Reader in their midst had come up with the word, clandestinely gleaned from one of the libraries. But why this particular name?

The vibrations suddenly rose up from my chest and seemed to hit my skull like a tidal rush filling a cave. I turned to leave. I had already absorbed everything I could and did not want my curiosity to alert suspicion.

The guards stood to one side for Hephzibah and then closed around us again. We returned to the boat and sailed out of the port into the deep, dark depths of the ocean once more. I imagined the great dome rising behind us like a swollen half moon and the elliptical Sphinx spinning within it like a miniature imprisoned planet.

46

I don't know which I dreaded the most; the part I was expected to play to the dinner guests or the dinner itself. I washed and dressed quickly and took care to wear my hair in the Water style, so that it looked short and sculpted to my head. I did not apply the cream left in the bathroom; it promised to give my features 'the luminosity desired by women everywhere', but I did not trust its ingredients, nor the intention of the giver, whoever that might be. Before leaving the room, I removed Homer's necklace and replaced it with the string of rubies Hephzibah had given me.

She came to fetch me. My sister was stunning in a silver diaphanous shirt, unbuttoned over a tight-fitting vest that revealed the half moons of her nipples. Her skirt hugged her thighs and ended in a burst of frills below her knees. She balanced on high buckled shoes which matched the sequinned blue of her skirt. Her sumptuous hair was pinned back like mine, but she had allowed loose tendrils to fall around her ears, which were decorated with clear, sparkling crystals.

She led me out onto a wide terrace overlooking a large pool of water lilies. Dragonflies skimmed the surface and soft music moaned from a corner of the lawn. Scented smoke hung in the air and we gathered around a polished mahogany table, which reflected the lights from the burning candelabra. Hephzibah surveyed the scene proudly.

'All for you, Jephzat,' she said. 'All for you, my darling sister. The great and the good of the Water Country are here to welcome you.'

'Jephzat, meet my father, the President,' Riffa said, emerging from his father's shadow. I instantly recognized the man I had seen from the nursery window. My arms were suddenly in the imprisoning grip of his massive, muscular hands. His lips stretched into a taut, uneasy smile.

'Hephzibah, you didn't tell me just how beautiful your sister is.' His voice was strangely high-pitched, feminine almost. 'And she learns quickly, too. She's only been here a short while and already she's beginning to look like a Water woman.'

I forced myself to smile gratefully as Bolgez pulled a younger man to his side. 'This is my other son, Gabriel. Fine figure of a man, isn't he?'

Embarrassed by the question, I avoided the eyes of the man I was to spend the rest of the evening sitting next to, and wishing that I wasn't. Unlike Riffa, Gabriel resembled his father. He had the same large head, but with fine dark hair cut close to the scalp and pomaded with pungent-smelling oil. His ears were too small and stuck out from his head like fins, and his lips were thin and slack. His skin had cold grey undertones, despite the warm candle-light. I fell back when he suddenly flung his arms around me and then steadied me. He scrutinized my face with hooded eyes.

'We've been looking forward to meeting you. Hephzibah has told us so much about you,' he said, in a Federese

I found easier to follow, and which indicated that he had been raised, or educated, elsewhere. His voice was deep and mellifluous, unlike his father's, and he kept an arm locked around my waist whilst speaking. I could see how many women would find him seductive, despite his looks.

Bolgez then introduced me to three top-ranking members of the military, all of them highly decorated for heroism. I could see that the pupils in their eyes did not react to changing light, and remained dilated. I sat next to one of the generals and noticed how intensely she observed me, as if she did not understand everything I was saying, and needed to read my face, body and lips for a full interpretation. I suspected that each of them had been 'enhanced'.

Bolgez pushed two more guests towards me. 'Meet two members of the Board of Directors. They've left an important meeting with the Federation to be here with us this evening.'

Naturally shy, I found it difficult to overcome my nervousness and initiate a conversation with them. Hephzibah did her best to put me at ease and Riffa smiled sympathetically at me from across the table. I had never seen my sister so confident before, she was flirting with everyone. One general, a man with wide shoulders and carefully manicured hands, hardly took his eyes off me, and asked me about 'post-war Olives'. I ignored the laughter that followed and answered with a proud defiance, saying that the war had had little effect on us, that it was business as usual, and that the Company had not been wise in goading its powerful neighbour.

'It's going to be a lot worse,' said the general beside me, summoning a waiter for more wine.

There was silence as we all watched her glass turn ruby red.

'That's true,' Bolgez squeaked, 'but this is not the time to discuss it.'

He asked me what I thought of Hephzibah's plans that I should stay.

'It's a wonderful idea,' I lied. 'I've considered it more carefully since Hephzibah first suggested it this morning and realize it would be a relief to get away from the backwardness of the Olive Country. I hope that I can be of service to you, and will assist Hephzibah and her new family in any way I can.'

Hephzibah smiled radiantly and raised her glass, seemingly impervious to the stilted quality of my speech. Everyone rose, and glasses clinked as my name resounded over the terrace.

Food was brought in on large silver dishes and an army of waiters served us attentively. As endless elaborate courses were brought to the table I looked up to thank the waiter serving me a simple plate of dressed crab. How I stopped myself from expressing my shock, I don't know. It was Lilith. Her pigtails had gone, replaced by short, oiled hair, which exaggerated her vulpine features. Instead of her eccentric dress she wore a figure-hugging waiter's outfit. She kept her head bent as she continued around the table, and I was glad that our eyes had not met; Hephzibah would certainly have noticed the slightest flicker of recognition between us.

The shock was overtaken by a relief that I was not alone, and a sudden fit of coughing which attracted everyone's attention. 'Pour her some more water,' Hephzibah commanded.

When my fit had subsided Riffa leaned over to me. 'Were you aware,' he said earnestly, 'that water has memory?'

'That's more than most of us have,' Hephzibah retorted, and everyone laughed.

But Bolgez only sneered at his son. 'I don't think the extraordinary capabilities of our water are of any interest to our honoured guest, do you, Riffa? We don't want to give away too many of our secrets.'

'But she's family,' Gabriel protested.

'Not yet,' Bolgez replied pointedly, ending my brief inclusion in their inner circle.

The waiters served more food, but still I did not dare look in Lilith's direction. The candlelight flickered in the warm night air, and sounds of the city rose over the sealed wall that surrounded us. Sometimes I found myself struggling to follow the conversation around the table as the voices of strangers from far away invaded my hearing.

'The good thing about minor Companies like the Olive Company – they were subsidiaries to start with after all – is that they have very little ambition,' Bolgez was saying. 'The bad thing is that they are like those little dogs that snap at your heels and, in their persistence, are far more effective than any large hound.'

'The Olive Company has only a very small presence in space,' added one of the generals smugly.

'Maybe, but it knows the value of real estate in the cosmos, as does the rest of the Federation,' Hephzibah said.

'We'll just have to make sure we are the first to make the biggest impact,' Bolgez said, and the rest of the table sniggered.

Riffa tapped a spoon on the side of his plate, 'The only thing that's holding us up is the ability to reproduce the formula. Exporting water in bulk into space is expensive and time-consuming.'

'But Jephzat is here to help us crack it,' Hephzibah said. 'That's why she's agreed to stay with us.' Everyone was suddenly staring at me.

Bolgez leaned over towards me, suddenly attentive again. 'Hephzibah has told me so much about you – about your work with your parents and how you might be able to help us.'

Before I could reply, Gabriel laughed and turned to me. 'You'd better pour some more of that olive oil over your salad, because it's going to be in short supply after tomorrow.'

What he said chilled me to the bone, but I started to laugh hysterically and found I couldn't stop. Everyone joined in but stopped when they saw tears beginning to stream down my face. For several moments the atmosphere of embarrassed silence was palpable. Then I felt a sharp pain in the fingertip of my left hand. I placed my napkin on the table and quickly excused myself. I had to go to the bathroom, I explained, and left the table hurriedly.

I heard Gabriel commenting on my entertainment value as I left. But I had to return to my room. The alarm from my bag that I had inserted below my fingernail had just alerted me to someone riffling through my possessions. I steeled myself to confront an intruder in my room. It was dark when I pushed open the door and saw the outline of a hunched figure. It was Kehmet, and she immediately made the sign that Lilith had given me as a password. I was safe. I relaxed on to the bed beside her.

'Where's Lilith?' she asked.

'Still downstairs serving.'

'We have to act quickly,' Kehmet said, opening my bag. 'They're going to flood the Olive Country tomorrow afternoon.'

I started to ask for more details, but at that moment Lilith rushed into the room.

'I've only got a few seconds before I have to get back,' she whispered urgently, and grabbed my arm. She pulled out the thin wire filament and fixed a small lens to her eye.

'I'm reprogramming it so that the Olive Company agents receive misleading information. It'll send them on a wild goose chase and keep them off our backs for a while.

'Everything is arranged,' she hurried on. 'You know what to do, Jephzat, and we are counting on you. We have Readers from all over the Federation prepared and at the ready. They know exactly what their roles are; some are at the Water Production Centre ready to assist you. Others are posted at the main Federation communication and military centres. The most important thing is that you get the water formula and bring it back here to us. Kehmet and Pedro are to go with you. Marcel will be on duty when you arrive. He's not one of us, but you'll know how to sweet-talk him, I'm sure.'

'But they can get to us from space. They have a complete technological arsenal up there, and can track everything we are doing.' I felt very scared.

Lilith sensed my mood, and began to shake my shoulders as if trying to wake me up. 'Don't underestimate

CHRISTINE AZIZ

the power of the Readers. We are stronger and cleverer than the Federation because we have the knowledge to be so. We know there is more to life than the propaganda it's feeding us. We have stepped out of its prison of ignorance. We know what it did to us, and what it keeps doing to us. And by the end of tomorrow we will no longer be slaves.'

She released my shoulders gently.

'Remember the books, Jephzat. Remember what they told you. If you don't trust us, then trust the stories.'

'It's just a tiny black ball,' I said as if in a trance. 'But we must get it. We must get it.'

Gabriel clapped and whistled as I re-entered the dining room, and when I sat down tried to pull my hand under the table onto his crotch. I snatched it away and caught Hephzibah smiling at us as if we were a couple of naughty children. As we ate in silence, I thought how jarring and noisy a meal was when eaten with silver cutlery and china plates compared to the gentle scraping of olive-wood spoons in olive-wood bowls. I tried desperately not to think of the villagers clinging to the olive trees as the water surged through the branches.

It seemed a long time before I could retire to my bedroom, but at least I had rebuffed Gabriel's advances for good. I knew I should rest while waiting to be summoned, and after undressing lay beneath the sheets in my second skin, my stomach churning with fear and anticipation. I dozed off after half an hour but was awakened by the sound of a baby crying. I thought it must be Mariam, and covering myself, walked into the corridor to investigate. The lights were low and from the gardens I could hear the sound of running water.

When I entered the nursery, Mariam was awake in her cot, and the nanny was in a deep sleep on the other side of the room. The baby raised her arms to me and I lifted her up, holding her close and singing to her. She stared up at me until her eyelids began to droop. I placed her gently back into the cot and, still singing, stroked her forehead and cheeks. She felt so soft and looked so peaceful that I did not want to leave her. My love for her felt over-whelming. But I tried to control my churning stomach as I realized I wouldn't be able to protect Mariam after our insurrection.

I was still preoccupied as I carefully closed the nursery door behind me. Standing outside to check that my niece hadn't reawakened, I heard noises from behind a shutter on the other side of the landing. It was slightly ajar and I crept over to it. In the faint light I glimpsed the back of a naked woman straddling a man on the bed. The woman arched her back and neck so that her hair streamed down her spine. Then I heard the man moan with pleasure. I stepped from the door, sickened but not surprised. It was Hephzibah and Bolgez. Back in my room I realized that the coupling of my sister with the man who ran the most efficient work camp in the Federation had only made me more eager than ever to complete my mission.

For the first time since I had left the Olive Country I felt elated, the prospect of revenge a formidable motivator.

Book V

*I have always imagined that Paradise
will be a kind of library.*

JORGE LUIS BORGES

47

The beginning of my life was spent living in a society you would consider feudal, but the reality is that I am living in a time far more technologically advanced than yours.

We have come a long way since the ailing American empire and its allies set up a base on Phobos, a Mars moon, in a vain attempt to escape the pollution they had caused on our planet. Tiny in comparison to our Earth, Phobos quickly became the most expensive real estate in the solar system, despite its waist-deep dust. We now know how to simulate gravity, which has developed interstellar travel even further, and there are small, settled communities on various planets. The galactic cities that Bolgez and Hephzibah dreamed of still do not exist, but our knowledge of the cosmos far outstrips yours. Of course the corporate empire treated our galaxy in much the same way as its predecessor did, as its own backyard where the washing is hung out, and the rubbish is dumped. Thank goodness more galaxies are being formed as I write. You wouldn't want to run out of real estate, would you?

But no matter how far our technology outstrips your understanding, we are united by one constant. It is still the unpredictability of death which connects our seemingly disparate worlds.

*

I was not prepared for the screaming and wailing that disturbed me at dawn. I was awake, prepared to leave and waiting for Kehmet. I had already applied the special communications system that ran like veins under my second skin, and I constantly stretched and flexed my muscles, anticipating the demands that would soon be placed upon my body.

I became nervous when I heard panicked footsteps running along the corridor. Had any of the Olive Readers been discovered? And where was Kehmet? I had managed to dress myself when the door was suddenly flung open and Hephzibah appeared, distraught and dishevelled.

'Bolgez is dead,' she screamed, flinging herself into my arms and sobbing.

'How? What happened? He was fine only a few hours ago at dinner.'

'I don't know. His maid took him his early tea and thought he was asleep. When she returned with his breakfast, he was still sleeping, which is unusual. She tried to wake him, then realized.'

She began to sob again, and I tried to console her, my mind racing.

'You'd better wash and get dressed,' I said. 'As the Company Mother, you have to remain dignified and in control. There are things that need to be done, and you will have to do them. Riffa and Gabriel don't strike me as particularly capable men.' I knew this was what she wanted to hear.

She shook herself, dabbed the tearstains from her cheeks and regained her poise. A glazed brightness obscured her eyes and I was suddenly reminded of the way she had looked after she killed Mariam.

'You're right,' she said. 'The directors will have to be informed. As the older son, Riffa will take over the Company until the Board officially elects him, which it is bound to do. Its members think he'll be easily influenced by them, but they'll have to count on me!' Now she looked triumphant. 'We also have to let all the workers know and start promoting Riffa as their new leader.'

I stepped towards her.

'Did you kill him, Hephzibah?' I asked quietly.

She seemed neither surprised nor offended by my question. She merely gave an ambiguous smile and I was aware that as a newly arrived stranger from a hostile neighbouring Company, the finger of accusation could easily be pointed at me.

'It will be found to be natural causes. I am sure of that,' she said without hesitation, as if reading my mind. 'I forget how well you know me. Didn't I perform well? Let's hope I can keep it up for the next few days. Remember what I said yesterday, about you helping me to run the Company. I bet you didn't think it would happen so quickly.'

I decided to stall her, but couldn't stop myself asking one crucial question: 'I suppose with the aftermath of his death to deal with you'll be calling a halt to the flooding?'

'No, of course not. It's become even more imperative that we press on. I don't want the Federation to think that Bolgez's successor is a spineless wimp.'

I did not want to waste my time begging her to reconsider. I had to dupe her into believing that my willingness to sacrifice anything for her sake remained intact.

'What about Riffa?'

'Oh, Riffa will effectively hand the reins over to me so that he can continue at playing being a cosmologist, or whatever it is he fancies himself to be.' She pushed her face into mine, a face full of malicious hope. 'There are people in the Company who want me to take over. They know I have the right ambitions to make the Water Company the centre of the universe. They know Bolgez was grooming me.'

'You do what you have to do,' I said quietly, as I realized I had lost for ever the little girl my sister had once been.

'I'll have to go and get ready,' she said, her voice full of excitement. 'Our parents will be arriving tomorrow. They're already in transit.'

I knew then that Mariam's death had been only the beginning.

When she had gone, Kehmet appeared in the room as though she had never left it, her skin still bruised from a reflected night.

'Let's go,' she said. 'We've got to take advantage of the situation. It's already chaotic out there.'

I told her that Hephzibah had killed the President, but Kehmet showed no surprise and with nothing more to say I fixed Homer's fire crystals around my neck. Ignoring Kehmet's pleas to remove them, I crept quietly out of the room.

I did not dare contemplate failure as we moved into the gardens. Lilith had told me, before my departure for the Water Country, that groups of dedicated Readers had spent years in deep subterranean tunnels preparing and rehearsing for this final confrontation. Their day had now dawned.

Like choreographed dancers, a small group of guards – Pedro amongst them – broke away from their comrades and discreetly escorted us out towards the sealed wall. Voices rose from the buildings behind us, and air buggies landed on the green lawns. The secure and rigid calm of the President's household had turned to chaos.

It was easy exiting the island. I informed the operatives I was acting under Hephzibah's instructions. They expressed their condolences then let us out, like birds from a cage. It was the part I had feared most; I had not forgotten the foaming moat we had to pass over.

Pedro and I exchanged looks, both realizing how quickly Bolgez's death was already working in our favour. Who would risk their newly insecure position by confronting me, the sister of the woman closest to the new President? There were fewer patrols than expected – we guessed everyone was watching their screens for news updates on the demise of the President. Voices moaned from around the city and the wail of sirens echoed relentlessly across the wide canals. A man's stern voice was being broadcast across the entire city, urging calm and uninterrupted labour. Some defied him, and there were already clusters of people on the banks of the waterways looking bewildered, or doing their best to appear grief-stricken.

We slipped into our boat, which formed part of the Presidential fleet, then slid noiselessly into the water. The pilot didn't see us leave, and continued his journey. We dived to the water bed, our suits alerting us to surveillance frequencies and laser triggers. I knew that many of the surveillance systems had already been doctored by our infiltrators to allow us to reach the Centre as easily as possible. Pedro led the way and we followed, moving easily through the weed that snared our faces like nets. Schools of tiny fish encircled us and I lost sight of the others. When they cleared, like a passing storm, I found myself being pulled by an eddy of water into the entry tunnel of a large building. I tried to swim against the pull of the water, but was being sucked towards the brightly lit opening. I heard a voice which shuddered through my skin.

'Don't panic! We're coming.'

I was about to be swallowed into the bowels of a building when someone wound an arm around my neck and jerked me back. I struggled and kicked as hard as I could, and we rolled in the water until I heard Pedro's voice. 'For goodness' sake. It's Kehmet. Stop resisting.'

We swam close together after that, and gathered around the pipes like sea scavengers. Kehmet pointed to the pipe I was to swim alongside and which would lead me into the Water Centre. It was a feed for the Olive Country supply, and I resisted an urge to turn around and swim the other way. As I swam, I led my mind to other places; I saw myself emerging from a reservoir overlooking terraces of olive groves, and Homer and Mariam reaching out with towels and a thick robe. All the time I sensed Kehmet and Pedro encouraging me.

By the time I reached the Centre, my body was exhausted, my muscles were on fire and I had begun to trail my legs in the water like a jellyfish. So it was with relief that I finally reached the end of the pipe, and began to force my way out onto the platform above me. Water gushed from the pipe with such force it slapped me back down towards the sea bed. Avoiding its vortex, I circled up towards the Centre's entrance and pushed my way through what appeared to be a sealed crack, like a scar. For several seconds before the opening closed behind me, water flooded in, but I hauled myself into a mercifully dry, dimly lit chamber. My body immediately began to swell, like a fast-ripening fruit. It was a pleasant sensation at first, associated with arousal and voluptuousness, but quickly became uncomfortable. Pedro was waiting for me with a tiny bitter pill which he forced into my mouth. It absorbed my saliva and I grimaced, but at least it would prevent the water replicating inside me until I exploded.

'So far, so good,' Pedro said tensely. 'You're doing fine. You know what to do now.'

I could tell he was nervous, and suddenly realized how young he was. Shaved hairless for his infiltration of Presidential security, his face looked soft and vulnerable, like a baby's.

'Have you taken care of the Centre's director?' I asked.

'Don't worry about him. He's the least of your worries. Everything's going to plan so far. We've seized the Federation surveillance centres.' His face broke into a broad grin of excitement. 'I think we're going to make it.'

'Have you heard what's happened to my sister?' I asked anxiously, unaware of the fierce battle that was already blazing around the dome between the Readers and the Centre's operatives.

'Don't worry about that. There's been exchange of fire. That's all I know.'

He held my arm and I asked if the Readers would remember their promise to me; not to harm Hephzibah or Mariam.

'Now's not the time to worry,' he ordered. 'We're close, Jephzat. Concentrate on getting through.'

He walked me around a ledge built at the base of the dome and expertly sliced through the membrane of an unfilled pipe. It ran from beneath the dome but had been sealed off. I wriggled inside, struggling against the out-flow, and clutched at its fabric as I inched my way forward. It would lead me eventually to the interior of the dome itself – the only way to get access to it.

I became aware of a slow, rhythmical pulsing that seemed to come from all around me. At first I thought it was noise from the pumps that drained the dome, but there was an unfamiliar, non-mechanical force to it. The waves of energy moved through my body as if taking over the function of my heart. It was a gentle force, and lulled me into a deep and unexpected serenity that both sur-prised and concerned me: it was as if the pulse of it was exorcizing all my recent turmoil. I experienced absolute peace for the first time since Mariam's death, and was suddenly reluctant to move away from this seductive, tranquil place. I felt my limbs grow heavy and torpor descend; I shook myself awake and tried to remember the titles of the books I had read. That gave me strength and moments later I pushed my way through the pipe's tight seal and found myself in the dome.

The pipe's seal closed behind me, and I did not hear the alarms that rang the moment I entered the embrace of the water. Such was my relief on getting through, that I found myself spinning around like a playful fish and corkscrewing through the water as I used to when swimming as a child. I filled a small phial with the water before allowing myself to float for a while, as if being held. And then I saw it.

The Sphinx was suspended before me, spinning slowly in its fixed orbit. It emitted a low sigh of supernal sound that broke through the water. I swam towards it, momentarily robbed of memory. As I swam I battled with its pulse, which was now strumming through my body with a great force. I was facing the biggest threat to my survival: I was forgetting how to be afraid. Like a brief spark, an image of trees drowning in oceans suddenly came to me and I kicked my legs into action. I circled the Sphinx several times, like a shark with its prey, getting nearer with each circuit. Then I reached for it and tugged. It was like plucking a ripened fruit from a tree.

I swam and swam; I do not remember for how long. I did not know where I had come from, or where I was going. I drifted down and bounced along the bottom of the dome, the Sphinx somehow guiding me. As I floated through the water I birthed stars, rode on the backs of meteorites, ranged our universe in the eye of solar storms, held the cooling crusts of planets in the palms of my hands and cradled galaxies in my arms. Not in fear, but with a deep longing, and for a brief moment I understood the infinity of the universe, unrestrained by language or human form.

It was Pedro who dragged me back to earth.

'What the hell are you doing?' he hissed. 'Do you think we've got all day?'

I felt as if I had been shaken from a deep sleep, and nodded, still feeling the faint throb of the calming pulse. I cradled the Sphinx protectively against my chest as if it were a newborn baby. It was no bigger than the full span of a human hand, and I could feel its full weight now that I was out of water – no heavier than a duck egg. I refused to hand it over to Pedro. As long as it remained out of its own self-propagating water, the Sphinx no longer had an effect on the body's own water content. I held it all the way back to the city. The Sphinx was mine.

I don't remember much of the return journey, except for the bodies drifting around us, and workers breaking out of the buildings and spilling out of the tunnels. Some surrounded terrified figures trying to escape and tore at them until blood curled like smoke through the water. A boat, its Water insignia already painted over, dived down and brought us to the water's surface.

I was not prepared for the crowds already lining the avenues and waterways. People were using anything they could find to paddle their way towards the Presidential home. Some waved flags while others held books up to us, cheering and crying and laughing. Women put their children on their shoulders as we passed, and men blew us kisses. Occasionally there were shouts of 'Maya, Maya,' and a thousand coloured scarves were thrown into the air.

By the time we reached the Presidential island the noise was overwhelming. People reached over as if trying to touch me through the boat's cover. Pedro and his colleagues formed a tight ring around me in case the crowds broke through, and I sat in the centre of the boat cradling my prize, already fearful of the implications of our actions. My head ached from the din around me, and surrounded by people, I felt the worst kind of loneliness. The dark sphere had ceased its calming pulse and clamoured now like a stressed human heart, as if mimicking my own.

48

From the moment I had stepped off the boat, it was clear that I was considered, by those around me, to be responsible for their new-found freedom. I sat on the terrace, listening to the celebrations of the crowds now gathering throughout the city. Once again, I picked up only fragments of speech that seemed to blow in from the outreaches of the city like swirls of dust. The words clamoured for attention, but I could not make sense of any of them. People waved from broken windows in the surrounding towers that looked down on us. Until now, any windows overlooking Bolgez's fortress island had been blacked out and sealed to protect his privacy. Now I waved back. I pretended a joy I did not feel – I had yet to find out how Hephzibah and Mariam were being treated by the Readers.

I gazed at the young olive trees planted along the terrace, soothed by their presence. Bodies were being laid out in the shade of the larger trees and covered with sheets. Occasionally someone would shout or announce the name of the latest Company to have fallen. Readers thronged the gardens, and I wished more than anything that Homer could have been among them. Instead I gazed across the makeshift mortuary and, placing my hand softly on his necklace, addressed him one last time.

'My sweet, sweet Homer. You'll be pleased to know that, as you predicted, the entire Federation, having been seduced into complacency by its own power, was overthrown by the three most effective weapons the Readers possessed – knowledge, surprise and daring. And thank you for inspiring me to take my part in it.'

Kehmet had advised me to rest and had disappeared with Lilith to have her tooth replaced by another of clear white enamel. I was sure that at the same time thousands of tiny images of Hephzibah and her Water family were being hurriedly removed. It was a ridiculous idea in the first place, I thought. So vain, and so suited to my sister.

I had made it clear that I did not want my family mistreated in any way. Lilith had merely nodded her head in acquiescence, and informed me they were being held in comfort in a part of the building that was suitable for family accommodation. I had then asked her about the Olive Country.

'It now belongs to the people,' she said. 'The President and directors had already left, fearing the flood. They were staying in the north, as guests of the Federation, and were happy to leave the workers behind to drown. Of course, the Federation had no plans to stop the Water Country. It was too afraid and preferred to let it destroy us, rather than risk a wider confrontation. It was also buying time until your parents came up with the water solution.'

'I suppose our library will be thrown open to everyone now,' I said, resenting the idea of people pouring into the library, spoiling its quietude, clumsily handling the books, perhaps even stealing them.

A cold drink was placed before me along with fruit, honey and slices of freshly baked bread, but I had no appetite. I felt a pair of warm hands rest on my shoulders. I knew instantly who they belonged to and whirled round. Sengita laughed uproariously as she pulled me up and hugged me to her, smothering me with kisses. 'I never thought I would see you again,' she said joyfully, swaying from her hips so that the bells on her waistcoat tinkled and her skirts shook. I felt my eyes water as I watched her grow more and more frenzied in her dancing. She was not wearing her wig, but I noticed a dark down of hair covering her skull, and the tattooed symbol on her forehead seemed more noticeable than before, as if a light shone on it. She held out her arms to me and I danced alongside her, holding the Sphinx aloft – our trophy of victory.

'So this is it,' she murmured reflectively. 'This is what gave the Water Country its power.'

She suddenly drew her hands back, as if scalded.

'This doesn't come from our Earth!' she said, looking very alarmed. She bent her head to the sphere, as if listening to it for guidance. 'How are we going to replicate this?' she asked.

'I think I know the secrets it holds. It's as if I've known all along. But that can wait. There's something else I must do first.'

I chose one of the Readers to accompany me. She was a young girl, dressed not in the Olive style, but as if from a manufacturing centre in the north, with her tight sleeves, high neckline and shorter, single-layer skirt. Her eyes were deep-set and her nose was flat and smooth, like a stone eroded by the elements. She appeared nervous and kept her eyes lowered. I asked if she would take me to my sister. She seemed too scared to move, and Sengita prodded her.

After a few moments' hesitation she led us to another section of the Presidential complex which I had not seen before. People greeted us as we passed. Some reached out and tried to grasp at my clothes or shake my hand, but Sengita brushed each of them away with polite smiles.

'You're popular!' she joked to me, just as the girl stopped outside a door and hesitated. Two armed guards relaxed against the door frame and greeted us as if we were old friends, which clearly annoyed Sengita. She corrected their posture, smoothed down their grubby clothes and tidied their hair before the door slid open and I was ushered into the room by a woman I recognized as Mariam's nanny. I turned to Sengita and instructed her to fetch me my bag.

Hephzibah sat in the far corner of the room beside a huge wall of glass that looked out over trees and a waterfall cascading over crystals. Heavy antique fabric framed the window and a soft evening light fell on to her hair, which now hung loose and tumbled around her shoulders. At her feet, Mariam lay awake in a small cot.

A familiar and much-loved scent filled my nostrils, and I realized that, intent on seeing my sister, I had not noticed the remaining walls, which were lined from floor to ceiling with books. I looked with bewildered surprise at Hephzibah, who by now was carefully studying my face and the Sphinx, which I held tightly in my arms. I walked over to the shelves and ran my fingers along the books, feeling a familiar rush of pleasure.

I felt Hephzibah's breath on the back of my neck.

'They all belonged to a famous twentieth-century actress and now they're all mine. The biggest collection of books on costume and costume design in the entire Federation.'

I swung round to correct her.

'You mean the "former Federation".'

She began to laugh, but in a joyless, empty way that chilled me and upset Mariam, who whimpered. The nanny attempted to pick her up, but Hephzibah rushed over and pushed her roughly away. She picked Mariam up and crushed her tightly in her arms.

'Don't you touch my child,' she screamed at the woman, who stared steadily at her with the confidence of one who was now on the winning side. 'Don't you dare. I don't want your filthy hands on her. Traitor. You betrayed us both. Don't come near us, do you hear? None of you. Stay away.'

I thought she would cry, but instead she fought to compose herself for a few moments and I watched, repelled, as she drew herself up to her full height and calmly walked towards me.

'I've got something to show you, Sister. It'll be a nice surprise.'

She leaned over my shoulder to breathe on to a corner of a shelf, and a section of the library swung open.

'Isn't it fun?' Hephzibah said, stepping into another room which immediately lit up. I caught my breath and gasped in horror. The long, low-ceilinged room was lined with what looked like erect, headless bodies. It was draped everywhere with antique textiles of all kinds; embroidered silks, gold-encrusted brocades, lightly quilted toile, lustrous lengths of velvet, delicate satins, bright, printed cottons. Scraps of cloth lay on the floor, and the dummies lining the aisle were dressed in a variety of strange costumes, all made in the most elaborate and exquisite fabrics. There were lace collars as delicate as cobwebs, and bodices stitched with thread as fine as hair and adorned with bows. Some skirts were hooped, others were layers of sumptuous velvet, or lengths of brightly coloured silk twined around the dummies like a cord.

Hephzibah walked me slowly down the aisle, explaining the history of the costumes and some of the sewing techniques used. It was as if the room remained her private domain, and nothing had changed. I was bemused by this sudden introduction to Hephzibah's new interest, and saw that the worktops were strewn with pins, scissors, tailor's chalk, paper patterns and bolts of fabric. It was as if people had fled suddenly from their work, abandoning their tools. I noticed splashes of blood on some of the cloth, and on worktops. Then Hephzibah placed Mariam gently in an empty sewing box on the floor and disappeared behind a heavy brocade curtain.

We waited for what seemed a long time.

When she reappeared, her small audience gasped. She was wearing a dress from another epoch. Hephzibah stood proudly before us, a surreal vision in a jewel-encrusted black velvet coat over what looked like a grey satin skirt fancifully embroidered in all colours. The waist of the bodice was elongated and pointed, making her look even taller and very slim. A collar of the finest intricate lace rose up stiffly behind her, and the sleeves were puffed and delicately cuffed. She wore a small coronet on her head, her fingers were heavily ringed and her chest roped with pearls. Embroidered pointed-toe shoes peeped out from under the wide skirt.

'Isn't it beautiful?' she said in a voice that was not quite hers. 'I'm not interested in what the peasants wore. I rescue and re-create the costumes of the old kings and queens, princes and princesses, emperors and empresses, tsars and tsarinas. They are the only ones worth bringing back to life.'

I shrugged my shoulders. Her privileged position allowed her to connect to the past in a way that appeared extravagant and self-indulgent when compared to my reading, or Miran's simple regard for his olive trees. Each one of us, in our own way, was seeking to heal our severed lineage. Her self-obsessed nochalance sparked a demonic fury. I placed the Sphinx on the worktop and grabbed at her collar, hissing in anger. It was not the force of my rage that made her step back, but its aberration.

'You spoilt, pathetic bitch. I'm not going to be there for you any more, Hephzibah, not in the way you want me to be. Do you understand that? Whatever is given to you is never enough. You want to take away bigger and bigger pieces of me until there's nothing left. You do that to everyone. You wanted to keep me here, like a prisoner, a slave, didn't you? But you can't. It's over.'

Hephzibah took a couple of steps towards me, but I held my ground.

'Do you know why I called your niece Mariam?' she hissed. 'So that when you arrived here – and I knew you would come running the moment I asked you to – you'd constantly hear the name of the woman you helped me murder. Every day you would be reminded of what you did for me, you'd be reminded of our little secret. It's the invisible chain that binds us together and a sacrifice you'd never be allowed to forget. But you got involved with these Readers instead and chose them instead of me.'

I did not regret my anger, but suddenly afraid of its consequences, I now stepped back.

'There was no choice, Hephzibah. And now I'm even more certain of it.'

'They're just using you, Jephzat. Don't you see that? You're useful to them as another figurehead, another Maya. These people don't care about you like I do. They just wanted to use you as my sister, and get the water formula from you. You're a fool. You always were. I'm the only one who cares for you.'

Mariam had started to cry and as I walked over to comfort her, Hephzibah moved across to the worktop and grabbed the Sphinx.

'We can do this together, Jephzat. You don't have to share everything with these people. They think just because they've read a few old books they know everything.'

'Give it back to me, Hephzibah.' I spoke softly, stepping towards her. She began to run in her cumbersome skirts and petticoats. I chased after her, Mariam now in my arms, the overdressed dummies falling as I pushed by. By the time I reached my sister, three Readers were already on top of her. She swung round to face me as they led her away struggling, and she shouted, 'What are you going to do with me, Jephzat? Kill me, or keep me in chains for ever?'

49

It was sometime before I could talk or face seeing anyone.
All I wanted to do was hold my niece close to me, but she
remained with Hephzibah. Restless and agitated, I finally
asked to be escorted to my sister. I could not look at her –
I did not want to witness her humiliation. But when I turned
my face to the window I could see her reflection. I told her
she was free to leave with Mariam, that she would be
provided with anything necessary to help her, but that I
never wanted to see her again. She nuzzled her daughter's
head, kissed her gently, but did not look at me before I left.

Sengita remonstrated with me afterwards. I was a fool to
let her go, she said.

'I was afraid of what I'd do to Hephzibah,' I told her.
'If I were able to countenance her execution, I could perhaps convince myself that it had very little to do with me.
I would not see the marks, the blood, the body. I would
not have caused the physical wounds, after all. But even if
I did not kill her, and even if no one else did, I would still
be guilty. I would be considering the murder of my sister
– not as I am now, as a possibility – but as a desire. I have
realized through Mariam's death that it is the intention
which also pollutes, not just the action itself.'

'You're not being rational, Jephzat! I don't understand a word of it! By letting her go free, you're doing what you've always done for that girl, and again you've sacrificed something of yourself.'

'What do I sacrifice by letting her go?' I asked quietly.

'You don't know yet.'

I sighed. 'But she's my younger sister. There is no choice between justice and love.'

Sengita smiled. 'That's your reasoning. You can't have one without the other, Jephzat. I can't be your conscience.'

Sengita had made me feel unsure. 'She's my younger sister. I am responsible for her wellbeing. She'll be fine. Hephzibah knows how to survive.'

And so I was learning not to let sadness capture me in the aftermath of loss. After Hephzibah's departure and Homer's death, I realized it was best to hold sorrow at bay as if placing great stones against the loose earth of the olive terraces, to prevent the soil from uncovering the roots.

And now I was ready to meet my parents. They had been taken to the tall tower where I had first met Hephzibah. Lilith was already with them, explaining what had happened in the Water Country, but left it to me to let them know that Hephzibah was safe.

The evening light was already turning the city to delicate shades of coral and mauve. Flags flew everywhere, with pictures of books, doves, swords and rising suns. Pictures of Maya appeared on sheets draped from windows, and slogans for freedom, peace and choice were scrawled everywhere. 'We want our past back!' and 'We want our homes back!' were two of the most popular. From the air buggy we could see streams of people making their way to the tower on boats, by foot, or crowding into usurped Company vehicles. I scanned the crowds for Hephzibah. When we alighted, the sound of whistles, drums and chanting rose in the air alongside the constant thrum of excited voices and the cries of children.

Kehmet was there to meet me a second time, but now she was dressed in looser, softer clothes and looking more relaxed. Readers who had played a leading role in the insurrection were waiting to meet me, she said. I was also expected to demonstrate the replication of the water formula.

'What are the crowds coming here for?' I asked.

Kehmet and Sengita looked at each other incredulously.

'You don't know?' they chorused. 'They're coming to see you and to celebrate our victory.'

People surrounded me, but once again, I would not let anyone take my bag, or the Sphinx.

'Anyone would think that ball was your lover,' Sengita jibed.

I was escorted into the lift, noting the colourful welcome signs everywhere within the building. We plummeted to the sixth floor, and stepped out into a large room, with water flowing between transparent materials above and below us. The whole place was infused with light.

My parents sat closely together on a sofa that seemed to swamp them. I could see that they were bewildered and confused and I rushed over towards them, moved by their obvious relief and pleasure at seeing me. My father leaped up and I felt his frail body shudder against mine as he wept quietly. We held each other for a long time before he allowed my mother to step towards me. She was hesitant, as if overwhelmed by events, and then held out her arms. She seemed smaller than when I had last seen her, and vulnerable, and I felt the rush of a new affection for her. I no longer looked upon her as the mother who disdainfully distanced herself from me, but as the woman who had chosen to bring me into the world out of love for my father. We embraced each other with a new and spontaneous warmth.

She touched my necklace of fire crystals.

'Hephzibah?' she whispered, fearful.

'Someone else. Hephzibah's safe,' was all I could say.

'We're free!' someone in the room suddenly cried, full of impulsive joy. 'We're free! The Companies are dead. I can't believe it.'

The whole room burst into a triumphant chorus. 'The Companies are dead!'

I began to shout above their voices and there was silence.

'We are free to discuss whatever we have discovered in the libraries, and now will be a time of great learning,' I announced. 'You can speak the languages of the Old Countries that you have studied secretly, you can freely use the words and names you have not dared, and the Martyrs, whose names have so far remained secret, shall be publicly recognized alongside Maya. Federese will no longer be the official tongue. We will reclaim our own languages.'

A roar from the crowd outside crashed through the room, as if it had heard me. But within the room everyone

CHRISTINE AZIZ

was silent, as if the result of their actions had only just sunk in.

A young Reader buried her head in her hands and began to weep. I turned to my parents and with a choked voice said, 'You will be able to return home now – your real home.'

They sat dumbstruck, then Sengita stepped forward to greet and embrace them. I could see it was a comfort to my parents for a familiar figure from the village to be there and, noting Manos's absence, father enquired after her. Sengita replied that she was looking after the house, trying to keep out villagers who wished to move in, now it no longer belonged to the Company. Dolores gasped at the first intimation that she might be a refugee.

I sensed my moment. The atmosphere around me had changed gradually from ecstatic to expectant. I had set my bag in the centre of the room and everyone watched, fascinated, as I pulled out a bronze bowl and gave it to Father. He turned it over in his hands.

'It's more delicate than the one I showed you,' he observed.

I told him it was also half the size and that I had found someone in the village willing to produce a copy of the actual bowl for me.

'But what are you trying to show us?' queried one of the Readers.

'I'm going to show you how water is created.'

'It's impossible,' Dolores exclaimed, moving closer to me. 'The Federation's top minds have applied themselves

332

to this problem for a very long time, and your father and I have dedicated our lives to it, all without success.'

I took a small phial of water from my bag and poured its contents into the bowl. It was barely more than a couple of teaspoonsful, but I considered it to be enough. As I did so I spoke of the myths of creation from the ancient stories and scriptures. Those few who were already familiar with them chose to remain silent, as I explained how the stories often spoke of sound as the precursor to the very beginning of the evolution of the universe.

'For many people of the Old Countries, it was their belief that their world was created by the action of sound and light. In these myths the sound of creation is often described as a great wind, a profound sigh or an expression of joy,' I said, and quoted a verse as an example. 'Out of the Supreme Silence emanated the Nada Brahman, the sound aspect and expression of God ... Out of Primeval Sound became manifest all creation composed of the five elements namely space, air, fire, earth and water.'

'What has all this to do with the formula?' Dolores interrupted, eager to get to the scientific facts. 'Are you saying the formula is based on somehow harnessing vibration?'

'Wait and see,' I said enigmatically, playing for time and trying to gather my thoughts before continuing.

I was cut short by an older woman. She confirmed that the Sphinx must have been a title given by a Reader. Only someone who had read translations of *The Book of the Dead*, or other writings from the ancient civilizations, she said, would be familiar with the word.

'The Sphinx was apparently a manifestation of a god

called Hu, or the Divine Utterance. He, or she, breathed life into what we know as space, but which Hu's people called the Cosmic Ocean,' she explained.

'A neutron soup,' Dolores corrected.

'Imagine, it's darker than night, and the air suddenly vibrates with the sound of the first word of creation.' The Reader held her breath and then breathed out slowly. 'Huoooooooo. The god doesn't stop until it has finally created the sun. Apparently the word Sphinx came later to mean "an enigma", or "riddle", which is exactly what this is.'

'So you had access to dictionaries, too?' I asked, curious to know how other libraries compared to the one I knew and loved so well.

'Not many, and I suppose what I have told you may not be strictly true. Without more information, the full truth can't be known. We're probably going back ten thousand years. But I am telling you as I remember it.'

'You mean, your library had books that old?' Pedro interjected incredulously.

'The original script was written on a wall somewhere, I think, and then on parchment called papyrus,' the old woman said, as if she were a teacher addressing her pupil. 'My information was culled from a translation. As you can tell, the subject fascinates me.'

'These stories are all very well, and very pretty, but I can't see what they have to do with the struggles we've had to replicate water.'

Dolores sounded and looked exasperated. So I hurriedly took up my explanation once more. 'I would prefer to use a mix of Sphinx water with river or well water, because it has gone through the hydrological cycle, moving from subterranean regions to the atmosphere and back again. In this process the water is "charged" energetically and mineralized. This is what makes earth water sweeter and more healing for us humans. This stuff from the Source is like distilled water. It's still sweet, but rather bland, as if it has been treated with sugar or honey, and it's bereft of any healing minerals. To be of real value to us, water needs to go through its proper development. What we have here is the blueprint which has yet to be adapted to the Earth's environment and go through its hydrological cycle.'

I saw Father fidget nervously, and I turned to address him directly. 'When you showed me the singing bowl you were trying to tell me something, weren't you? Dolores, you told me that the vibrations are believed to generate the precise frequencies needed to produce standing waves. We have known for some time that water has memory and that everything on this planet and in our cosmos has its own sound imprint, its own vibration. When it was discovered that the cells continued to react in extremely dilute solutions, it showed how memory could be understood as the resonance of things once heard.

'So I began to think that perhaps the formula was a simple one; a vibration, a sound, that was imprinted in the water it produced. To put it crudely: once the vibration is imprinted in the water, it becomes like a tap turned full on, and the more water it produces, the more diluted is the message of the Source, and the stronger its replicating powers become. Even though the Water Company knew the principle of water memory, dilution and material potency, it didn't know or understand the nature of the material it was dealing with. It applied its latest technology to its mysterious discovery but could not discover what it actually *was*. That was the stumbling block to its research. None of us knew what it was we were trying to duplicate. And the water refused to give away its secret: its origins remain far beyond our human understanding still.'

I picked up the bowl and allowed it to pass around the room.

'Of course, the singing bowl is nothing more than an entertaining illusion – the standing fountain gives the impression that the water content of the bowl has increased. In fact, it is created by vibration that forces the water up into a fountain.'

Then I pulled out the Sphinx and held it in outstretched arms so everyone could see it. I allowed my father and Dolores to touch it, but no one else.

'It feels empty,' Dolores said, surprised, and shook it gently.

'I don't know this material,' Father said, intrigued by the black fabric of the sphere.

I placed the Sphinx in the singing bowl. It fitted perfectly and sat on the water. I spat on the palms of my hands and began to rub the two handles. The sound was barely audible at first, but eventually the humming of the bowl began to fill the room. My hands began to tingle and I heard a higher-pitched sound, like an echo to the hum, but which seemed to support the water itself. We watched as the water began to rise around the orb, which remained still and silent. Several onlookers gasped.

The water rose further and began to splash suddenly, as if the bowl were unleashing a storm. The Sphinx began to spin of its own accord until it was resting on the surface of the water, which by now was level with the bowl's brim.

As I watched the ball spinning, I felt as if I was being pulled into the bowl by an irresistible force. The Sphinx spun faster, the water grew calmer, and a few drops fell to the floor. I stared around the room. Everyone's attention was focused on the bowl and its humming, which had now all but blotted out the sound of the crowds outside.

'I don't think the researchers stumbled on the Source by accident. I think at least one of them knew what he or she was doing. Unlike light waves, sound waves do not travel through a vacuum. To travel and be heard, they need matter. That's why sound can be heard through a wall. In empty space there is no air, and what we humans know as sound is actually vibrations travelling through the earth's atmosphere. But there are gases in space and these can propagate sound waves, although we humans can't hear them.

'I think that the original space station crew were probably passing through an interstellar gas cloud when their equipment picked up this strange unearthly sound. It was not a recording, a copy, that they took back to earth, but the sound or vibration itself. They had stumbled upon what people of those ancient civilizations would have called a sound, or word of creation. Perhaps it was one of the five mentioned in the scripture, responsible for the creation of water. It was, in effect, stolen from the universe and remains here until we decide what to do with it.'

My father remained silent, his expression inscrutable, gazing at the Source, as I continued.

'In the full spectrum of sound this is likely to be an overtone of the universal sound current which runs throughout everything,' I said. 'You may think I've gone mad and am deviating from all that you have taught me,

Father. But if you think of the wonderful sounds of nature – isn't it possible that every breeze, every rustle of a branch is combining to make a harmonic overtone of the sound current? Does bringing in this, which people may not know, help the sequence? It's an intruder.

'It is as my biological mother, Maya, constantly reminded us. She once wrote: "The very fabric of our world is dependent for its existence upon the subtle and varied harmonies created by all living things. In the microcosm of nature, loss of one sound results in dissonance, which activates in us a yearning for harmony. We live in noisy underground cities and towns and yet long to be outside for the restorative sounds of nature." '

Father and Sengita looked across at me proudly, anticipating my solution for replication, but I knew then what I had to do.

I picked up the Sphinx as if it was a fragile, newborn creature and held it like a nursing mother. I stepped towards the large glass doors, knocking the bowl and spilling its contents over my feet. The doors instantly parted for me and I found myself on a large balcony that ran the full length of the building. It had been planted with lush, tropical gardens. I was aware that several people stood behind me, and that above me, throughout the building, people were leaning out of windows and waving, desperate to catch a glimpse of what was going on.

When they saw me the crowds gave a loud roar. 'Maya, Maya,' they called wildly. Below me, boats were packed together on the small lake, and people crammed every vista. They were holding lights, and the carmine city flared before me, awaiting the moon. I stood with the Sphinx in my hands. The crowd grew silent, waiting for

22

Figures could be seen climbing up the steep slopes from the banks of the estuary. Those with free hands were holding them to their ears to protect themselves from the strange, unsettling sound that still vibrated through the air. Others were hanging on to what looked like a rope, but was in fact a thin hose. The first arrivals aimed its nozzle at the burning building and attempted to extinguish the fire with a fierce jet of water.

We all shuffled gingerly forward to get a better view.

'Bit like trying to stop a plague with a spoonful of sugar,' one old man observed, his eyes red and weeping.

'I think we should give them a hand,' another volunteered, and took off down the path, a cloth held tightly to his nose and mouth.

Others quickly followed, and I wondered whether to join them. I alone knew the purpose of the cylinders and the noxious substances they contained. I tried to call the volunteers back, but no one could hear me above another explosion, which sent those with the water pipe reeling backwards. I began running towards the fire to warn people of possible larger explosions.

'Doesn't seem to be doing much good,' shouted the woman who was directing the water. I told her to stop; there was no one trapped in the building, and there was

Fortunately there were more explosions, which stopped people in their tracks for an instant and then had them running with me back towards the house, where we stood in a group, spluttering and coughing, our faces covered. We gazed up at the flames that seared the sky. Smoke billowed out over the estuary and an eerie green light spread from the fire. Homer drew me to him as I sobbed helplessly; there was nothing anyone could do now to save a lifetime of my father's work.

fruit. The cylinders' seals had been broken so that their contents had leaked out. The few items of electronic equipment Father was permitted to use were gone. Only his sound valve lay intact on the floor.

I searched for any of my father's notes, but found nothing. They had either been stolen or had dissolved in the viscous liquid that covered the worktops and dripped in thin ropes to the floor. Not knowing how much of his work in the laboratory was devoted to researching the water formula, I wanted to salvage as much as I could, but my lungs began to burn and my eyes were stinging. I rushed towards the door, noting that two of the cylinders were beginning to glow with extreme heat while the remaining three were collapsing in on themselves. The delicate balance of elements that had preserved them as miniature worlds imitating the atmospheres of planets millions of light years away had now been transformed into an acrid chaos of toxins.

Outside I pushed through the pines and scrambled over the bank, and did not look back even when I heard the explosion. I felt a rush of hot air hit me from behind with such force that I was thrown to the ground. The heat stripped the pines of their needles, scorched the earth and filled the air with smoke that stung my eyes and throat and obscured the path. I staggered through undergrowth, relying on my instinct to lead me back to the house. Through the swirl of smoke I saw figures running towards me and heard voices. Someone grabbed my hand and ran with me towards the house. I yanked myself away and tried to run back and stop those heading for the laboratory.

'Don't go there! Come back! It's dangerous. There's nothing you can do,' I yelled.

alert. There was so much to do, and now that I was stronger I had to get busy.

I dressed hurriedly and crept down the stairs. Manos and Homer were in the kitchen, but I did not want them to notice me. They would only try to persuade me back into bed again. I wanted to go to the bunker but knew I would have to wait until they had gone. Instead, I headed for Father's laboratory, which was some way from the house and hidden by a thick clump of pine trees and a large bank of rocks. The building was a rounded single-storey mound with porthole windows and covered with bougainvillea. A great deal of attention had been paid to the security of the building, so I was surprised to find the door already open. Only my parents' breath and mine was recognized on the sensor. Perhaps Father had forgotten to set it before his sudden departure. I stepped inside and knew instantly that something was wrong. I could smell rotting vegetation, and I began to choke on the air, which was thick with fumes. A thin, low-pitched sound vibrated above me through the laboratory and I covered my ears.

I left the door wide open and, protecting my nose and mouth with my shawl, rushed through the small lobby that preceded the main laboratory. The benches had been upturned and receptacles smashed to the floor. The five cylinders which had been secured to the ceiling in special drums designed to withstand both implosion and explosion had crashed to the floor and been smashed open. Inside the cylinders Father had tried to re-create the hostile atmospheres of planets beyond our galaxy. The drums protecting the cylinders had been designed to resist pressure of any kind, but each one had somehow been crushed open to reveal the cylinder lying inside, like the seed of a